Bringing Out Their Best

Bringing Out Their Best

A PARENT'S GUIDE TO HEALTHY
GOOD LOOKS FOR EVERY CHILD

Wende Devlin Gates

Bantam Books
New York ▪ Toronto ▪ London ▪ Sydney ▪ Auckland

BRINGING OUT THEIR BEST
A Bantam Book/November 1992

Library of Congress Cataloging-in-Publication Data
Gates, Wende.
    *Bringing out their best : a parent's guide to healthy good looks for
every child / Wende Devlin Gates.*
        p.   cm.
    Includes bibliographical references and index.
    ISBN 0–553–37034–0
    *1. Grooming for boys.   2. Grooming for girls.   3. Children—
Health and hygiene.   4. Beauty, Personal.   5. Child rearing.   I.
Title.*
RA777.G38   1992   92–24210
649'.63—dc20   CIP

Published simultaneously in the United States and Canada

*Bantam Books are published by Bantam Books, a division of Bantam
Doubleday Dell Publishing Group, Inc. Its trademark, consisting of
the words "Bantam Books" and the portrayal of a rooster, is Registered
in U.S. Patent and Trademark Office and in other countries.
Marca Registrada. Bantam Books, 666 Fifth Avenue, New York,
New York 10103.*

PRINTED IN THE UNITED STATES OF AMERICA
HCR   0   9   8   7   6   5   4   3   2   1

CONTENTS

FOREWORD

Our folklore is full of adages reminding us not to "judge a book by its cover," but the fact remains that appearances *are* important and, quite understandably, parents are concerned about the external appearance of their offspring. There is a fine balance here, however. To the extent that these concerns are limited to a desire to maximize the child's natural features, they are healthy. However, when concerns about external appearance become an obsession and regarded as an end unto themselves, they can become counterproductive, even though well intentioned. Thus, over many years of seeing children (and their parents) because of concerns regarding their growth, I have observed families with appropriate and healthy concerns and, on occasion, families whose concerns were likely to be harmful because they conveyed displeasure or dissatisfaction over something that the child was powerless to control. Fortunately, in my experience, these are the unusual and exceptional situations; nonetheless it serves to remind us of the critical need to balance appropriate concerns regarding external appearances with truly realistic expectations.

As a physician, it is frequently my responsibility to provide this balance; as an "expert" who is consulted regarding normal variations of growth, it is occasionally my task to restore the equilibrium between what families desire for their children and what is medically appropriate. It is precisely this sense of balance that Wende Gates seeks to provide in this book, and I believe that she has succeeded admirably.

Myron Genel, M.D.
Professor of Pediatrics,
Yale University School of Medicine

I N T R O D U C T I O N

"We find a delight in the beauty and happiness of children, that makes the heart too big for the body."
—Ralph Waldo Emerson

How fortunate we are to have our children! We watch them grow, nurture their minds and spirits, and help keep them healthy, fit, and attractive. During this process, we so delight in their beauty and happiness, we practically burst with pride, our hearts made "too big for the body."

But keeping children healthy, fit, and attractive is, as every parent knows, not always simple. Children too often run into problems that threaten their fitness and good looks.

What kinds of problems? Here are a few of the questions parents asked when I began researching this book. You may have similar questions.

"Annabelle has chicken pox. How can I help prevent scars?"

"What can I do for my overweight 11-year-old? She feels awful about herself, but I can't get her to lose weight."

"As a working mother, I can't cook every night. How can I be sure my two sons are getting adequate amounts of the right foods?"

As any parent will attest, these questions are not frivolous or vain. As adults, we know that if we look good, we feel better—and the very same credo applies to children. More and more we are learning that the way a child looks, or thinks he looks, affects the way he feels about himself. Kids, as a matter of fact, are made even more aware of their appearance by other children who lack the maturity to temper their judgmental and often hurtful remarks. It's truly a "jungle out there" at school and on the playground.

Problems such as unattractive teeth, poor fitness, being overweight, and poor personal hygiene all stand in the way of a child's socialization, and can undermine his or her confidence to do and be his or her best in school, sports, and social life. Along with helping children develop other important aspects of personality and character, part of our duty as parents is to help children maintain healthy good looks so that they can present their very best selves to the world. The rewards in self-esteem and self-confidence can last a lifetime.

Today there are more remedies and preventive measures available than ever before to insure children's good health and good looks. Children today do not have to suffer the way you and I may have had to with cavities, acne, some disfiguring birthmarks, and sexual discrimination in physical education, for example.

Our children do, however, face *new* threats to their health and appearance. A rapidly depleting ozone layer puts your child at a greater risk for skin cancer than when you played outside all summer. TV-viewing, video games, and fewer physical-education classes are all partly responsible for the fact that children today are heavier and less fit. Good nutrition is often sacrificed when working parents don't have time to prepare proper meals. My hope is that this book will make parents aware of the forces working against the good health and fitness of children so that they can take the proper steps to prevent or remedy problems—and maybe even learn a thing or two about their own health and good looks!

To achieve this, I have brought together the expertise of pediatricians, dermatologists, dentists, sports-medicine doctors, psychologists, nutritionists, fashion consultants, and children's hair stylists. They shared my belief that beauty is a word that truly applies to all children—especially in the eyes of their parents! A crooked smile, skinny legs, and even tragic disfigurations don't dampen our perceptions that all our children have beauty.

I have confined the focus of my book to ages 2 to 12, post-babyhood and pre-adolescence, since infancy and adolescence require very different information. This age group was of special interest to me—my own children were 3, 6, and 9 when I started this book. During the six years it took me to write this book I asked hundreds of parents for information on how they coped with their children's health and appearance-related problems. I also feel fortunate to have been able to ask the many medical experts I consulted the questions we all might like to ask our pediatricians or dermatologists or dentists, but feel they don't have time for. These experts are busy with medical care for children, but the quasi-medical questions such as "What is the safest way to have my daughter's ears pierced?" or "Is it safe for my children to drink diet soda?" need expert advice, too. This book provides the answers to these questions and hundreds more.

The children photographed in this book are children of friends or relatives, including my own children. All were a joy to work with, and I feel fortunate to have had such an enchanting subject. A few parents are also seen in this book, and they made great models, too!

I've watched many children grow and flourish during the years I've worked on this book. It has been said many times, but it's worth repeating that the precious years of childhood seem to fly by so quickly—they're gone before we realize it. I, for one, would give anything to capture my children's sweet young years in a vessel to store and be able to bring out like a living drama when I have the time and ease to appreciate it. We are all so busy during the child-rearing years, that we never seem to have enough time to fully enjoy our beloved children.

I have hoped to celebrate the beauty of the whole child in this book. I hope, too, that I've helped parents to see and to bring out their children's very best during this wonderful and magic time called childhood.

For my daughter, Julia Wende, with love

CHAPTER ONE

All About Your Child's Hair

Ah, the natural beauty of children's hair. If we adults had that shine, the silkiness, the natural streaks, half the hairdressing establishments would go under! The other half, however, would still be at work. For no matter how pretty the color and texture, children of all ages still need good haircuts as well as a regular at-home hair-care routine. Combining these two with good nutrition and some preventive hair-care measures will ensure the healthiest and best-looking hair possible for your child.

Fortunately, most children after age 2 or 3 care about the way their hair appears, and parents can channel this interest into good everyday habits. Your 3-year-old daughter may shriek at the mention of her twice-weekly shampoo, but she is also learning that her hair, when freshly washed and caught up in a bow, evokes a positive reaction from her parents and her friends at playgroup. Boys, from age 3 or 4 on, seem to walk taller after getting a good haircut. (If it's one they hate, tears may freely flow, embarrassing the guilty barber!) A well-groomed head of hair, even at age 2 or 3, instills a sense of pride and satisfaction in children and allows their natural beauty to shine.

■ Whose Hair Is It, Anyhow?

Hair is an emotionally charged subject, and deciding how the child's hair is worn can become a symbolic fight for power in the parent-child relationship at many junctures during the growing years. Most children develop a strong sense of how they want their hair to look early on, but when a 7-year-old expresses a wish for a tricolor Mohawk hairdo, we are caught between showing respect for our children's preference for how they want to look and encouraging realism and practicality. "Orange spikes might frighten Great-Grandma, dear.")

Having a good argument on hand when a child desires an outlandish hairdo is not as difficult as trying to influence our kids to wear their hair in a style we like when they want another. Some children are so intent on wearing their hair in a certain style that the parent may judge the child's wishes too important to undermine. An example is the girl who desper-

■ ■ ■ ■ ■ ■ ■ ■ ■

A DAZZLING ARRAY OF CHILDREN'S HAIR COLORS AND TEXTURES. THE SHAPE OF THE HAIR SHAFT AND HOW FAST OR SLOW HAIR GROWS DETERMINES THE DEGREE OF CURLINESS. COLOR, THICKNESS, AND CURLINESS ARE ALL DETERMINED BY HEREDITY.

ately wants to wear her hair extra long, halfway down her back, when her mother prefers a shorter cut. A possible solution in this case is a promise from the girl that she take extra time and care to keep her hair clean, brushed, and tangle-free, and, if she is younger, a promise to be patient and not to complain when her hair is brushed. Another parent might feel her child's haircut choice is simply so unaccept-able to her own sense of style that she will insist her child choose another.

As children grow older, a parent might find herself in an age-old dilemma: the more she disapproves of a style, the more the child desires it. There comes a time when kids want to move away from the parent-approved look, toward the antihero look of a rock star or TV hero.

Hairstyles are not important to all children, but for those kids who have strong opinions, lend an ear. In the end, both parent and child may have a say in the decision.

■■■■■■■■■■■■■■■■■■■■■■■■■■■■■■

How Does Children's Hair Differ from Adults'?

Whether its owner is 5 or 50, human hair has the same makeup. True, a child's head of hair is usually shinier than it will be when she grows up. It's also thinner in diameter and grows faster than an adult's. But the difference ends there.

You may already know that hair itself is dead, like a fingernail, but grows from a very alive follicle just under the scalp. The hair shaft is made of three layers enclosed in a fibrous sheath. Each one is structurally unique. The inner layer, or *medulla*, has large cells containing keratin and re-flects light in its own fashion, creating your child's own unique "sheen." The middle layer, or *cortex*, is made up of scales that give a child's hair that enviable shine when freshly shampooed and brushed. The outer layer is called the *cuticle*. Hair specialists speculate that since children's hair grows very fast, the cuticle doesn't suffer the daily abuse of brushing and exposure to the elements for so long a period and is, as a result, shinier.

While the basic makeup of hair is exactly the same, the number of hair follicles each child is born with, the diameter of each hair, the color, and the shape of each hair shaft is different, which is what gives each head of hair its own unique look. Even growth rates and growth styles differ from child to child. Straight-haired children have round hair shafts that grow out of hair follicles at even rates, and wavy-haired ones have oval-shaped shafts that grow in long, bending cycles. Kids with kinky hair have hair shafts that are flat when seen in cross section, and bend from side to side in short cycles when growing.

◼ Follicle Folly

The fact that the number of hair follicles is fixed at birth and there will never be any more or less may be a little-known one, since many parents in various cultures shave their infants' heads to "stimulate the scalp and make the hair grow in thick," as one Italian friend suggested. Fifty years ago, my husband's aunt went so far as to not only shave her children's scalps, but also cut their eyebrows and eyelashes!

Dr. David Orentreich, assistant clinical professor of dermatology at the Mt. Sinai School of Medicine, states, "When you shave hair, you don't affect the roots one iota. All you're doing is removing all the dead hair shafts. Hair is going to shed and grow in beautifully anyway." What shaving does, he says, is allow the hair to grow in at a uniform rate, perhaps making the baby's hair appear thicker.

◼◼◼◼◼◼◼◼◼

ALTHOUGH IT HAS NEVER BEEN CUT, HAYLEY'S HAIR HAS UNEVEN LENGTHS DUE TO FRICTION FROM SLEEPING IN THE CRIB AND SHORTER OR LONGER GROWING PHASES IN DIFFERENT AREAS OF THE SCALP.

Hair thickness depends on two factors, the most important being the thickness of the diameter of the individual hair shaft, and then, to a lesser degree, the number of hair follicles. Your child's hair quality is almost completely a matter of genetics. Gulping extra vitamins and adding special foods to your diet during pregnancy will do nothing to improve your child's hair quality. And only a devastating illness or injury can adversely affect hair-follicle development in utero.

Children with red hair are born with the fewest number of hair follicles and their hair shafts are usually the thickest in diameter, giving redheads like the main character in *Annie* a thick, full head of hair. Blondes are born with the most hair follicles on their scalps—about 140,000—while brunettes have approximately 120,000 and redheads only 90,000.

Color Changes

OVER THE SUMMER THIS BOY'S HAIR COLOR CHANGED FROM LIGHT BROWN TO BRIGHT BLOND. BECAUSE THE DIAMETER OF CHILDREN'S HAIR IS SMALLER THAN ADULTS', THEIR HAIR IS MORE SUSCEPTIBLE TO THE SUN'S OXIDIZING EFFECTS.

While the number of hair follicles remains fixed, hair color usually undergoes numerous changes in childhood, and, to a lesser degree, all throughout life. One first-time mother was amazed to see the dramatic change in her daughter's hair color in her first five years of life. She watched her little girl's dark shock of hair present at birth fall out, then grow in blond and straight. At age 3, her hair grew dark blond. By 4, it had become browner and thicker, eventually developing waviness by age 5. (According to children's hairdressers, a child's hair texture is usually established by age 5.)

This wide color swing is not unusual; hair usually lightens a shade after the hair present at birth falls out, then darkens a shade or two in the following years. Changes are less dramatic between ages 5 and 10, but as puberty begins, hair transforms again, usually darkening, coarsening, and if hair is wavy or curly to begin with, becoming curlier or frizzier.

Why do we see so many color and texture changes in our kids' hair in the twelve years of childhood? In a word, hormones. Until the age of 18, a special "human growth hormone," or "HGH," is produced in large amounts, accelerating the hair growth cycle. (HGH output slows down as we age.) A child's hair will grow about 2.5 millimeters per day, while an adult's rate has slowed to .45 millimeters a day. HGH also influences the melanin (thus determining hair color) and the gradual thickening of each strand of hair.

Not only is children's hair growing at a faster rate than adults', but more hair is growing at any given time. This is how it works. In normal hair, each strand goes through a three-stage growth cycle: anagen (or the growing stage), which lasts from two to six years (although babies and toddlers have a much shorter anagen phase, so that the whole head of hair is not in this stage at the same time!); catagen (or regressive stage when growth slows), lasting up to two weeks; and telogen (the resting phase), taking three to six months, after which hair falls out.

In adults, 85 to 90 percent of hair is in the anagen or growing phase at any given time. In children, however, more than 90 percent of hair follicles are in the anagen phase, giving children a full head of hair, compensating for its thinner diameter.

■ ■

Good Nutrition—Great Hair

Hair is the first place on the body to show nutritional deficiency. Because nature assigns hair growth a low priority for available nutrients, especially protein, the rest of the body takes up most of what is at hand, and if there is a shortage, the hair goes without. If a child is malnourished, both hair and nails suffer and become brittle and lackluster. Hair may even fall out.

Parents and caretakers are usually careful about children's diet, so that this is of very little concern for most babies, toddlers, and young children (and of great concern for underdeveloped countries and areas in our country where adequate food and nutrition are not available). If children are getting enough calories and protein, hair and nails will grow strong even if their diet is not perfectly balanced, so don't worry about the child who is currently refusing all vegetables or has been on a steady diet of peanut butter and jelly for the last six months. An unbalanced diet is rarely the cause of thin or unshiny hair.

What will cause hair loss? Severe deficiency and actual overdosing on vitamin A or D. Deficiency of these vitamins is usually caused by illness. Extreme obesity can also cause hair loss because of the havoc it wreaks with hormone levels. And severe caloric restriction, such as in cases of anorexia among older children, can change the quality and slow the growth of hair.

Also affecting children's hair are colds, toothaches, fever, and even emotional stress. Sometimes a stripe in the hair will appear approximately three months after a high fever or major physical trauma, such as blood loss. Since hair cells are the most rapidly dividing ones in the body, hair is extremely responsive to physical stress.

Can parents help achieve "super hair" for their children with the right nutrition? No. Not even vitamin supplements will change the quality of hair. Aside from the damage caused by abuse from blow-drying, hot rollers, or constant braiding or cornrowing, your child's glorious shiny curls or thinner head of hair are a direct result of genetics.

Because hair can be a barometer for health problems, any dramatic changes in your child's hair color or texture should be reported to your pediatrician or dermatologist. The simple formula for your child's healthy hair and nails is good nutrition. Keep pumping in those green leafy vegetables, whole grains, and low-fat yogurt, Mom and Dad. Your child's head of hair is the crowning glory to his or her general good health and good looks.

■■■■■■■■■■■■■■■■■■■■■■■■■■■■■■■

Establishing a Hair-Care Routine . . . the Earlier the Better

There is a point at which even naturally great-looking, well-nourished hair will go unnoticed. To keep your child's hair at its glorious best, your child (and you, if your child is young) must be willing to participate in a daily hair-care routine. Some children respond better than others to the rituals of hair care. One young mother, Edna, shampoos the long hair of her 4-year-old daughter, Lindsay, then styles it, often with a blow dryer, *every single day*. She then adds a pretty hair accessory. Although many of us would find this exercise too time-consuming for an everyday routine (and maddening with an unwilling child), this mother and daughter thoroughly enjoy the hour together. Lindsay has cooperated since she was a baby. They talk and fuss, Lindsay often taking a brush to her mother's hair. It is an evocative scene, a favorite subject immortalized by painters throughout the centuries.

Kathy Hess, a New York hairdresser, has been cutting children's hair for over fifteen years. She feels that parents and children today don't have time for such elaborate care. Her advice is music to working parents' ears: "I suggest keeping hair-care routines to a minimum, whether it is for an adult or for a child," she says. "Twenty minutes a day on your hair is too much. I believe if you have a decent haircut and you use good products, there is no reason you or your child can't simply wash and wear without curling, crimping, or styling with a blow dryer."

Whether you decide to devote a lot or a little amount of time to your child's hair care, two rituals *must* be observed: daily brushing to keep hair smooth and tangle-free, and frequent shampooing. Bangs should be kept short enough so children's vision is not impaired. Messy, unclean hair, especially among older children, will possibly act as a social barrier. This lack of personal care can get in the way of other, more important, aspects of their social and emotional development—especially when peers start judging each other at age 4 or 5 and then again with a vengeance at age 8, 9, or 10. Parents should let children, from infancy on up, know that having a clean, healthy, attractive head of hair is going to make them feel and look better. Parents should help children become increasingly independent in their own hair care, certainly by age 7, although parents will want to counsel kids on hair care all the way through the teen years.

TYPICAL OF MANY 2- TO 5-YEAR-OLDS, LINDSAY TOOK THE SCISSORS TO HER OWN HAIR AND CREATED AN UNUSUAL STYLE OF BANGS. MANY PARENTS ARE DEVASTATED WHEN THEY FIND THEIR CHILD HAS HACKED AWAY THEIR LOVELY BABY LOCKS. NEW, SHORTER STYLES ARE OFTEN REQUIRED TO CORRECT CHOPPED-UP HAIR.

The Shampoo

When asked how she shampooed her four young children's hair, Kathi, 36, said, "The fastest way I can." There is a logical process, though, which even Kathi probably observes. Read on for some tips that may help you and your child actually enjoy the shampoo ritual.

Until children reach the age when they feel comfortable shampooing in the shower—anywhere from age 4 to 11—shampoos are most easily accomplished in the bathtub amidst rubber duckies and other toys. Keep hand soap out of the tub until *after* the shampoo, since these suds will leave a residue and dull your child's hair when rinsed in it. Shampoo your child's hair a few minutes before getting out of the tub, because sitting around in a bathtub full of shampoo and/or conditioner may cause urinary-tract infections for both boys and girls. *Then* use hand soap for the rest of the body.

Remember that your choice of shampoo is important. Choose one that gives your child's hair luster and manageability. It should also get his hair clean—free of skin debris, hair-product residue, dirt, and Play-Doh! (If you don't already have a favorite shampoo for your child, see the chart on page 16 for one tailored for your child's hair type.) Some parents prefer a no-tears baby shampoo for toddlers and young children, although some hairdressers feel these shampoos tend to strip too much oil from the hair. The dermatologists I interviewed do recommend baby shampoos, because these products have the fewest sensitizers, or ingredients that may cause allergic reactions. Baby shampoos are perfect for any child who has a skin condition or a sensitive scalp. By the way, you should know that most shampoos are extra thick and concentrated. You can save money by diluting almost any shampoo with water. Simply take a clear plastic bottle and pour in one half of the shampoo. Fill to the top with water. This gives you twice as much shampoo and makes it easier to apply.

If your child's hair is becoming greasy as he or she approaches puberty, use a shampoo that's more emulsifying, or "sudsier." If your child's hair is thin and flyaway, use a shampoo designed for "dry" hair. Adult shampoos are fine for children, but, if you like, why not try some of the baby and child shampoos that are new on the market? There are lots of wonderful new kids' products now available. "Herbal" or "natural" shampoos are also a good choice. They are often milder than other shampoos and are usually excellent for children. Supporters of herbal beautifiers claim that plants such as rosemary, thyme, cucumber extract, chamomile, and aloe have been used in households for generations and have stood the test of time with respect to safety for children as well as adults. Dr. Sidney Hurwitz, a dermatologist at Yale University School of Medicine, warns, however, that poison ivy is "natural," too. "Don't be fooled by the word 'natural' or 'herbal,'" he says. "Ingredients in these shampoos can be just as irritating as the ingredients in other shampoos."

Keep experimenting with shampoos to find several you like for your kids. And change their shampoo occasionally. Children's hair, like adults', can get used to a shampoo and then resist it, leaving hair less than shiny bright.

Your older children may also need your care in checking that they get all of the shampoo and/or conditioner out of their hair. When their hair looks dull, limp, or stringy, it is a

Suds Success

The following six steps will smooth the way to a perfect shampoo.

1. Take a small amount of shampoo and massage it in your hands to bring it to body temperature. Shampoo straight out of the container may feel icy to a young child's scalp.

2. Gently apply warmed shampoo to the crown of his head, carefully avoiding any spills over the forehead into his eyes.

3. Work shampoo into his hair. If he enjoys it, massage his scalp a little. From age 18 months on, you can ask him if he would like to wash his own hair, starting with his own massage at the crown of the head. Remind him that the shampoo should reach his front hairline and temples to get his hair completely clean. Keep the suds fairly "dry" so that shampoo doesn't drip into his eyes.

4. Rinse with clean, warm water, if possible, using a hand-held shower or a container filled with warm water from the faucet. Some children steadfastly insist on lying down, with only their faces above water, and rinsing their hair in the bathwater. This is fine if the water is clean and the child gets out of the tub soon after this rinse, as mentioned

above. If your child tends to have ear or fungus infections ("swimmer's ear"), submerging his head in the bathwater should be discouraged. If your water faucet is high enough, rinsing can be accomplished there, although most children don't like the awkward angle at which they must remain. A second lathering is not usually necessary unless Junior has been rolling in the mud all afternoon.

5. Should parents use a conditioner after the shampoo? "Of course," say the experts. Dermatologists and hairdressers alike agree that children should use a conditioner after every shampoo or every few shampoos. Conditioners reduce static, add body and shine by coating the hair with protein, cut down on breakage, and, best of all, make your child's hair easier and less painful to comb—with fewer tears from tangles.

6. Pamela Plummer, manager of Shooting Star hair salon at FAO Schwarz in New York City, recommends running a wide-toothed comb or a "pick" through your child's hair as you apply conditioner. This gets rid of tangles before the final combing. Rinse well after applying conditioner. Use the wide-toothed comb once again after rinsing. Brushing wet hair should be avoided, since it increases breakage.

sure sign that they are not rinsing well enough. Remind them that all products must be completely rinsed out. Some older children might even enjoy an old-fashioned lemon- or vinegar-and-water rinse. (One-half lemon or two tablespoons vinegar in 8 ounces warm water in a plastic container.) Remind kids to take care not to get the rinse in their eyes.

Use the following ideas to help keep soap suds out of your child's eyes:

■ Use a hand-held shower for rinsing.

■ Have your child hold a washcloth on his forehead and tip his head back during rinsing.

■ One mother found the following solution: Marilyn sudsed up her child's hair in the bathtub and transferred him to a kitchen countertop and a towel. While her son was lying on his back, Marilyn supported his head and used the sink sprayer to rinse his hair. This allowed her body to be closer to him, giving him more security.

■ Use a "shampoo hat," which can be found in notions catalogs. This ingenious cap allows parents to wash hair without fear of getting soap or water in kids' eyes.

A SHAMPOO HAT, FOUND IN NOTIONS CATALOGS, PHARMACIES, OR CHILDREN'S STORES, CAN HELP KEEP SOAP OUT OF KIDS' EYES DURING SHAMPOOS.

Easing into It

Giving a young child the perfect shampoo is a breeze if they are *willing.* The cooperative ones allow their hair to be sudsed up and never make a peep during rinsing. For the more reluctant ones, usually of toddler age, the fear of getting water or soap in their eyes makes the shampoo a threat to their very existence: Mom approaching the child in the tub clutching the shampoo bottle is transformed into the Wicked Queen offering Snow White the poisonous apple!

These fears can get in the way of keeping hair clean if they are not dealt with early. Even when a parent attempts the following remedies, the child may still hold on to this "shampoo fear," and growing out of it (usually by age 8 or 9) is sometimes the only answer. Most parents can find success, however, by following the instructions on page 13.

DON'T	DO
Let the child's fears get you upset. Your anger and anxiety will spill over from you to your child. The gentler and more patient you are, the more quickly this problem will find a solution.	Let your child know exactly what you'll be doing, describing each step aloud a moment before you actually do it. Remind her how nice it feels to wash one's hair. You may also let her try to wash her own hair.
Proceed with haste and exasperation, using force to accomplish the shampoo. This might create fear and distrust in the child.	Play-demonstration to help her anxiety. If she has a washable doll, show her how you wash its hair. Let her wash its hair next. Perhaps she has watched *you* shampoo in the shower.
Accept your child's refusal to shampoo. Act confident and calm and gently persist in 'attempting to wash his hair. He will sense the clarity of your mission and nine out of ten times will back down and allow a shampoo.	Hold your child firmly and support her body while you are shampooing and rinsing her hair. Children are often insecure in a slippery tub full of soap suds and water. If she is old enough, ask your child how she would feel most comfortable getting shampooed and rinsed. Some children will end up in Mom's or Dad's lap, or outside the tub, getting water everywhere! Once she gets used to the idea that her hair can be washed painlessly, she'll probably stay in the tub.

■■■■■■■■■■■■■■■■■■■■■■■■■■■■■■■■

How Often Should I Shampoo?

Parents report shampooing as often as every day to every ten days. Age, of course, is a factor. Babies can have their hair washed every time they are bathed. A 3-year-old whose time is mostly spent at nursery school, or at day care, may not need a shampoo for four or five days, whereas an active 10-year-old who plays soccer or other gritty outdoor sports may need a nightly shampoo. Girls age 9 or 10 or older boys who are entering puberty may be producing more oil and some body odor and may feel more comfortable shampooing every night. Opt for a mild shampoo in this case.

Dermatologists have as widely varying opinions about shampoo frequency as parents. Dr. Neil Sadick says, "When you wash your hair, more shedding occurs than during a normal day. Combing or brushing the hair after a shampoo

■ ■ ■ ■ ■ ■ ■ ■ ■

LIGHT-HAIRED CHILDREN MAY SPORT GREEN STREAKS IN THEIR HAIR BY SUMMER'S END— CHLORINATED WATER WITH COPPER IS THE CULPRIT. WASH YOUR CHILD'S HAIR WITH A CHLORINE-REMOVING SHAMPOO SUCH AS ULTRA SWIM, MATRIX'S ALTERNATE ACTION, OR PAUL MITCHELL'S THREE AFTER EACH SWIM TO RESTORE HAIR TO ITS NATURAL STATE.

SAFETY ALERT

Maintaining a Safe Environment in the Bathroom

The bathroom can be a dangerous place for children. The most dangerous of all scenarios is an electrical appliance near a bathtub full of water. My recommendation is to keep hair dryers out of the bathroom when children are bathing until children reach their late teens. Even then, adults, as well as children, have been electrocuted by a plugged-in hair dryer slipping off the sink or a holder into the shower or tub. The Consumer Product Safety Commission estimates that seventeen people, most of them children, die every year from electrical shocks caused by hair dryers that have gotten wet.

Luckily, many hair dryers, including most Conair and all Clairol Inc. dryers, are now made with a "ground fault circuit interrupter," which shuts off the dryer when it gets wet. The Underwriters Laboratories Inc., a nonprofit group that sets standards for the electrical-appliance industry, set January 1, 1991, as the date of compliance for this shutoff feature. Check your dryer for this safety feature. (See page 18 for more hair-dryer safety information.)

Whether or not your hair dryer was made before or after 1991, always unplug it and place it out of reach after each use in any bathroom in the house when there are young children around. Many countries in Europe don't even allow electrical outlets in bathrooms precisely because of the danger they pose.

Make the bathtub safe from kiddie slips and bumps by using a nonskid rubber bath mat or textured bath decals for safe footing. To cover those often-dangerous bathtub spouts, cylinder-shaped foam-rubber products can be purchased at many children's and bed-and-bath stores. Because of hard surfaces in a bathroom, a fall there can have more serious consequences than anywhere else in the house, so keep floors and surfaces as free of toys and other objects as possible. Rubber-lined bathroom rugs that prevent slips are also wise investments.

also increases mechanical breakage of the hair. It is not necessary to shampoo more than once every three or four days or when hair feels oily." Other doctors feel that washing your child's hair every day can be healthy for the scalp. Dr. David Orentreich says, "It removes dead scale, helps prevent dandruff, and doesn't strip away oil as many people expect."

How frequently you wish to shampoo your child's hair is up to you, your child, and your various needs and lifestyle. Generally speaking, it is probably not wise to shampoo more than once a day or less than once every seven days.

■■■■■■■■■■■■■■■■■■■■■■■■■■■■■■■■■

Your Child's Hair Type: Which Shampoo and Conditioner Are Best?

The chart on the next page can be referred to off and on for many years. Your child's hair texture will probably change— or may become a combination of types. When baby hair grows out, a new hair texture will often grow in at the same time, resulting in a combination "baby-fine" and "average" hair type. Or at age 10 or 11, an "average" hair type may suddenly become an "oily" hair type. "Coarse" hair is any hair that doesn't shine; it is often curly. (Redheads usually have coarse hair.) Unless a medical condition exists, children don't have "dry" hair. "Oily" hair usually develops only among older kids. Active children who play outdoors frequently and engage in sports every day can also follow tips for care of "oily" hair.

■■■■■■■■■■■■■■■■■■■■■■■■■■■■■■■■■

Styling Products—Are They Right for Kids?

Gels, mousses, hand-pumped hair sprays—they're all fine for kids, according to the hairdressers I interviewed. Kids' hair—unprocessed and healthy—can handle any of these products. They're also water-soluble and wash out easily. Some gels or mousses, when used every day, may interact with the sun to cause a color change. Have your child use these products just for special occasions.

Shampoos and Conditioners—Which Is Best for Your Child's Hair Type?

	BABY-FINE OR WISPY	AVERAGE HAIR	BLACK HAIR	COARSE HAIR	OILY HAIR IN OLDER CHILDREN
SHAMPOO (pH balance, a number assigned to shampoos that measures the alkaline level, should be rated anywhere from 3 to 7, assuring mild alkalinity. Most shampoos fall into this category.)	Mild, herbal, or baby shampoo.	Shampoo of choice.	Mildest black or other shampoo of choice on market. Experiment with richer shampoos as child grows.	"Moisturizing" and herbal shampoos.	Shampoo of choice, but shampoo more frequently. Experiment with "oily" hair products.
CONDITIONER	A mild conditioner "plumps" fine or wispy hair. Condition after every shampoo or once every two or three shampoos.	Conditioner of choice. Condition after every shampoo or once every two or three shampoos.	Conditioner designed for black hair after each shampoo. When child is older, hot-oil treatment or other "pack" conditioners for ten min. once every two to three weeks.	Rich conditioner after each shampoo. Older child may try "pack" conditioner.	Rinse with cider vinegar, or lemon juice (2 tbs. to 8 oz. water). Use conditioner once every three shampoos or apply conditioner to ends only. If your child's hair is short, a conditioning shampoo may be substituted.

■   ## Home-Grown Hints for Children's Hair Care

A wad of bubble gum enmeshed in your 6-year-old daughter's shoulder-length hair? Kids forcing you to take out a second mortgage by going through a bottle of conditioner a week? No problem. Below are some helpful hints for some down-home problems.

■ Use creamy peanut butter to loosen up that bubble gum or other sticky substances buried in your child's tresses.

Apply directly to hair-gum ball and use your fingers or a wide-toothed comb to gently pull the object out of the hair. If you're fresh out of peanut butter, you may substitute mineral oil. A shampoo is in order.

■ Condition your child's hair with any of the following: mayonnaise; warm olive or vegetable oil; mashed avocado; or a whipped egg. Shampoo well to avoid smelling like a salad.

■ Use club soda to lift out copper and chlorine from your child's hair left greenish from the pool all summer.

■■■■■■■■■■■■■■■■■■■■■■■■■■■■■■■■■■■■■■■

All About Blow-Drying Your Child's Hair

If time is short and your daughter's hair is long and thick, hand-held hair dryers can be very handy. But don't blow-dry every time she washes! Relying on blow-drying after each shampoo can result in hair breakage or at least brittleness or lack of shine. One dermatologist warns that wet hair can be further damaged if it is blown dry and combed at the same time. Dr. David Orentreich says, "When hair is wet, it is very elastic. While blow-drying and combing, you stretch the hair and heat it at the same time. This results in permanently stretched and deformed hair which is thin and very susceptible to breakage."

Blow-drying your child's hair is fine on occasion—once or twice a week should be the limit. Dr. Orentreich recommends air-drying first, or at least towel-drying, then blow-drying when the child's hair is just slightly damp. Heat should be set on a warm temperature—never hot. If your daughter is as unhappy with the heat on the back of her neck as my daughter is, switch to a cool setting. To avoid hair damage, keep moving the dryer all around the child's head instead of drying one section at a time. Use a vent brush with a ball-tipped bristle to allow aeration and make detangling easier, or simply use your other hand to fluff the child's hair. If your daughter has very long hair and will cooperate, you can ask her to bend over when finishing off drying, flipping her hair inside out to create a fuller look.

If hair is tangled, simply apply a small amount of creme conditioner to the tangle, then brush. You can even try a protein-rich moisturizing mousse to give your child's hair a fuller, glossier look and make it easier to style. "Don't tug your child's hair when styling," says Dr. David Orentreich. "Special care must be taken for children's finer hair."

■ Introducing Your Child to the Dryer-Dragon

Like shampooing, blow-drying can be an anxiety-fraught process for children who are fearful, especially children like 18-month-old Ali, who is going through a noise-sensitive period, not uncommon for children her age. For her, sounds from vacuums, food processors, and doorbells can produce tears of fear and perhaps even pain (children's eardrums can be very sensitive to loud noises). A hot, noisy blow dryer near Ali's head at this stage would terrify her. For now, Jan, Ali's mother, gently towel-dries her hair and keeps Ali in a warm area while her shoulder-length hair air-dries.

After Ali grows out of this fear period, Jan can test Ali's reaction to the blow dryer by watching her reaction to her own blow-drying process. This learning by example, mentioned in the shampoo section, is the best way to introduce blow-drying and other body-care methods to children. If she is not afraid, set the blow dryer at room temperature or a comfortable warm setting and let her feel the air with her hand about four inches from the end of the nozzle. Let her watch you blow-dry a washable doll's hair. If it's convenient, arrange a trip to a children's hairdresser to let her observe other children getting their hair blown dry. She may allow a hairdresser at a salon to blow her hair dry before she lets you—one of the many ironies of motherhood! Keep asking at home—and one day she'll be willing.

Before using your own hand-held hair dryer on your child or buying a new one, consider this checklist for safety points:

■ Check whether or not your dryer has a "ground fault circuit interrupter," mentioned on page 14. This device shuts off electricity when wet. (Most were installed after Jan. 1, 1991.) And again, never leave the hair dryer plugged in. I've already mentioned hair-dryer safety in a bathroom, but a child can easily turn on the dryer in any room, causing it to vibrate, move, and possibly burn the child.

Unplug and place dryers out of reach when they are not in use. If you drop the hair dryer at any time, have it checked professionally before using it again. A malfunctioning dryer can burn and possibly explode. Always test the dryer yourself for a few minutes before drying your child's hair.

■ If you are using an old hair dryer, check for a screen that covers the air-intake port. Children's hair can be easily sucked into this fan—it may have happened to you! This can be a painful experience, and it's one that can be easily avoided. Most models now include the safety screen.

■ 1000 watts should be the maximum power for your children's hair; 1000-watt dryers will help keep Mom's hair from overdrying, too.

■ If you are buying a hair dryer, try to find the quietest machine available. This is obviously easier on children's sensitive ears.

■ Cords should be long enough to give you flexibility with your wandering little one. While some children will sit patiently during blow-drying and styling, others, especially younger ones, may get fidgety. Look for the "UL" or "Underwriters Laboratory" seal on your hair dryer. The Underwriters Laboratories organization tests for the safety of all cord electric appliances.

■■■■■■■■■■■■■■■■■■■■■■■■■■■■■■■■

No-Tears Brushing

Lucky is the parent whose child loves having her hair brushed! Brushing and combing stimulate blood circulation in the scalp, remove loose hair scales, and help distribute oil on hair shafts. Less fortunate are the children and parents who find hair-brushing a painful experience. Peter, a 35-year-old divorced father, gets upset and angry when his 7-year-old daughter flees the room as soon as she sees him reach for her comb and brush. "Lizzie's long hair is a mess all weekend," Peter complains. "She'll hardly brush her own hair and definitely won't let me do it. She says it hurts too much. What's wrong?"

Lizzie's not being just obstinate. Many children, unlike adults, experience pain when hair is brushed—especially if their hair is long, thick, and curly. There are physical reasons for this. Dr. Neil Sadick explains that a child's scalp is more sensitive than ours because it is softer and more pliable. Also, since hair textures are constantly changing during childhood, baby hair can tangle with newer textures. These two factors can make hairbrushing an unhappy experience for children until they reach age 10 or 11, when the scalp cuticle has toughened sufficiently to withstand more pressure and more pulling. But until then, what's a parent to do? Here are some pointers.

■ Start with the proper equipment. The hairdresser's favorite seems to be a rubber-based brush with either natural bristles or nylon. Natural bristles are preferred, although plastic or wooden brushes with nylon or synthetic bristles can be fine as long as the bristle ends are rounded. Sharp ends can break hair and irritate a child's sensitive scalp. Test a child's brush in your palm before buying it. If it feels spiky to you, don't buy it. Opt for a softer, more pliable brush, making sure that the bristles are long enough to reach your child's scalp. (Soft-bristled baby brushes are fine for infants up to age 2 if there is little hair growth.) Black children and children who have tangle-prone hair need a brush with flexible widely spaced bristles that catch less hair and don't tug. Combs for children should follow the same rule. Avoid sharp ends and choose a wide-toothed comb for less hair trauma and breakage. Keep these brushes and combs clean by soaking and scrubbing them in warm water, a few drops of shampoo, and a few drops of ammonia or a tablespoon of baking soda. Rinse with warm water and let air-dry. Each family member should have his or her own brush and comb. Neither a borrower nor lender be!

■ When you want to brush your child's hair, approach him gently in a pleasant, comfortable setting. Don't try to wash the breakfast dishes, answer the phone, and brush your son's hair all at the same time. Dr. David Orentreich suggests that younger children may have fantasies about hair we're not attuned to and may view hairbrushing as an attack. "When you brush a child's hair, you can't necessarily use the same pressure. Remember that our scalps

■ ■ ■ ■ ■ ■ ■ ■ ■ ■

BRUSHING FOR BLACK CHILDREN IS MADE EASY WITH A HAIRBRUSH OR COMB THAT HAS WIDELY SPACED BRISTLES THAT CATCH LESS HAIR.

are not as sensitive as children's, and you must take this into account when brushing."

■ When brushing tangled hair, try one of the following techniques. Hold your hand on the crown of the child's head to stay the hair. This minimizes pulling directly on the scalp. Brush downward to tease out the tangles. You might also try to section off hair in the back and gently brush the nape of the neck first, working upward, section by section. Take care not to bear down on the scalp with a brush or comb. This can cause abrasions or at least hurt the child's scalp, making her all the more brush-shy!

■ A good haircut and shaping will help keep hair tangle-free. Conditioning after shampooing will also keep hair more manageable, as will "detangling" hair products. If you hit a snarl while brushing, spray diluted conditioner on the tangle. Never pull or yank at the tangle. This will cause hair loss, pain, and balking next time hair has to be brushed!

■ Let the child try his hand at brushing as he grows. He'll apply just the right pressure. Remind him to brush the back of his head, which he doesn't see as he looks into the mirror.

■ Even though a parent may be as careful as possible, a child may still run when she spots a brush. One 8-year-old girl's mother finally had to resort to cutting her daughter's hair short after years of struggling with her Alice in Wonderland–style hairdo. "It was time for a change anyhow," says her mother, "and now she actually enjoys brushing and styling her hair."

■■■■■■■■■■■■■■■■■■■■■■■■■■■■■■■■■

A Hundred Strokes—Myth or Must for the Under-12 Set?

One dermatologist recommends brushing children's hair minimally—only to keep hair well-groomed. He warns that brushing increases hair breakage, especially when wet. Brushing or combing with a wide-toothed comb is the only sensible way to groom children's hair, according to this doctor.

Our other expert, children's hairdresser Pamela Plummer, feels this rule applies to children only until age 5. Before 5, children's hair is fragile and their scalp too tender to brush with any regularity. After age 5, however, 100 strokes a couple times a week is great for kids, according to Pamela. "Brushing helps coat the hair with oil that fills in the tiny holes and cracks in the hair shafts," she says. "This helps keep hair shining."

Certainly wait until age 4 or 5 to start a hair-brushing routine of more than twenty strokes. One hundred strokes for a child requires great patience and seems excessive, to my way of thinking. Twenty-five strokes once or twice a week should be adequate, and only if you and your child really enjoy this grooming.

■■■■■■■■■■■■■■■■■■■■■■■■■■■■■■■■■■■■■

Fun Hair Styles

■ The Ponytail

Younger girls seem to like higher ponytails, while older ones tend to favor ponytails gathered at the nape of the neck. Ponytails are sheer simplicity. Simply start with clean, well-brushed hair and gather to the point where you want it to sit. Secure the ponytail with a covered rubber band or other pretty hair accessory. No plain rubber bands, please! These will break or damage hair. Avoid pulling hair too tightly. This can cause "traction alopecia," or hair loss due to pulling.

■ Ponytail Variations

■ Leave out one band of hair on either side of the head to wrap around the ponytail.

■ Braid the ponytail and secure the end of the braid with a covered rubber band or other accessory. High ponytails look pretty for this style.

■ Braid two small sections of hair, beginning at the temples. Catch them back with the rest of the loose hair in a ponytail.

■ Part your child's hair in the center from the forehead back to the nape of the neck. Create two small high ponytails, braid them, and wrap around in a wheel. Secure with hairpins or bobby pins. This is a "pinwheel" ponytail.

■ The Alice in Wonderland look. Part your daughter's hair from the top of the ear across the center of the head to the other ear. Pull the hair above the part back, and fasten just below the crown of the head. This section falls over the rest of the loose hair to mix with it. A classic!

THIS 8-YEAR-OLD NATIVE AMERICAN BOY OF THE SHINNECOCK TRIBE ON LONG ISLAND WEARS CLASSIC BRAIDS.

■ Braids

Most of us know how to make simple braids: simply divide hair into three equal parts and alternate them left over center, right over center, and continuing until all hair is braided and held with an elastic, barrette, or other stay.

Your child can wear one braid in back, or one braid on each side, Native American style. You can also use braids to "kink" your child's hair, making eight to ten braids all around the head, and having your child sleep on them overnight to create a Pre-Raphaelite look.

The French Braid

One of the prettiest and most popular braids is the French braid. It takes a little practice, but if your daughter is cooperative, you can weave a beautiful look in just minutes. Here's how.

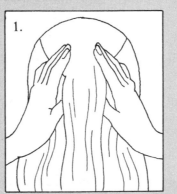
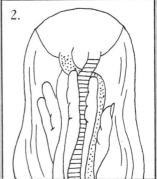

1. As always, start with clean, brushed hair. Facing the back of the head, create a triangular section at the top of the head, using a comb or your fingernail, bringing one point of the triangle about two inches below the crown. Separate this hair from the triangle into three equal sections.
2. Braid once. Hold these three sections with your right hand, palm facing you, placing one section between the thumb and forefinger, one between the forefinger and the middle finger, and one between the middle and ring finger.

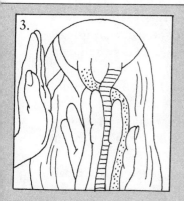
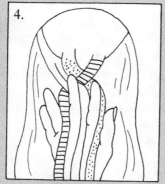
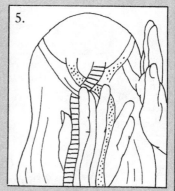

3. With the pinky fingernail of your left hand, slice a section of hair about ½ to ⅓ inch wide below the original triangle on the left side. Pull this hair into the left section of braid.

4. Cross this larger section over to the middle spot, replacing the original center section, which moves over to the left.

5. Shift the three sections of hair to your left hand, in mirror image of your right hand. Gather a slice of hair from the right side and add to the section that is now on the right. Place this thicker section across the center so it now rests in the center position.

6. Continue this process all the way down the head, making the lower slices a little thinner than the ones before. When there is no more hair left to gather, continue with a regular braid until all hair is gathered.

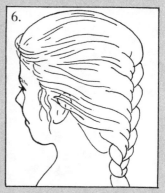

If a looser braid is desired, hold hair away from the head when braiding. Pull out some loose hairs at the temple, if you like.

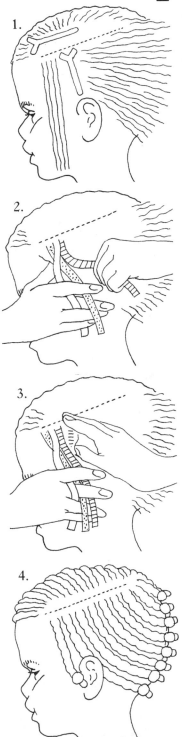

1.

2.

3.

4.

Cornrow Braiding

This style, made famous among white Americans by Bo Derek in the movie, *10*, has been a favorite among African Americans for years. Its origins are African—each tribe had distinct braids, and varying styles within the tribe indicated status.

Creating uniform braids requires practice and patience, but the results can be beautiful on a child. Take care not to braid so tightly that hair is pulled and causes pain. Children's hair and scalps are more delicate than adults' and damage may result from continual pulling. Make rows looser than you would for an adult and give your child's hair a rest from time to time. Cornrows may be left in for five to seven days by using a cotton scarf at night to prevent loosening. Adults often have "extensions" of synthetic or human hair added to their braids, but this is not recommended for children since extensions require special care.

The following are the most basic instructions for cornrow braids. Once you know how you can braid hair in any design or direction you like.

Comb through clean hair. Add a pomade to make hair shiny, if desired. Create a part on one side so that the final effect will have braids originating from this part. If you'd like a look more like Bo Derek's, simply start all cornrows from the face, ending up in the back of the head.

1. Separate a small "row" of hair starting at one side of the head. Hold rest of hair back with clips.
2. Take top section of row and separate into three sections to braid. Instead of braiding left over center, right over center as seen in the French braid (page 24), the sections are crossed UNDER the center section, left UNDER center, right UNDER center.
3. After making first braid, gather a small strand of hair from the left side of the cornrow and add to the left section. Pass this under center section. Now gather additional hair from the right side and add to the right section. Pass hair under center section.
4. Continue braiding until all the hair in the row is caught up in the braid. Secure with a tiny barrette or other fastener. Braid the next row in similar fashion, ending up with about 18 braids around the head. As I said above, you may

experiment with the direction of the braids and their width as well. Have fun!

■■■■■■■■■■■■■■■■■■■■■■■■■■■■■■■■■■

Styling

Parents are often at a loss when trying to choose hairstyles for their younger kids and trying to help guide older ones. Will a child with curly hair look good in bangs? How does one handle flyaway hair? What style will help hide ears that stick out? Matching up hair types and face shapes to flattering hairstyles is a challenge, since both are changing as your child grows. But it's a fun challenge. You'll enjoy trying new styles for each stage, helping your child look his best.

I've put together some of the most-asked questions on hairstyles and have suggested some answers with the help of hair experts. See if they help you.

Q. *My 3-year-old daughter's hair is wispy and always looks flyaway. What styles will make her hair appear fuller and more orderly?*

A. Try the following dos and don'ts:

DON'T	DO
Keep your daughter's hair long unless she is absolutely desperate for it. Long hair is not flattering to wispy hair.	Have her hair cut in layers or graduated lengths. Keep hair at a short or medium length.
Have her hair cut in a blunt style. This accents the light, flyaway texture.	Give her bangs if hair is not too wispy. This adds attractive variation and style.
Shampoo her hair too often. Hair shafts of wispy hair are usually thin, and frequent washing strips the hair of oil. Follow shampoo with a rich conditioner.	Use a variety of pretty hair accessories such as headbands, barrettes, and ribbons. These adornments give a polished and fun look to hair that is difficult to manage. A word of caution: wispy hair is more fragile than other hair types and is especially at risk for breakage and even hair loss. Make sure that hair accessories don't pull.
Despair. Wispy hair will thicken with age and will eventually be easier to style.	

Q. *Both my son and my daughter have inherited my square jaw. What are the best haircuts for this face shape?*

A. Hairstyles for children with a square jaw follow the same rules as those for adults. The trick is to create fullness and/or variation at the sides of the face to soften the severity of this face shape. Avoid styles, such as ponytails, that pull hair straight back. For your daughter, some feathering or layering around the face would be flattering. An ideal style for your son is a modified bowl cut, with some layering at the sides. When he gets older, tell the hairstylist or barber to keep some fullness around the sides of the face. To avoid highlighting the square shape of the face, part the hair at a slightly lower point than normal to create a focal point other than the top corners of the square of the face.

Q. *Because Heather's hair is always in her eyes, I'm considering bangs for her. Besides, I love bangs on 5-year-old girls! I have hesitated before because her face is quite round and full, and I fear bangs will accent her face shape. What do you think?*

A. Not if they're cut properly. Bangs flatter almost all little girls, regardless of face shape, according to Ed Schulte, who has styled children's hair for thirty years. "The look is in the cut," says Ed. "If a child's face is round, the hairdresser should cut lighter, more feathered bangs to create softness around the face. A straight cut across the forehead will definitely accent a round face shape. Rounded bangs, creating a circular look around the face, are also out for Heather. Find a good hairstylist, and he or she can make bangs look terrific on almost any shaped face."

Q. *My 9-year-old daughter, Erin, loves her long, brown hair. But she is on the top swim team at the YMCA and must practice four nights a week, in addition to two competitions on weekends. This means lengthy shampoo and blow-drying sessions for her long hair after each dip in the pool, adding at least one half hour onto these practices and meets. Any suggestions?*

A. Have you tried tucking your daughter's hair in a bun under her bathing cap to keep it dry? This works for a small percentage of girls and helps keep hair out of their eyes. If this doesn't work, a medium- or short-length haircut will certainly cut down on washing and blow-drying time. You and Erin should weigh the importance of the activity against how much Erin wants her long hair. If she cuts it shorter now, she can grow it long again if she loses interest in swimming next year. If she decides to try for state champion, however, Erin should seriously consider a short haircut.

Q. *My 7-year-old son loves to wear his hair very short. This would be fine except for the fact that this short cut reveals three cowlicks at the nape of his neck—all on the right side! He doesn't seem to care, but I do. What style would best camouflage these odd-looking whirls? What are cowlicks anyway?*

A. "Buzz" cuts or short haircuts have always presented problems for those who have cowlicks. A cowlick occurs in an area of the scalp where the hair suddenly grows in a circular direction or in a concentrated mass. The word "cowlick" is from the notion that "the hair looks as if it had been licked by a cow," according to Webster's New World Dictionary. One is able to spot these on babies, often in fascinating designs, such as the common double cowlick, one on each side of the crown of the head, looking almost like the beginning of horns.

   The most common sites for cowlicks are on the crown of the head, the beginning of the front hairline, and the nape of the neck, usually at one side or the other. If there are multiple cowlicks, it's best to have children wear hair long enough to weigh down the cowlick. Since your son's cowlicks aren't in an obvious spot and he loves wearing his hair short, why not let him? If he wears his hair longer in the future, always remind the barber about the cowlicks so he won't cut too short and allow the cowlicks to bush out or create a bump in his hair. Hair-dressers agree that a cowlick located at one side of the front hairline is a natural site for a part.

Q. *Young children seem to have these perfectly framed foreheads that look so pretty when exposed by pulling the hair back with a headband or when it's wet. Older children and teens seem to lose this look. Why?*

A. There is an abundance of visible hair on a child's forehead that does give a child's face a beautifully "framed" look. Between the ages of 10 and 15, androgen levels gradually increase and "male pattern balding" may begin for both boys and girls. Dr. Neil Sadick explains: "During adolescence, everyone begins losing their hair. The front hairline in all males and approximately 80 percent of females changes as some of these hair follicles become inactive. The entire face is reshaped during this time."

Parents of young girls often instinctively understand that the lower, more symmetrical hairline is short-lived. Many eschew bangs for their daughters, maintaining that their foreheads and hairlines are too beautiful to be hidden. "Emily will never again have this perfect framing for her round little face," says Lee. She's correct. After adolescence the hairline is usually changed forever.

Q. *Both my son and my daughter have been cursed with my husband's ears, which stick out. Which hairstyles are effective in covering them up?*

A. Protruding ears can be a problem. Here are some tips on hiding them.

For girls: Girls have more flexibility than boys for ear-covering styles. Any style that covers these ears—especially the tops of the ears—will help camouflage this cosmetic problem. A layered cut is often a mistake, as ears can often be seen peeking through the layers. Fine hair is also often a problem, especially when hair is pulled back. For thicker hair, though, ponytails are great at disguising this problem. Blunt cuts, particularly short bobs, are very effective in hiding big ears. If hair is too long, ears may start to show through again.

For boys: Ask the barber to cover the tops of ears when cutting and styling hair. Longish hair, including a bowl cut, is great. Never "whitewall" or shave above ears. Short buzz looks may simply be out of the question for boys whose ears stick out.

■ ■ ■ ■ ■ ■ ■ ■ ■ ■ ■ ■ ■ ■ ■ ■

A PROFESSIONAL HAIRDRESSER SHOWS A YOUNG MOTHER HOW TO CUT BANGS AT HOME. IF YOUR DAUGHTER WANTS BANGS FOR THE FIRST TIME, I SUGGEST THAT YOU HAVE THEM DONE PROFESSIONALLY. THE HAIR-DRESSER WILL SHOW YOU WHERE THE BANGS SHOULD START, USUALLY ABOUT TWO INCHES IN FRONT OF THE CROWN.

LEFT, ISABELLA'S HAIR HAS BEEN SHAMPOOED AND BLOWN ALMOST DRY. HAIR SHOULD BE SLIGHTLY MOIST AND WELL COMBED BEFORE THE CUT. IF HAIR IS WET, CUT BANGS SLIGHTLY LONGER SINCE THEY WILL SHRINK WHEN DRY.

BELOW, TO START, PULL HAIR BACK FROM FACE TO LEAVE ONLY BANGS, CREATING A TRIANGULAR SHAPE ABOVE THE HAIRLINE. MAKE SURE HAIR FROM THE TEMPLE AREA IS PULLED BACK. THESE HAIRS SHOULD NOT BE PART OF THE BANGS. HOLDING HAIR BETWEEN THE MIDDLE AND FORE-FINGER OF THE LEFT HAND, CUT THE LONGEST STRANDS TO EVEN THE BANGS.

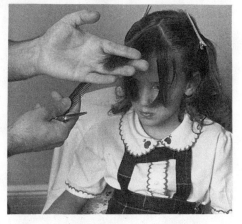

AFTER COMBING HAIR AGAIN, CUT BANGS FROM ONE SIDE TO CENTER. THEN CUT FROM OTHER SIDE TO CENTER. IF THERE ARE ANY COWLICKS ON THE HAIRLINE, CUT FROM ONE SIDE TO THE COWLICK, AND THEN CUT FROM THE OTHER. OR DO A SIDE BANG, BRUSHING HAIR AWAY FROM THE COWLICK ON EITHER SIDE. HERE, BANGS ARE CHECKED FOR EVENNESS.

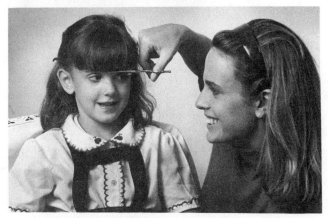

TRIM ANY STRAY HAIRS AFTER BANGS ARE DRY.

■ The Bowl Cut—Do It Yourself at Home

The straighter the hair, the better your son will look in this classic "bowl" style. Hair with a little wave will look cute, too, but kids with curly or frizzy hair would do better to try another style. Boys seem to outgrow the bowl cut after a certain age (6 or 7), but children as young as 18 months can wear it.

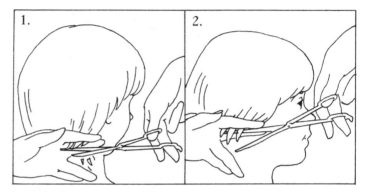

Here's how you can do this cut at home: Wash, condition, and towel-dry your child's hair. Hair should be damp when cut—not wet. Hair stretches when it's wet and shrinks up as it dries. Keep a mister nearby filled with warm water and a teaspoon of conditioner—or use a detangler (Johnson & Johnson's No More Tangles is excellent). Use a wide-toothed comb.

Seat your son on a stool or chair in front of a mirror—this will give him something to look at while you cut. If this is impossible, try to place him in a spot where there is visual diversion—in front of the TV, or in front of a poster he likes. This will be especially helpful for squirmy toddlers. Toys may also help. If he's very young and of very limited patience, do the haircut in two or three different sessions during the day. Talk as you go along, telling him what you're doing.

1. To begin, comb hair straight down on all sides, using the crown as the center pivot. Starting with the back, tip head forward and take hair between the forefinger and middle finger of the left hand, with scissors held in the right. (If you are left-handed, use the opposite hands, of course.) Lift this hair to check the natural hairline. Never cut above this line. Move fingers below this line and trim.

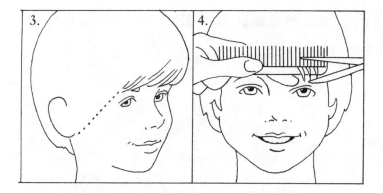

2. As you trim toward the sides, angle the cut about ¼ inch toward the ears. Comb again from crown to check evenness on both sides. Use caution not to poke or cut ears or face with the scissors. Blunt-edged scissors are recommended for younger children.
3. Using the earlobe and the eyebrow as visual anchors, cut hair toward the bangs, from low to high.
4. Bangs are cut at the center, just above eyebrow level. (Don't cut too short! Short bangs can be disastrous. Better too long than too short.) If necessary, finish off trim at temples, using a forty-five-degree angle and curving down to the sides.

■■■■■■■■■■■■■■■■■■■■■■■■■■■■■

Finding the Right Part

How can you find where your child's hair parts naturally? Simple. After a shampoo and conditioning, comb hair straight back. Place your hand on the crown of your child's head and push it forward toward the forehead. You will see a deep split in the hair. *Voilà*—the natural part. A cowlick on one side at the front hairline will usually determine where the part will be.

You can change the part to the opposite side from time to time if you like. One cannot "train" a part as such, because the direction hair grows—the follicle angle—cannot be changed. The way hair is cut can help hold hair down, though, if a change in parting sides is desired. Barrettes and other hair accessories can help keep hair in place to accommodate the new part while hair grows.

■■■■■■■■■■■■■■■■■■■■■■■■■■■■■

Hairstyle Changes: Talking to Your Child's Hairdresser

Hairdressers and barbers are usually skilled in the fine art of communication. (And if he or she isn't, run, don't walk, in the other direction!) You and your child must do your part in letting the hairdresser know exactly what you want for your child, especially if the haircut is a new one. I am always amazed at how sensitive children are about their haircuts. You and your child will be happiest with your child's haircut if you think about the following:

STORE HOURS
Monday · Saturday
10 a.m. · 6 p.m.
Thursdays 'till 8 p.m.
Sundays
12 noon · 5 p.m.

■ Depending on the age of the child, discuss what style they want before going into the salon. Discuss your lifestyle and how much time you're both willing to put into a hairstyle that requires a good deal of care.

■ Ask the hairstylist what he or she thinks about your style choice. He may have input you had not thought about.

■ Discussions on hairstyles often require a little give-and-take, but be firm if you and your child know exactly what you want.

■ You can also bring in a picture of a new hairstyle you'd like for your child. Listen to the barber's advice, though, if he feels your child's hair type will not cooperate with the chosen style.

■■■■■■■■■

JULIA WANTS A SPECIAL HAIRCUT FOR HER FIFTH BIRTHDAY. THE SALON OF CHOICE? SHOOTING STAR SALON AT FAO SCHWARZ IN NEW YORK CITY, AN EXCELLENT PLACE TO GET BIRTHDAY PRESENT INSPIRATIONS AS WELL.

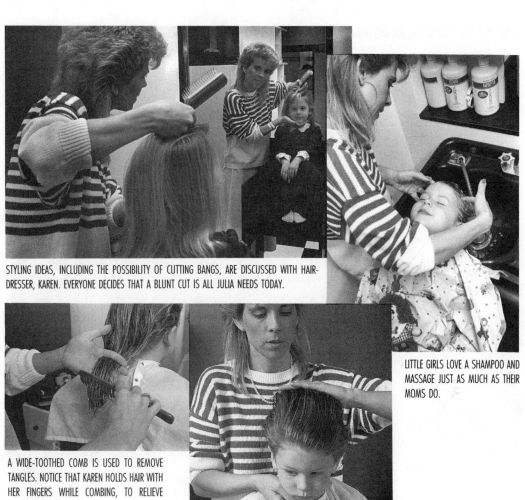

STYLING IDEAS, INCLUDING THE POSSIBILITY OF CUTTING BANGS, ARE DISCUSSED WITH HAIR-DRESSER, KAREN. EVERYONE DECIDES THAT A BLUNT CUT IS ALL JULIA NEEDS TODAY.

LITTLE GIRLS LOVE A SHAMPOO AND MASSAGE JUST AS MUCH AS THEIR MOMS DO.

A WIDE-TOOTHED COMB IS USED TO REMOVE TANGLES. NOTICE THAT KAREN HOLDS HAIR WITH HER FINGERS WHILE COMBING, TO RELIEVE STRESS ON SCALP.

KAREN FINDS THE NATURAL PART BY PUSHING JULIA'S WET HAIR FORWARD FROM THE CROWN.

IT WAS A WONDERFUL PARTY.

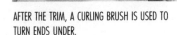

AFTER THE TRIM, A CURLING BRUSH IS USED TO TURN ENDS UNDER.

■■■■■■■■■■■■■■■■■■■■■■■■■■■■■■

A Bleached Blonde at Four? What Parents Should Know About Coloring Children's Hair

Two or three times each summer, Beth gives Rachel a lemon-juice rinse, then scoots her out to splash in her wading pool. Rachel has golden blond hair and could easily play Goldilocks for the school play. Says Beth, "*My* mother kept my hair blond till I was about 10 with this method. Rachel's hair is blond till almost Christmas each year with just a little help from me and nature's own ingredients—lemon and the sun!"

Is it safe to color your child's hair? Experts agree that using chemical processes—stripping, then peroxiding or dying a child's hair—is very unwise. The fumes can be irritating to the scalp and eyes, and the dyes can be absorbed through the bloodstream. Experts also agree that children's skin and hair tones are in such beautiful and delicate balance that coloring a child's hair can create an odd color disharmony. Why would anyone bother? Indeed, the hairdressers interviewed had very few requests for hair-color changes for children, even among child actors.

Although very few parents would chemically color their child's hair, interviews with many parents and hairdressers reveal that the lemon-juice rinse combined with the sun is still a very popular cosmetic practice—especially for girls ages 2 and up. It's a practice that has its fans and its critics. Dr. Neil Sadick warns parents that lemon juice is very drying. "Any acidic substance applied directly to the hair can cause damage to the hair shaft." Hairdresser Kathy Hess reports that she has seen some brassy results among teenagers who had applied lemon juice directly from the bottle. "It's like taking a bottle of peroxide and pouring it on your hair—you have to know how to handle it," she says.

Pat Paz, a New York hairdresser for children, recommends a patch test. "Take a small strand of hair and apply diluted lemon juice to that area—use a half a lemon or one tablespoon of fresh lemon juice to eight ounces warm water for younger children. Leave rinse on for two hours in the sun to see how this patch of hair responds. If hair lightens to a pretty color, try this rinse for the whole head—but only once or twice a summer.'' Ms. Paz warns that using the rinse too often will dull and dry the hair and may even result in an orange or brassy look. She also recommends that lemon-and-sun sessions be followed with a shampoo and conditioner.

THREE LITTLE GIRLS, AGES 7, 7, AND 6, TRY A LEMON-JUICE RINSE TO LIGHTEN THEIR HAIR TO AN EVEN BLONDER SHADE. KATHI POURS DILUTED LEMON JUICE ON ANNIE'S HAIR AFTER A STRAND TEST EARLIER THAT DAY. THE OTHER TWO GET A TURN, TOO.

AFTER BEING OUT IN THE SUN WITH THE LEMON-JUICE RINSE IN THEIR HAIR FOR TWO HOURS A DAY, FOR TWO DAYS IN A ROW, THE GIRLS BELIEVE THEY NOW LOOK MUCH BLONDER. HMMM.

Pamela Plummer of Shooting Star Salon is an outright fan of lemon-juice rinses—but not in combination with the sun. "If used properly, lemon juice can be a great beauty aid for kids—especially older ones who have oily hair," she says. "After a shampoo, a lemon-juice rinse can help control oil, cut soap, and result in more shine. It's great for blondes or dirty blondes—to help create blond highlights. All hair has different tones and colors. Lemon juice helps bring them up!"

To Perm or Not to Perm

The popular 1940s and '50s rage—using permanent waves on little girls' hair—has not stood the test of time. Changing fashion and growing public concern about chemicals in the products we use have turned most families against the permanent process. But there are exceptions—and some parents today are still perming their children's hair.

"We occasionally get requests for body waves for children," says Pat Paz. "But we don't do it." She explains that children have sensitive skin and can have allergic reactions to the permanent lotions that contain ammonia, as can adults. The ammonia is also irritating to the eyes. "The cosmetic companies specifically warn us not to use the permanents on anyone under 13 or 14," she notes.

Karim Ahmed, a scientist formerly with the Natural Resources Defense Council, warns that permanents are particularly damaging to children's delicate hair. "The chemical substances used in permanents actually break down the structures that hold the fibrous protein of the hair shaft," he says. "This destroys the texture of the hair and results in dry, lifeless hair. A month after the permanent wears off, the child's hair may look like straw." Mr. Ahmed notes that not much is known about the damage caused by absorbing a permanent's chemical substances through the scalp. "My recommendation," says Ahmed, "is don't!"

Some black parents wonder when they can begin using "relaxants" on their children's hair. Latrinda Johnson of Savvy Hair Salon in Norwalk, Connecticut, feels that parents should wait until their children are teenagers and can assume the responsibility for their own hair. "Once one begins using a relaxant," she says, "you have to continue, because growing it out can be long and difficult." Ms. Johnson is particularly concerned because relaxants contain the chemical equivalent of lye—which is strong and potentially irritating. "It's best to let children's hair grow naturally until they are in their late teens and older," she says. *"Then* they can change it."

Hot Rollers and Curling Irons

For a special occasion, it can be fun to curl your daughter's hair. Mothers have curled children's hair for centuries—with rags, tissue paper and bobby pins, rollers made of steel, plastic, foam, whatever! Now that many households sport hot combs, electric rollers, and curling and crimping irons, parents can have their little girls looking like Shirley Temple in minutes. But precautions must be taken when using these electrical devices on a young child. (See blow-dryer section for other safety tips on electrical devices.) Read these tips before using hot rollers on your child.

1. Protect the scalp! Heat rollers to moderate instead of full heat. Rollers should never be uncomfortable to the scalp. If your child objects to the hot rollers or curling iron, don't force the issue. Wait a few months and try again.
2. Use papers to protect the hair ends. These can be purchased at most drugstores or beauty-supply stores.
3. Use electrical curling devices in moderation, no more than two or three times a month. Since children's hair is thinner and more fragile than ours, curlers can cause damage.

You and your daughter can create fun looks in minutes. Use rollers and combs and irons in much the same way you would on yourself or another adult, remembering that children's hair probably curls faster than your own. Experiment a little. Each child's hair curls differently and requires a little practice.

■■■■■■■■■■■■■■■■■■■■■■■■■■■■■■■■■

What Can Happen to Children's Scalp and Hair—Some Medical Problems and Solutions

Nature doesn't play favorites with hair and scalp problems. Children seem to be just as subject to them as adults, with the exception of dandruff! Most children under 12 are happily free of this common adult problem. Herewith, listed and detailed for easy reference, are five of the most common hair and scalp disorders among children. It's best to consult your pediatrician or a dermatologist if any of these occur.

Ringworm (or tinea capitis). Ringworm is not caused by a worm, but a parasitic fungus. Because it is highly contagious, whole classrooms and camp groups have become affected before ringworm has been brought under control. The fungus can be transferred from child to child through sharing of towels, bedclothes, and other objects. Keep these items separated. Pets or other animals may also be guilty of transporting the fungus.

How can you spot ringworm? Look for scaly, red, balding patches, round or ring-shaped, on the head. (The fungi actually eat the keratin of the hair shaft!) If left untreated, ringworm can scar the scalp, destroying hair follicles so hair can never grow again. Treatment includes keeping the affected area dry and applying a topical antifungal preparation. There are also pills, known generically as "griseofulvin," that can be prescribed. Brand names include Grispeg and Fulvicin. Your doctor may also use ultraviolet light on the affected area.

Cradle Cap (or seborrheic dermatitis). Cradle cap is normally confined to babyhood, a result of overactive sebaceous glands, then often reappears as "seborrheic dermatitis" in adolescence when glands are again overstimulated. How frustrating, then, when a child of 5 is still plagued by these scaly, yellowish-brown patches on her scalp that appear once or twice each year. Pediatricians and parents see cradle cap or a version of this seborrheic dermatitis sometimes persisting up to ages 5 and 6. The suggested course of action: a trip to your pediatrician. The doctor will probably prescribe a dandruff shampoo for children 18 months and older and a washing routine to remove the crust safely and hygienically.

Traction Alopecia. You've probably seen cases of traction alopecia on little girls at your child's school. There is balding at the frontal hairline (especially the thinner areas at either side where hair is parted), caused by ponytails, braids, cornrows, headbands, and even excessive brushing. The stress on the hair follicles caused by these styles results in traction alopecia. Black children who wear cornrows or "rasta" braids are particularly at risk, since these styles are often worn for long periods. If your child wears these styles and you notice any thinning of hair at various sites on the scalp, discontinue this style at once. Allow the hair to hang free and use no hair accessories at all. This thinning will correct itself if caught in time, but continued traction stress can severely damage the hair follicles and result in permanent bald spots.

Trichotilomania. When one mother noticed a bald patch on the side of her 9-year-old daughter's head, she raced her off to the dermatologist. After a few tests, the wise doctor determined there was nothing physically wrong with the child to warrant this hair loss. He did begin to suspect a condition called trichotilomania, in which the child (as young as toddler age) or teenager or even adult consciously or unconsciously pulls out hair as a nervous or stress-related habit. Ninety percent of the sufferers are girls—often preadolescent. Doctors report that these children frequently deny pulling their hair, and parents are unaware of it as well. A talk with the dermatologist helped Ann realize her daughter was twirling her pencil in her hair at school as a kind of nervous gesture. Once the girl became aware of the destructiveness of this habit, she was able to stop. If your child is pulling at her hair—especially at one section—point this out to her in a gentle manner. This will increase her awareness that she is causing scalp and hair problems.

Trichotilomania is a mild form of self-mutilation. In severe cases, psychiatric help is needed to address family problems before the disorder is arrested. One little girl stopped when her mother went back to work!

Head Lice. After having almost disappeared for a generation or two, head lice have made a comeback among schoolchildren today. This return is probably due to the restricted use of DDT in the United States since 1972. Since our generation rarely experienced lice infestation as children, first-time parents are shocked when they find that lice notices from school are practically as frequent as report cards. And when a parent first spots that dreaded bug on her child's tender scalp, the reaction is almost universally the same: shrieks of disbelief followed by subsequent (and uncalled-for) guilt and shame!

Admittedly, the word "lice" has a bad image. We picture unclean people scratching away at their heads—hardly an appropriate image for our kids. This public perception needs updating, since these pests are passed among families that have the highest cleanliness standards. Our children are particularly susceptible to infestation: not only are lice more attracted to children than adults, they also prefer girls.

Lice, or "pediculus capitis," are hard to detect, since they are only $\frac{1}{10}$ to $\frac{1}{8}$ inch long and present no cosmetic problem other than intermittent head-scratching. Once in a while, a rash will appear at the back of the neck. A number of summers ago, my son had his neck rash misdiagnosed on two different trips to the pediatrician. Blaming the heat for this rash, the doctor treated his neck with a cortisone cream. I finally discovered his problem when, seated one evening in a movie theater, I felt my scalp move completely independent of my efforts. By that time, our head lice were large enough to be saddled. The only family members who escaped the cruel infestation of these bloodsuckers were my bald husband and my then one-year-old, nearly bald, daughter!

If I had known or even thought to look for nits, or egg cases, attached to individual hairs, I could have identified our lice problem immediately. Resembling flakes of dandruff or pieces of dirt, nits won't move when blown. They are small and silvery or white opaque, and feel like tiny grains of rice. Nits and the hatched lice are best observed under a bright light with a magnifying glass, because nature has given the head louse the ability to take on the color of the child's hair, believe it or not.

Other signs of lice are scabs on the scalp from scratching, and sometimes a body rash from sensitization to the parasite. In severe cases, a swollen lymph gland in the neck or under the arm can spell a lice problem. If any of these symptoms are present and you do spot nits or live lice, talk to your pediatrician for his advice. School nurse Terry Nagler has compiled the following steps.

1. Call your pediatrician for his advice. The doctor will probably suggest an over-the-counter lice shampoo called NIX. Follow any lice shampoo directions carefully.
2. Use a warm vinegar rinse (one cup of white vinegar to one cup of warm water) to loosen nits so that they may be removed more easily. A new prescription lice shampoo contains a conditioner that makes combing and nit removal even easier. Ask your doctor about it.
3. Since shampoos do not kill all nits, they must be physically removed from the hair shafts. While hair is still wet, comb with a fine-toothed nit comb, often included in the lice shampoo package, or else available at drugstores. Be aware that lice combs are not always successful at removing all nits. You will probably have to use tweezers or your fingernails to get rid of the most tenacious egg sacs.
4. Continue to inspect family members for two weeks. Reapplication of shampoo is advisable seven to ten days after initial treatment, if necessary.
5. Eggs also accumulate under children's fingernails. When you shampoo, be sure to also cut your child's nails and scrub them thoroughly with a nail brush.
6. Wash all combs, brushes, and hair accessories in hot water and lice shampoo for twenty minutes. Be especially careful not to share these items at this point.
7. Wash all clothes, bed linens, and towels in your washing machine in hot water.
8. Dry-clean scarves, hats, coats, pillows, blankets, etc., or seal them in a plastic bag for thirty days. Seal up stuffed animals and cloth-covered toys as well. Some experts report that these items can be run through the dryer for about thirty minutes with just as effective results. On furniture and car seats, use a special lice spray available at most pharmacies. After spraying, vacuum well.

All these precautions may seem excessive, but if you don't get rid of all the nits, you could still be in trouble! Just two live nits can start the whole life cycle all over again. One mother whose daughter, Missy, kept getting lice even after repeated shampoos and combing complained to the school nurse that the child's classmates must be reinfecting her. The school nurse pointed out that practically every strand of hair on her daughter's head must be checked and *every* nit removed. She explained that prescription and other lice shampoos are insecticidal, but not ovicidal. The eggs can sometimes withstand the poisonous shampoo and happily hatch a week later. She also reminded the child's mother that combing alone will not always remove all nits, since children's hair is so thin. When the mother and the nurse sat down to properly check Missy's hair, they picked out more than thirty nits! Her lice problem promptly disappeared.

CHAPTER TWO

Your Child's Skin

Its Beauty and How to Protect It

Childhood is the one time everyone has beautiful skin. Once the baby stage is over, diaper rash, blotchiness, and infant acne are a thing of the past. And because the sebaceous glands are not fully developed, pimples, acne, and body odor loom somewhere way off in the future. Sun has done no terrible damage, and skin tones are delicately even. There is nothing quite as lovely as a child's complexion after exuberant exercise, glowing with health and beauty. But without proper health habits, a child's skin can suffer, possibly becoming pale and mottled, with dark bruiselike shadows under the eyes. Beautiful skin is a product of the balance of important elements that must be tended to throughout childhood: good nutrition, adequate sleep and rest, lots of exercise, and a low-stress environment. Let's look at these beauty boosters.

Diet. Many dermatologists now believe that diet has little to do with most skin ailments, including acne; however, food sensitivities are reported by parents all the time. One mother began to notice an orange cast to her 18-month-old's face. He was getting too many carrots in his diet, which produces "carotonesis," a pigment-affecting skin ailment. Excess carotene from oranges, squash, or carrots can often cause this discoloration.

We do know that good nourishment is essential for all-over good health and energy. By helping your child avoid too much sugar, salt, fats, etc., and get the right vitamins and minerals to nourish the youngster's largest organ—the skin—you'll help her look and feel good. Remember that water, and plenty of it, is essential for the skin's hydration and suppleness.

Remember, also, that smoking around your children will have the same physiological effect that causes premature aging of the skin among smokers—constriction of blood vessels in the face. Their skin tone can turn sallow, like that of smokers. Breathing secondhand smoke also slows down children's blood circulation and adds to retention of waste material, not to speak of the diseases to which you may be predisposing your child.

■ ■ ■ ■ ■ ■ ■ ■ ■ ■

CHILDREN ARE BLESSED WITH EXQUISITE SKIN, BUT SAFEGUARDING ITS BEAUTY REQUIRES GOOD HEALTH HABITS, INFORMED SKIN CARE, AND PROTECTION FROM THE SUN.

Sleep. One look at a 9-year-old after that first slumber party is proof positive that a child's skin is extremely sensitive to the effects of too little sleep. Inadequate rest means a slowed circulation and less nourishment to the blood. The result? Dark circles under the eyes and dull, sallow skin. Enforcing bedtimes is not the easiest task, especially when children start sleepovers or want to watch TV on weekends till late at night. Do your best to help the kids get their "beauty sleep." Their skin will show the healthy results!

Exercise. Although nursery-school children may appear to be in perpetual motion, most of them spend a lot of time sitting around. By the time they reach elementary school, they are already way behind in the amount of exercise needed to keep physically fit, according to numerous studies. Exercise brings a beautiful glow to a child's skin, just as it does to an adult's. It increases the circulation of the blood, which brings nourishment to the skin and helps build new cells. Exercise also helps get rid of impurities through sweating. Encourage a regular exercise program for your child for good health and great skin.

Stress. We don't often realize our children are under stress until they exhibit some kind of physical ailment such as a rash, eczema, or asthma, traceable, at least in part, to stress. Some of our emotions show up on the skin immediately—blushes, paleness from fright, etc. Stress and other emotional distresses can cause temporary color and texture changes in the skin, and later on may worsen acne. Help your child relieve stress by encouraging discussions and getting him involved in image-strengthening activities. (Regular weekly chores can help enormously in building self-confidence!) Exercise is also a great stressbuster. One of the best tension-relievers, for parents as well as children, is a nightly snuggle at bedtime—reading books, talking over the day, holding your child close to you.

■■■■■■■■■■■■■■■■■■■■■■■■■■■■■■■■■■

Great Starts for a Lifetime of Proper Skin Care

Helping your child develop a good skin-care program that includes proper diet, good hygiene, protection from the sun, and a knowledge of his or her skin type, can go a long way in preparing the child for a lifetime of intelligent skin care. With adolescence around the corner, and its accompanying urge for independence, children will have some solid habits and information to fall back on when dealing with their own bodies, including the proper care of their skin. Now is a perfect time to help your kids get started on a skin-care routine that can last the rest of their lives. As we adults know, beautiful skin takes hard work, but what a payoff!

■■■■■■■■■

CHILDREN LOVE TO COPY THEIR MOTHERS—ESPECIALLY IN THE BEAUTY AND MAKE-UP DEPARTMENT. WHEN THEIR MOTHERS WOULDN'T LET THEM USE THEIR COMMERCIAL FACIAL MASKS, THESE THREE 9-YEAR-OLDS MADE THEIR OWN. THEY MIXED PLAIN YOGURT, DRAINED PINEAPPLE PIECES, MASHED AVOCADO, HONEY, AND COCONUT, WITH A LITTLE DRY OATMEAL TO CREATE A STIMULATING MASK THAT WAS SURE TO MAKE THEM LOOK MORE BEAUTIFUL. YOUR CHILDREN MAY USE ANY COMBINATION OF THE FOLLOWING: AVOCADO, HONEY, CREAM, STRAWBERRY, MASHED BANANAS, AND EGG WHITES. THE MASK CONSISTENCY SHOULD BE DRY ENOUGH TO SLATHER ON, AND WET ENOUGH TO SPREAD GENTLY ON THEIR CHEEKS. THIS CAN BE A MESSY ACTIVITY, SO DO PROTECT CLOTHES. ASSIST THE CHILDREN IN REMOVING THEIR MASKS—CHILDREN MAY RUB TOO HARD. IF YOUR CHILD IS ALLERGIC OR HAS SKIN SENSITIVITIES, AVOID THESE MASKS OR CHECK WITH YOUR DOCTOR BEFORE USING THESE INGREDIENTS ON THE FACE.

WHEN APPLYING THE MASK, TAKE CARE TO AVOID THE EYE AND EAR AREAS. LEAVE MASK ON FOR THREE TO FIVE MINUTES. WASH RESIDUE OFF WITH WARM WATER.

THE GIRLS' SKIN IS RADIANT. ALL THREE LOOK MONTHS YOUNGER!

■■■■■■■■■■■■■■■■■■■■■■■■■■■■■■■■

Informed Skin Care

Proper diet, exercise, sleep, and relaxation are only part of the skin-care picture. Children need schooling on protecting the skin from the terrible harm the sun can wreak on the skin (described in detail on pages 61–64), and a knowledge of the proper skin-care routine for various types of skin and those commercial products that can aid them. We are lucky to live in an age when children's special body needs are being met by cosmetic companies. These made-for-kids products are not always necessary, since most skin problems can be remedied by products already on the market.

■■■■■■■■■■■■■■■■■■■■■■■■■■■■■■■■

Cleanliness Routines

A child should wash her face or have it washed, depending on the child's age, at least twice a day. Hands should be washed as needed, always before meals and before bedtime. Younger children will need help washing their faces to avoid getting soap in their eyes. Use a "dry" wet washcloth with a little soap to clean, making sure you wash behind and in the ears. Be careful not to get water inside the ear canal. As a child grows, teach him or her to be aware of ear cleanliness, since children face the special problem of secreting more ear wax than older people. Do not use a Q-Tip to clean your child's ear canal. Once a child approaches the teens, he can use a cotton-covered Q-Tip on the outside of the ear canal only. To avoid injury to the delicate middle ear, even adults should not probe inside the ear.

Special "baby" soaps are not necessary after age 2. Skin all over the body has reached its fullest thickness by then (aside from the areas that will expand with developing hair), so that washing with any pure soap such as Ivory suits most children's needs. If you like, check out the number of skin-care products made especially for children—soaps, cleansers, moisturizers, etc. Avoid using deodorant soaps, heavily perfumed soaps, or other special adult-needs soaps, since they may be too harsh and drying for children's skin.

A bath or shower can be a daily routine, although twice

■ ■ ■ ■ ■ ■ ■ ■ ■ ■

CHILDREN USUALLY LOVE BATHTIME. BUT KEEP
BATHS SHORT IN WINTER TO PREVENT DRY SKIN,
AND RESTRICT BUBBLE BATHS TO A ONCE-IN-
A-WHILE TREAT. BUBBLE BATHS ARE SOMETIMES
RESPONSIBLE FOR URINARY INFECTIONS.

or three times a week is usually sufficient if a child is not
terribly active. Older children involved in sports may feel
more comfortable if they shower or bathe after practices or
games.

Young children usually love bathtime—as do most parents as they learn that a warm bath relaxes children for bed.
Don't let children soak too long, especially in the winter
months, for this can have a drying effect on children's skin.
Be wary of bubble baths, as many are too harsh and may
cause skin irritations or even, in girls, urinary-tract infections.
Bath oils smell delicious and may help keep skin from drying
out, but doctors warn that bath oil not only coats a child's skin
but also the bath surfaces. This makes getting out of the tub
dangerous, especially for a young child. If your child's skin is
dry, see the following section on dry skin.

As a child begins puberty, a nightly or every-other-night
bath or shower is especially important, as hormonal changes
create new body odors, some not so pleasant! One mother was
shocked when she realized her 11-year-old daughter had a
particularly offensive underarm-odor problem. With the help
of a deodorant and a doctor's explanation, the mother relaxed.
He said that underarm odors among preadolescents are often
unusually strong, because when puberty is at its beginning
stages, hormonal output is often not completely regulated.
Body odors will improve as hormones settle down.

Older children usually have strong opinions on the

"right" deodorant or other body-care items, and this desire to assume responsibility for personal care should, within reason, be indulged, even though the products may cost more than your own!

■■■■■■■■■■■■■■■■■■■■■■■■■■■■■■■■

Problem Skin

■ Dry Skin

Even little kids can get dry skin. How? From an inherited tendency toward dry skin, from aggravating conditions such as too much soaping and bathing, and from an overly dry atmosphere and winter weather. When oils are removed, skin—even young skin—has trouble holding moisture and the deeper layers of skin have trouble moving moisture upward. Here's how you can help the child who suffers with dry skin.

■ Cut down on baths and the use of all soaps except non-drying ones such as superfatted or glycerine soaps. Avoid soaps with drying antibacterial agents and alkaline. Dermatologists suggest that a child with dry skin take no more than two or three baths a week, each no more than ten minutes long, without soap or bubble bath. Bathwater should be comfortably warm. If your child has very dry skin, use only a cetyl alcohol lotion; this type of lotion is marketed under brand names such as Cetaphil.

■ Gently apply a hypoallergenic lubricating cream, such as Eucurin, to the dry areas right after the bath and several times during the day. Try one of the moisturizers made especially for children, which are usually alcohol-free. If your child has hay fever or other allergies, avoid the scented moisturizers. Baby products are excellent for dry skin, because they lack fragrances and preservatives. Many children have to use moisturizers all winter long, because dry skin can last for months.

■ Great for skin, plants, and furniture are the handy cold-water humidifiers. Keep this machine pumping mists of fresh water in his or her room all winter long, if need be, but use extra care in cleaning humidifiers regularly, since they have been shown to harbor bacteria and mold. Steam-heated apartments are in special need of humidifiers. Make sure your house or apartment is not overheated or over-air-conditioned.

■ Avoid cold temperatures and wind. Excessive sunbathing can also cause dry skin.

■ Make sure the child with dry skin gets plenty of water and eats a well-balanced diet.

■ "Ashy Dryness" Among Black Children

Black parents have been moisturizing their children's skin for centuries to cover an ashy look or cast to the skin. The limbs are most often affected, but the face, too, may have a grayish tinge, often accompanied by a thin, grainy scale on the surface of the skin. This condition gets worse in winter, when skin gets drier from the cold combined with the drying effect of home heating. White people suffer from the same dryness, but because their underlying skin is light in color, the dry horny cells on the outer layer of skin do not show up. Oil secreted from the sebaceous glands will also be more visible on black skin.

Moisturizing the skin helps. But hydrating the skin—patting water on, or soaking in the bathtub before applying moisturizer—is even more effective. The dry outer layer of skin takes in the water, and the moisturizer acts to trap moisture. Be careful not to overlubricate the skin, or an undesirable shininess or greasy look may result. This may clog pores as well. Keep humidifiers running all winter and avoid harsh soaps. Soaps and moisturizers formulated especially for black skin are plentiful. Experiment to find the ones best for you and your family.

■ Oily Skin

This condition almost never occurs until the onset of puberty. If it does, see your pediatrician or dermatologist to determine its cause.

■ Pallor

Skin tones and coloration are as varied as shades of hair. Some children seem to have more pink in their cheeks, while others seem to have sallow undertones or a paleness to their skin. Grown-ups can alter their color with foundation, blusher, and other makeup, but unless children are actors or models, there's no need to change their natural skin tones. If you are having the family photographed, your child may look pale next to Mom, who may have more makeup on than she would normally. Borrow a trick used by magazines specializing in children: add blusher to your child's cheeks. Babies may also need this extra color to prevent a washed-out look for a special photo.

MEDICAL ALERT
Allergies and Your Child's Skin

If your toddler has one of the symptoms on the list below, he or she might be allergic to one or more of the allergens in our environment including various foods and chemicals. Common food allergens are milk, eggs, corn, wheat, and various fruits such as bananas and grapes. Common chemical allergies often result from aerosol sprays, carpets, cigarette smoke, and pesticides.

Pediatric allergist Doris Rapp, a pioneer in identifying allergic reactions and previously unrecognized allergens asks parents to be aware of the following symptoms:

• Red earlobes
• Red cheeks
• Dark eye circles
• Bags under the eyes
• Wrinkles under the eyes
• Glassy, glazed eyes
• A "spaced-out" look
• Wiggly, restless legs
• Dislike being touched or cuddled

When children get older, other allergic symptoms can include dry skin, hives, and itchy rectum. Other symptoms such as intestinal problems, wheezing and coughing, and aggressiveness and anger are also seen in allergic reactions. Many doctors are reluctant to accept the possibility that these symptoms could be allergic reactions.

A further note on cigarette smoke: A child's skin will react to passive smoking (breathing smoke exhaled by smokers) much the way a first-hand smoker's does. The skin can become sallow-looking and the child can suffer with teary eyes and irritated sinuses. Children often develop allergic reactions to cigarette smoke, giving them the look of cold-sufferers.

If parents cannot quit or can't smoke outside the house, they should at least confine smoking to one room the children don't use. Install a good ventilation system to further rid these cancer-causing fumes from the children's home. Your children's good health is your responsibility!

■■■■■■■■■■■■■■■■■■■■■■■■■■■■■■■

How Skin Texture Changes During Childhood

"I can't get over the softness of my baby's skin," said Christie, a first-time mother on leave from her job in banking. "I can spend hours stroking her dear little cheeks, silky back, and tummy. I used to spend my free time with spreadsheets and financial reports. Now it's Lila's skin. What's wrong with me?"

Nothing, according to anthropologists. Parents are as drawn to the feel of their babies' skin as they are to their delicious scents. Indeed, studies have shown that without cuddling and stroking, premature babies fare poorly when compared with those who get plenty of physical touching. Hospitals regularly encourage parents to cuddle and feed their premature infants, for, like most other mammals, a human baby's central nervous system is positively stimulated by gentle stroking and handling. According to some studies, girls are slightly more responsive to touch than boys.

So it is with feelings of wistfulness that Christie and other parents watch their babies' skin become firmer in texture as they grow. A 6-year-old still has soft, pliant skin, exquisite to the touch and beautiful to the eyes, but hormones, physical growth, and exposure to the environment are changing the child's skin every day. By age 11 to 14, puberty has begun its dramatic transformation and baby bumpkin's soft skin is a sweet memory.

How dramatic is this change? Observe an 11-year-old girl holding her newborn brother to study the contrast in their skin. Unless their coloring is radically different from one another, the older girl's skin is probably firmer, darker, and covered with more hair. The baby has silky skin, fine body hair, and is fairer now than he will be eleven years hence. What happens to skin, the body's largest organ, from infancy to adolescence?

First we have to understand that skin plays an enormously important role in human health. It helps regulate the body's temperature, warming when outside temperatures fall, and cooling when they rise. It helps eliminate impurities in the body and serves as a durable, elastic barrier (if only partial) to environmental elements, protecting us from infections and external injury. Skin also protects us from dehydration and hemorrhage. Both painful and pleasant sensations are communicated through the skin, as it is richly endowed with sensory nerve endings.

As a child grows from a vulnerable infant to an independent school-age being, her skin is changing to respond to a different, less-protected environment. Her skin will "toughen" as she grows. This "firming up" process during childhood is caused mainly by hormonal changes. A newborn's dermis, or second layer of skin, contains almost no elastin or tissue protein, which makes skin feel almost liquid to the touch. Under the influence of hormones, including "human growth hormones," or HGH, both the dermis and the top layer of skin, or epidermis, grow and thicken. During the childhood years, HGH causes the dermis to become more fibrous as more elastin and collagen, another protein substance in the skin, are produced. An infant's skin secretes less sebum than older children's, and it takes a full eleven or twelve years until the sebaceous glands are fully developed.

New York dermatologist Dr. David Orentreich talks about the environment's role in this "firming" process. "A newborn's skin is soft because it has been exposed solely to the environment of the womb," says Dr. Orentreich. "As the child grows and is exposed to the sun, wind, heat, and cold, the skin reacts. The skin is especially sensitive to sunlight," he explains. "Exposed to the ultraviolet rays of the sun, the skin goes through a process called 'actinic degeneration' in which it becomes leathery and some of the softness is lost. The more skin is protected against the sun and wind, the less damage it will suffer and the softer and healthier it will remain."

Hair-growth changes also affect the "feel" of skin. Hair is a part of skin, as we know, and by the time a child reaches age 7, increasing amounts of androgen (the male sex hormone produced in both boys and girls) cause more bodily hair growth. As hair follicles become more active, the skin surrounding them must enlarge in order to supply the follicles with more nutrients. Skin must grow thicker to support the changes going on with the increased growth of body hair.

And why does skin darken throughout childhood? Dermatologist Michael Fenster explains that skin thickens with growth, increasing the number of pigment-containing cells (the skin's coloring agent) to increase the concentration of pigment. "The second reason a child's skin darkens," says Dr. Fenster, "is the daily exposure to the sun and the cumulative effect of this sunshine." Black children have greater protection from the sun because of their skin's extra pigmentation, which tends to reflect rather than absorb sunlight. But black children, too, must guard against sun exposure. (See page 63.)

■■■■■■■■■■■■■■■■■■■■■■■■■■■■■■■■

Nails

One of the many delightful observations we make of a newborn baby is his or her perfectly formed nails. They, like hair, originate in the epidermis, or outermost layer of skin, during fetal life and are fully formed at birth. Fed throughout life by the dermis, or second layer of skin, nails, like hair, are influenced by diet, health, and disease. Indeed, many illnesses, as well as vitamin and food deficiencies, can be "read" in the nail. Anemia, lupus, psoriasis, and thyroid, liver, and lung disease may be detected in the nails of adults by the trained eye. These conditions rarely reach the point of showing up on children's nails, according to dermatologists I interviewed, but rather exhibit themselves in other parts of the body well before the child's nails. Children's nails *will* show horizontal white lines, furrows, or depressions, after a fever, infection, or serious illness. White spots on the nail bed (the skin under the nail) are usually the result of an injury.

Harder and stronger than hair, nails grow more slowly than hair, at a rate of about $\frac{1}{8}$ to $\frac{1}{4}$ inch per month, compared to the $\frac{1}{2}$-inch growth rate of hair. Toenails grow one-half to one-third more slowly than fingernails. Some studies show that nails grow faster in the summer, and that the middle and fourth fingers grow faster than the others. Nails on the right hand may grow faster than nails on the left, perhaps due to stimulation. Children's nails vary in their strength and resistance to breakage, just as adults' do. The individual quality of nails is determined largely by genetics, health, and environment.

Nail Hygiene

Are dirty nails ever kosher? Only immediately after a session of serious mud-pie manufacturing. Aside from romps outside or gardening chores, when children's (and adults') nails inevitably get dirty, you can help your child by teaching him or her that keeping nails clean is a social and health "must."

Nails, like hair, have evolved in our culture into objects of pride. A little effort spent on finger- and toenails will pay off well in social rewards and health habits for the future.

How can you instill good nail-grooming habits? Here are a few tips.

■ Start young. Help your 2- to 5-year-old use a nailbrush when washing hands or in the tub. Some children *hate* nailbrushes because the bristles hurt the skin under the fingertips. If you don't choose a soft-bristled nailbrush, you run the risk of nailbrush phobia! Make your child aware of her toenails, too. If your children truly hate nailbrushes, have them soak a little longer and ask them to use lots of soap when cleaning. As your child grows, encourage him or her to use their own nailbrush to keep nails sparkling clean. Do nail inspections regularly, especially before meals, school, and activities such as ballroom-dancing class!

■ Cut your child's nails in an oval shape with either nail scissors or an emery board, remembering to keep nails long enough to protect the delicate nail bed underneath the nails. Make sure to round off any sharp edges left from nail scissors with a file or emery board. To prevent breaks and snags, always file nails in one direction. Children's nails are more fragile than adults', and sawing back and forth will weaken them. For younger children, use nail scissors with blunt tips to prevent accidental jabs or cuts on squirmy little hands.

■ Toenails should be cut horizontally with a clipper or nail scissors. Ingrown toenails often result from rounding off the toenail shape, which will allow the nail to grow into the skin and cause painful ingrown toenails. Shoes create further pressure on toenails, so be watchful of growing feet and tight shoes.

■ Manicures

If your daughter loves a polished look (and how many of the 3- to 6-year-old girls—and even boys—love to copy Mom doing her manicure), make sure you or another adult are around to help paint her nails. Nail polish and especially nail polish remover are very toxic. Use a nonacetone nail polish remover. It's less drying to children's nails and less irritating to the skin around them. Use any nail polish remover in a well-ventilated area, since the fumes are very strong. Listed here are some steps for a child's manicure. (As your child grows, she can assume responsibility for her own manicure.)

■ Set up a little manicure salon in your bathroom, kitchen, etc., complete with a towel, a bowl of warm water with a small amount of shampoo, nail scissors, an emery board, nail polish remover, nail polish, cotton balls, and perhaps a tape of soft music for ambience. You can even give her a hand massage first, using a bit of hand lotion warmed up in your hand. (Wow, who does this for *us*?)

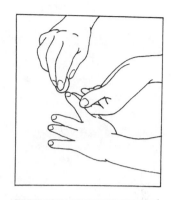

■ Clean your child's nails with soap, water, and a nailbrush. Liquid detergent may be more effective than hand soap. Remove all old nail polish with nail polish remover and cotton balls, sweeping it off the tip of the nails.

■ Dry nails with a towel or even a hair dryer to make sure nails are completely dry before filing, because wet nails are especially weak.

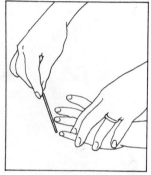

■ Cut or file nails in an oval shape. File off corners.

■ Children do not need to have their cuticles, the skin at the base of each nail, pushed back or cut. Many dermatologists feel that adults as well should leave these normal protective coverings alone. Vigorous pushing back or buffing of the cuticle may cause ridges or depressions in the nail.

■ To polish: apply a base coat of clear nail polish to prevent absorption of the color polish. The made-for-children nail polishes are generally safer than the adult products, although some of these often peel off easily. When painting toenails, use a cotton ball to separate the little "piggies." When applying, tap polish off so you'll work with only the amount of nail polish you need. Sweep polish up the center of the nail toward the tip. Use two more strokes on each side to complete each nail (your child's nails may be so tiny that you may have covered them in the first sweep). Allow to dry. Apply color coat next, using the same technique. A second coat of color is usually unnecessary.

A note of warning: Manicures and pedicures with color nail polish should be a once-in-a-while treat rather than a routine. Nail polish doesn't allow nails to "breathe" properly, and these cosmetics are harsh and could cause allergic reac-

tions. If you see any signs of rash or other skin irritations on
fingers, face, or other body parts that could have been
touched by the polish, discontinue use and talk to your doctor. Your child's skin could react to resin in nail polish. Be
aware that nail-polish products, like hair products, can cause
skin reactions. If your child is insistent on a manicure (and
how willful young children can be), introduce her to the
aesthetics of "buffing." Buy her a buffer at the drugstore and
show her how to create her own gleam by gently rubbing and
buffing her nails (avoid the cuticle, as I said above). You can
even finish off with a white pencil used on the underside of
nail tips. She may forget all about that sparkly magenta polish
she had her eye on at the drugstore!

Nail Biting

This annoying habit is one that researchers estimate affects
one-third of all children between age 6 and puberty. Because
chewing nails seems to suggest a lack of confidence, or anxiety, many of us feel a strong impulse to discourage this habit
in our children. And cleanliness presents a real health problem, too—including one that I never found in the medical
literature, but rather from a few parents I interviewed. One
mother from Atlanta, Georgia, told me about her 3½-year-
old daughter who complained that it hurt when she urinated.
The diagnosis: worms. The child was a nail biter and did so
during and after playing outside, where she picked up worms
despite her mother's attempt to keep her hands clean.

How can we get our children to stop biting their nails?
Using a bitter-tasting medicine to coat nails is not generally
successful in discouraging nail biting, but you may wish to
give it a try. Another way to break the habit is distraction.
Since nail biting is often done while watching TV, or while
concentrating on some task, you can mention to your child
that he is biting his nails, then ask him if he would like to play
catch or draw with you. Rewards for avoiding nail biting may
or may not work. One woman I know said she stopped biting
her nails at age 8 when her mother promised her a pretty
watch. At 8 years old, she may have been simply ready to quit
and her mother's reward may have been well-timed, so to
speak. If your child is older, try talking to him and appealing

to his good sense. By age 7 or 8, girls discover that torn, bitten nails are unattractive. They begin to notice that other girls can wear nail polish and have pretty nails and they can't.

Changing a habit takes internal pressure and a personal decision to stop. None of the above methods is very effective. It may be helpful to know that most habits such as nail biting, thumb sucking, and hair pulling are outgrown, usually when the child is ready to abandon it. Peer pressure—when both boys and girls get teased about their chewed-up nails—is most effective, certainly more than parental pressure. The best advice may be to ignore the problem while making sure hands and nails stay as clean as possible.

■■■■■■■■■■■■■■■■■■■■■■■■■■■■■■■■■■■

Sun and Skin Damage Among Children: The Hottest Topic Around—and the One You Can Do the Most About

Rosina, a 40-year-old mother, watches her two beautiful daughters, 5 and 8, play in the sand on a beach in South Carolina and reminisces about her own childhood in Uruguay. "We would arrive at the beach in our bathing suits at nine in the morning and play till dinnertime," she laments. "We never heard of UVA rays. Now the children are loaded with lotion, wear broad-brimmed hats, and must go inside at lunchtime. My mother always told me that children needed lots of sunlight for good health. What has changed?"

Plenty. First of all, to correct Rosina's and others' misconception, children need only a few minutes of daily exposure to the sun to produce required amounts of vitamin D. Even without the sun, an adequate diet should provide all the vitamin D necessary. The harmful effects of excessive sun exposure—skin cancer and premature aging of the skin and even a weakening of the immune system—far outweigh this small vitamin D benefit.

Secondly, we live in a vastly different world from the one thirty years ago, one in which the stratospheric ozone layer, which normally screens the earth from most of the sun's

■■■■■■■■■

ZINC OXIDE PROMISES THE MOST PROTECTION FROM THE SUN. DURING MIDDAY HOURS, USE IT ON VULNERABLE AREAS SUCH AS THE NOSE AND CHEEKS.

ultraviolet radiation, has been dangerously depleted. According to the Environmental Protection Agency, each 1 percent decline in the ozone layer could bring as much as 5 percent more skin cancer. The culprit in this depletion? Chlorofluorocarbons, a group of industrial gases released into the atmosphere. (CFC's are used as a spray propellant in the production of plastic foams and are released as a by-product of refrigerants and air conditioners.) International treaties have been drawn to stabilize the rate of emissions of CFC gas and eventually reduce them to one-half of the 1986 levels. But many scientists remain skeptical about our ability to repair the damage already done.

This is all to say that children are at a much greater risk for developing skin cancer and possibly melanoma, the potentially fatal form of skin cancer, than ever before. One doctor reports that in the 1930s, one in 5,000 Americans developed malignant melanoma, and that today this ratio is one in 150. He speculates that if the rate goes unchecked, an estimated one in 100 individuals will be developing malignant melanoma by the year 2000.

Fortunately, skin cancers among children are rare and, if found early, are almost 100 percent curable, even melanomas. What many parents don't realize is that almost all skin damage is done by the time the youngster reaches the age of 20. In those first twenty years, children receive 80 percent of their lifetime exposure to skin-damaging ultraviolet rays, and this damage is cumulative and can't be undone.

We have excellent sunscreens today to protect our children from skin cancers tomorrow. A study done by R. S. Stern, M. C. Weinstein, and S. G. Baker at Harvard University Medical School shows that regular use of a sunscreen with a sun protection factor (SPF) of 15 during the first eighteen years of a child's life might reduce the lifetime risk of skin cancer by 78 percent. (Consult your pediatrician about the use of sunscreen for infants 6 months and under.)

The importance of regular use of sunscreens becomes even more apparent when we understand that even one bad sunburn during childhood or adolescence can do far-reaching damage—much more so than severe sunburns later in life. Not only are the cells peeled off, but damage may be done to the DNA in the cells underneath. (DNA is the part of the cells that transmits genetic and heredity patterns.) Dermatologist Dr. Norman Orentreich explains: "Exposure to an hour's sunlight is far more damaging to a 5-year-old child for example, than to a 45-year-old adult, because the child's cells will be dividing many more times than the adult's. If you have an injury such as a sunburn hitting a specific aspect of the DNA, and that cell has to keep dividing for another seventy years, making copy after copy, the chances for error are obviously greater than for a cell that may divide for only thirty more years. You would expect a child to heal faster from an injury. But now we believe that the cancer results when the clone of abnormal cells takes over from an injury and continues replicating itself in this mutated fashion."

Do all children have to take special precautions in the sun—even the dark-skinned ones? The answer is yes—each and every child must be protected against the sun. Even black children, who have the most melanin, or dark pigment, which protects the deep layers of the skin, can get bad burns if allowed to stay in the sun too long. Light-skinned children of northern European extraction are at the greatest risk of premature aging and skin cancer. (See the box on page 64 for more information on which children are at higher risk for skin cancer.) A helpful pamphlet from The Skin Cancer Foundation called "For Every Child Under the Sun" lists the following characteristics for those in danger of getting skin cancer. (To get a free copy, send a stamped, self-addressed, legal-size envelope to The Skin Cancer Foundation, P.O. Box 561, Dept. K, New York, NY 10156. The pamphlet has been endorsed by the American Academy of Pediatrics.)

A final word about protecting kids from harmful sunlight: it is hard enough for a parent to get an older child to apply and reapply sunblock when he goes out for an afternoon of play at the beach or on a baseball field. You must also make sure other adults who care for your children—other parents, baby-sitters, camp counselors, coaches, teachers— are also diligent about keeping sunblock on your child, especially if he is fair-skinned. One mother, Libby, was dismayed when she came to pick up her redheaded 5-year-old, Jonathan, from a friend's home. The little boy was lobster-red. "I didn't realize he'd sunburn so easily," said the dismayed mother of Jonathan's friend. "I took them to the beach at two

BLACK CHILDREN HAVE EXTRA MELANIN IN THEIR SKIN, WHICH HELPS PROTECT IT FROM THE SUN'S POTENTIALLY DAMAGING RAYS. BUT EVEN BLACK CHILDREN CAN GET SUNBURNS AT MIDDAY IN SUMMER OR IN WARM CLIMATES. USE A SUNBLOCK IF CHILDREN ARE OUTDOORS FOR LONG PERIODS.

Who Is at Risk for Skin Cancer?

Children are at special risk for sunburn and skin cancer if they have:

- fair skin and/or freckles
- blond, red, or light-brown hair
- blue, green, or gray eyes
- a tendency to burn easily and to tan only slightly (or not at all)
- a tendency to burn before tanning
- a family history of skin cancer
- residence in a warm, sunny climate
- long periods of daily exposure or short periods of intense exposure
- a large number of moles

Source: Adapted from "For Every Child Under the Sun," The Skin Cancer Foundation, New York, NY.

P.M. and never thought he would burn." Libby had thought they were going to be inside or in the friend's shaded yard all afternoon and didn't think to mention Jonathan's fair skin. Another mother, who had on one occasion asked her 6-year-old daughter's day-camp counselor to reapply her sunblock after swimming, arrived to find her daughter with a nasty sunburn a second time. "I was so upset with the counselor, I took my daughter out of the camp that afternoon," said the mother. "It just wasn't worth having my daughter get a painful and dangerous burn like that." This counselor was careless, but extra steps, such as reminding caretakers of a child's sensitive skin with a note, are often necessary to help everyone remember that sunblock must be applied and reapplied to protect our children's skin. Give other adults your sunblock with your name written on it, along with careful instructions about where to apply the lotion and how often to reapply.

■ Sunglasses

While you're taking care to protect your child's skin, think about getting sunglasses for your child as well. Overexposure to ultraviolet rays can damage the eyes and lead to cataracts. The Food and Drug Administration has approved a rating system for cosmetic, general-purpose, and special-purpose sunglasses to let consumers know how much protection the sunglasses provide. When buying sunglasses, ask the salesperson for help in determining which degree of screening will best suit your child's need and read accompanying literature. Different percentages of UVA and UVB rays are screened according to what glasses will be worn for—the beach, boating, skiing, playing tennis, etc. The use of these sunglasses and their potential for getting broken and harming the eyes during an activity must be weighed against the general protection against the sun they provide.

■ Screening Out the Rays—Decoding Familiar Terms

Confused by the various initials in sun-protection lingo? Read on to understand important terms.

SPF means "sun protection factor," a rating used by cosmetic companies to classify sunscreens. At this time, ratings range from 2 to 50. A person who could normally withstand one hour of sun before burning could, by wearing a sunblock of 10, stay out in the sun for 10 hours before burning. SPF ratings generally apply to UVB rays (see below). Most Caucasian children need an SPF of 15 to protect against harmful summer sun rays.

PABA, or para-aminobenzoic acid, is a sunscreen developed during World War II by the American Army. Because it can be irritating to the skin, cause allergic reactions, and stain clothing, many sunscreen companies have stopped using it in their sunscreen products. If your child's skin is sensitive, choose a sunscreen that is PABA-free. Try a patch test if you're uncertain. Sunscreens that are creamy stay on longer, and ones that are waterproof are a must around pools, lakes, beaches, etc.

Ten Steps to Sensible Sun Protection

1. Keep infants and young children out of the sun as much as possible during the first year of life. A bad burn in a small infant can be very serious.

2. Watch the time and avoid the sun between 10 A.M. and 2 P.M. (11 A.M. to 3 P.M. daylight savings time). If your child is at high risk, try to schedule gym classes, tennis lessons, or visits to the park for early morning or late afternoon, so that the child is inside when the sun's rays are strongest.

3. Cover up your child with a sun hat, long-sleeved shirt, and long pants. Choose tightly woven fabrics and double layers when possible. For the newborn, a carriage with a hood is preferable to an upright stroller. With an infant or toddler, use a canopy stroller or get an umbrella attachment.

4. Use a sunscreen with an SPF of 15 or more, and remember that using a sunscreen should not be an excuse for overexposure to the sun. Sunscreens offer relative, not absolute, protection.

5. Beware of reflected light. Many surfaces—sand, cement, snow—can reflect harmful radiation. Merely sitting in the shade or under an umbrella does not guarantee protection. Be careful on cloudy days, too, when up to 80 percent of the sun's radiation reaches the ground.

6. Be especially careful at certain altitudes and latitudes. For every 1,000 feet above sea level, radiation increases 4 to 5 percent. And the closer you are to the equator, the stronger the sun's rays. Take special care if you live in or visit warmer climates.

7. Don't even consider artificial tanning devices such as tanning salons, reflectors, and lamps for your children. Radiation from these light sources can be dangerous. Obviously, tanning pills are to be avoided, too. Toxic side effects have been attributed to some of their ingredients, and they are illegal.

8. Don't mix sun with certain medications. Photosensitivity— an adverse reaction to sunlight characterized by rash, redness, and/or swelling—can be a side effect of certain medications. Consult your physician or pharmacist before letting your child go out in the sun while under medication.

9. Examine your child's skin regularly, as well as your own. Watch for any new raised growths, itchy patches, non-healing sores, changes in moles, or new colored areas. These could be signs of skin cancer.

10. Set an example for your child. The principles outlined here apply to people of all ages. If you use these simple measures to protect your own skin, it is more likely that your child will adopt sensible sun-care habits.

Source: Adapted from "For Every Child Under the Sun," © 1986, The Skin Cancer Foundation, New York, NY.

UVA rays are sun rays. They're dangerous because we don't think to protect ourselves or our children from them. They are year-round, longer, and less energetic. They can penetrate glass and plastic, and, with long exposure, can penetrate our deeper layers of skin to cause permanent damage. Children are not immune to their effects, and high-risk children should be protected with a daily sunscreen if they are outside a great deal, or are exposed to the sun on a long car ride.

UVB rays are the energetic ultraviolet light from the sun that is strongest at midday and during the summer. There are fewer of these rays than UVA rays, but they are more likely to cause burning and tanning. The UVB rays cannot pass through glass or plastic. Children must be rigorously protected from these rays with a sunscreen that has an SPF of at least 15.

■■■■■■■■■■■■■■■■■■■■■■■■■■■■■■■■■■■■■■

Common Childhood Skin Problems—How to Guard Against Their Scarring Effects

While we admire the beauty of children's clear, smooth complexions, most parents have seen at least a few skin problems on their children, whether it's eczema or birthmarks, cold sores, impetigo, or chicken pox. Many of these problems can affect the beauty and clarity of your child's skin, so speedy and careful treatment is often necessary to prevent or minimize scarring. While we know that most skin troubles affecting children leave no lasting marks, being aware of the ones that do will help you know when to seek attention from an expert.

Chicken Pox

These are the most common scars among school-age children, and if your child escapes them, he is lucky indeed. If stretch marks are the "badge of motherhood," then chicken-pox scars are surely the "badge of childhood." We can spot these scars—usually at the center of the forehead—even in closeups of actors and actresses on TV or at the movies.

No cure currently exists for this highly contagious childhood disease, although a vaccine is currently being tested. The ailment is caused by a virus akin to herpes simplex or herpes zoster (also called shingles). Parents sometimes hear the argument that kids should be exposed to chicken pox because if they miss getting it as a child, they might be hit with the virus as an adult when the attack is likely to be more severe and includes the possibility of pneumonia. Most doctors advise against purposely exposing a child to any infectious disease.

Flat red spots are usually the first sign of chicken pox. The "pox" soon turn into raised red spots, then blisters, then breaking blisters, and finally crusting blisters. There may be only a few on the body, or, in cases such as my son's, hundreds of blisters. (We stopped counting at 450!) A fever sometimes accompanies the disease. As you may know, you should never give your child aspirin when he has the chicken pox or flu. Taking aspirin during this time has been associated with Reye's syndrome, a rare but dangerous disease. Consult your pediatrician about which medication your child should take during the chicken pox.

There is no way of telling how badly your child will scar from chicken pox, or if he or she will scar at all. Sometimes a

SOME CHICKEN POX SCARS CAN BE PREVENTED IF INFECTION IS AVOIDED. CHILDREN SHOULD WEAR CLEAN, WHITE GLOVES WHILE SLEEPING SO THAT SCRATCHING POX IS DIFFICULT.

light case will produce scars. On the other hand, some children emerge from a severe case completely pock-free. Dr. David Orentreich reports that adults are left with far more extensive scarring than children. Blisters are more inflamed, which makes for more damage to the skin.

Is there anything parents can do for their children to prevent skin damage? Surprisingly, most of the scarring has to do with genetics. "Everyone has a different tendency to scar," says Dr. Orentreich. "This tendency may be inherited—if you or your parents scarred from chicken pox, chances are your children will also scar, possibly in the same site on the face."

Scarring will occur because of a child's "end organ sensitivity." Although two children may have cases of chicken pox that are exactly alike in severity, only one will scar. The latter child's "end organ"—the collagen here—collapses under the assault of the blister while the other child comes through scar-free because his skin has a lower "end organ sensitivity." How badly one scars may also have to do with the secondary infection of the blister, excessive inflammation, and even premature drying.

You can't do anything about your child's genetic predisposition, but there are some important steps you can take to prevent these added problems. Some of these steps require patience and vigilance, but avoiding lifetime scars are certainly worth the effort! If your child gets sick with chicken pox, try the following.

■ Encourage your child to avoid scratching at the blisters. This is a cardinal rule for avoiding infection at the blister site. If your child complains of feeling uncomfortable and itchy, give him a bath containing any of the following: ½ cup of baking soda; four tablespoons of cornstarch; or a cup of colloidal oatmeal (available at many pharmacies). Or ask your doctor to prescribe an antihistamine that will alleviate the itch and act as a mild sedative.

■ Cut your child's nails as short as possible and, at bedtime, have him wear white cotton gloves, which can be purchased at the drugstore, to keep him from scratching himself in his sleep. White mittens for younger children are also available.

■ Many doctors recommend keeping blisters moist because they feel that accelerated drying might encourage scarring. They suggest dabbing each blister with a little Vaseline-based antibiotic ointment. (The antibiotic guards against secondary bacterial infection.) Dr. David Orentreich says, "Every area on the body needs moisture to live. When water is removed, collagen is destroyed and scarring occurs. The longer the crust remains over the area under assault, the longer the area will have a chance to replace cells and avoid scarring." While calamine lotion is often prescribed to lessen the itching of chicken pox, and thereby cut down on the chances of secondary infections, it also has a drying effect that may not give the blisters adequate time to heal. Half of the doctors I interviewed felt it was better to use calamine lotion to prevent itching, while the other half felt it was too drying. Many doctors recommended the following compromise treatment: Have your child take cornstarch baths (four tablespoons to a tubful of water) to alleviate itching; ask your own doctor whether you should follow by applying antibiotic ointment. (You can also ask your doctor for the oral antihistamine mentioned above.) If blisters are extensive, remember that the most important area to protect against scarring is the face.

■ Insist that your child avoid picking at scabs. Dr. Orentreich says, "The premature removing of a scab means a new one has to form. This may lead to scarring, or deeper scarring, as the case may be."

If all these preventive measures have failed, and your child gets scars, what can be done? Doctors recommend that you wait at least two years to see whether the scars fade—it takes that long for the proper healing to take place. When they do, you and your child may feel they are insignificant.

On the other hand, some adults or teens are very much bothered by the deep pocks caused by chicken pox. There are three popular methods to lessen and even erase these scars: dermabrasion, collagen injections, and a procedure called "punch-graft excision with elevation," in which the scar is actually punched out with an instrument, then built up again with a graft of skin taken from behind the ear. These treatments are not recommended for children until after age 14.

A surprising complication of chicken-pox scarring happened to at least four children I know. Instead of the typical concave pocking, the scarring was convex, resulting in a bump on the pox site. This is known as a "keloid" scar. These minor keloids resulting from chicken pox are actually hypertrophic (overgrown) scars, which can be injected with cortisone if they are unsightly in later years. One teenager I heard of had her small chicken-pox keloid scar worsened to a large one when a doctor tried to excise it with a surgical knife. He hadn't recognized the first keloid scarring. Keloids are scars gone wild—and they can worsen as time goes on.

According to some sources, keloid scarring is ten to twenty times more common in black people. If keloids run in your family, let doctors know about this fact before any surgery is performed, because there are precautions doctors can take to prevent these scars from overgrowing. Be aware that earlobes are a common site for keloid scars (certain areas of the body are more prone to keloids than others), so be careful to have your child's ears pierced by a surgeon, and think twice about having it done at all if there is a family tendency to keloid scarring.

Cuts and Bruises: How to Be Sure Your Child Comes Away with the Least Possible Damage

Even a small cut can cause an unattractive scar if not treated with proper first aid. When your child gets a cut, make sure it's not gaping open and check to see whether any fatty tissue is protruding. If either of these is the case, take your child to the doctor immediately, since stitches are probably in order. Any cut on the face should also be discussed with your doctor.

Check the following points to help keep your child scar-free:

■ Wash the cut with soap and water. All soaps act as a disinfectant. Irrigate the wound with fresh water and allow the force of the water from the faucet to dislodge any dirt.

■ Use a sterile gauze pad or sterile cotton to dry the cut.

■ Disinfect again with hydrogen peroxide for extra protection against infection. Infection can cause permanent scars. Apply an antibiotic ointment.

■ Cover with a sterile bandage or gauze until bleeding stops. Then expose the cut to the air.

■ Keep the cut dry and watch for any infection. Call the doctor if any redness or any oozing occurs.

■ Facial and Other Severe Cuts

When Jill brought her 9-year-old son into the emergency room with a nasty cut on his cheek from a bicycle fall, the doctor on duty in the small hospital told her he could clean and sew it up, but if she wanted a plastic surgeon to look at it, she was out of luck. The plastic surgeon in this resort area was not taking calls for the weekend. Jill, a registered nurse, was very concerned about the scar the cut would leave when it healed, and she knew she had about six hours before the cut began to heal on its own. She opted to have the cut cleaned there, and then drive to a larger hospital three hours away. After the plastic surgeon repaired the cut, he told Jill that her instinct to find a specialist for her son's facial laceration was correct and definitely worth the ride.

How will you, as a nonexpert, know when to request a plastic surgeon if your child gets a bad cut that may result in a noticeable scar—either on the face or on other areas of the body? Certainly, you should take into account the advice of the emergency-room doctor. Dr. Guy Rowley, director of the Emergency Department at Grant Hospital in Chicago, says that a dialogue between the emergency-room physician and the parent is crucial in determining the course of action. He says that parents can do three things if they are uncertain: call the family pediatrician to get his advice; request a conversation with a plastic surgeon; and/or have the ER doctor talk to the plastic surgeon. Dr. Rowley admits that it is sometimes difficult to get plastic surgeons to come to the hospital in many instances, especially if the need for a plastic surgeon is in question.

Also, the talents of plastic surgeons vary, and most emergency doctors are as capable of repairing minor cuts as any plastic surgeon. It is fair to say, however, that plastic surgeons on the whole are more skilled in leaving the least possible scar when they sew up a cut. That's their business. If a parent such as Jill decides to drive to another medical center with her hurt child, Dr. Rowley suggests that she at least have the emergency-room doctor cleanse, but not debride (irrigate, scrub, trim off the loose shreds of skin) the wound. This is part of the repairing process that should be left to the plastic surgeon. Wet, sterile compresses can be held to the wound while traveling to the plastic surgeon. As I said earlier, cuts should be worked on within six to eight hours. A gaping cut losing a lot of blood must obviously be repaired immediately. The emergency-room doctor must advise you on your fitness to travel any distance.

Even if the finest plastic surgeon works his best magic on a wound, the cut may still scar. Some scars—especially on the face—may have to be "revised," or operated on again, if the healing is unattractive. Dr. Bill Weston recommends waiting at least two years before revising a scar to give the wound adequate healing time. Dr. Neil Sadick, however, reports that bad scars that will need dermabrasion (planing, or abrading the skin with a dermabrasion machine) should be revised within six months of the scar injury. If dermabrasion can be postponed, however, most parents elect to wait till the child is in his teens or older, since the procedure can be somewhat uncomfortable and requires the child's full cooperation.

Revising a scar can be done by methods other than dermabrasion as well: cortisone injections; collagen injections; a treatment using various acids; a combination of collagen injections and dermabrasion; and grafting. These methods are not always successful, and they should be considered very carefully. Always obtain at least two opinions by board-certified plastic surgeons before proceeding with an operation.

Acne (Blackheads and Whiteheads)—in Children?

If you thought (as I did) that children are relatively immune from acne until puberty, read on. The following questions and answers will let you know all about early acne and what you can do about it.

Q. *My 8-year-old daughter has pimples, and a friend suggested we see a dermatologist. There is no sign she has an early start on puberty. How can a child so young get acne?*

A. Dermatologists report that by age 7 or 8, children can indeed get acne. By then, children are already producing small amounts of sex hormones. Androgen, secreted from the testes in boys and adrenal glands in girls, is the main culprit in acne. These sex hormones cause oil glands to enlarge and increase their oil production. Some children's oil glands overreact to the hormonal stimulation, oil clogs beneath the skin, and pimples result. Babies sometimes get "newborn acne" at 4 to 6 weeks of age, probably resulting from exposure to the mother's androgen while in utero.

Preadolescent acne is so common, reports one dermatologist, that it is one of the major causes of scarring in children! Dr. Bill Weston, in his book *Practical Pediatric Dermatology*, says that "The onset of adolescent acne occurs between the ages of eight and ten when the early lesions of acne develop in 40 percent of children, primarily on the face. Eventually, 85 percent of children (teenagers) will develop acne." These early lesions are "precursor" bumps of acne—blackheads and whiteheads—and are usually seen only on the face. The more severe "cystic" acne doesn't usually happen until the age of 13 or 14.

Q. *What treatment is recommended for a child with acne? Is it different from that for a teenager?*

A. Most dermatologists treat acne in children, teenagers, and adults with topical medicines such as benzoyl peroxide and retinoic acid creams in child-size dosages. Soap-and-water cleaning will not be adequate for the child who suffers from acne. The usual course of treatment for acne is the following:

1. Wash one to three times a day, as your doctor has directed, with a prescribed cleanser. Follow with a lotion, cream, or gel containing retinoic acid or benzoyl peroxide applied to the affected areas. This process rids the face of grease and dirt, and stimulates cell turnover. Don't wash too often or the skin will compensate for its loss of oils by becoming even more oily.

2. Keep hair clean, washing at least every other night. Although your child may want to cover her pimples with bangs or loose hair, she must understand that hair on the face may aggravate her skin condition. Also, keep hair free from creams, gels, hair sprays, and other dressings.

3. If your child plays sports, make sure he takes a shower right after returning home—no homework, video games, or TV first.

4. Remind your child that picking or squeezing can lead to scars.

5. Many dermatologists now believe that diet plays no role in acne, while others claim that chocolate, milk, cheese, nuts, and seafood should be avoided.

Q. *My son is 6 years old and has numerous white bumps on his cheeks and the backs of his upper arms. If they are scratched or squeezed, white matter comes out. Does he have acne?*

A. No. His age and the fact that the bumps on the backs of his upper arms are similar to those on his cheeks is the tip-off that your son probably has another common childhood skin condition called "keratosis pilaris," a hereditary problem that affects dry areas of the skin such as the cheeks and backs of the arms, thighs, and buttocks. According to Dr. Weston, most people of northern European ancestry have this condition. The skin becomes dry, then scales, and finally plugs up. Parents can help by gently rubbing the area with a loofah sponge to slough off dry skin. This may help prevent new bumps from forming. Otherwise, let them alone. Picking and squeezing won't help, since the pimples will eventually return and continued squeezing may cause scarring.

■■■■■■■■■■■■■■■■■■■■■■■■■■■■■■■■■

Rashes

Eczema and impetigo are two rashes particularly unsightly and particularly common in children. Remember that all rashes must be seen by a doctor to confirm their diagnosis.

■ Eczema (atopic dermatitis)

This red, scaly, itchy rash appears in patches and is often "weeping," or oozing fluid. Babies get it on the cheek area, children get it in the folds of the elbows and knees and on the back of the neck, and during the teens and adulthood, eczema affects the hands. The condition frequently shows up in families that have a history of hay fever and asthma. Eczema is not an allergy, however, but an inherited type of sensitivity.

Continual scratching can lead to scarring, thickening of the skin, and/or pigmentation changes that often last for years. Color variations from eczema are particularly noticeable among black children. Excessive scratching among black children will cause a darkening of the skin and a bumpiness, like many insect bites, at the eczema site. Special care must be taken to get children's eczema under control as soon as possible; hydrocortisone cream is usually the treatment of choice. Dr. William Dvorine, in his book *A Dermatologist's Guide to Home Skin Treatment*, says, "About 50 percent of all children with eczema will outgrow it by adolescence. Another 25 percent will lose it during adolescence and the remaining 25 percent will continue to get it off and on for most of their lives." There is hope of permanent relief for 75 percent!

The child who suffers with eczema should be under the care of a dermatologist who will prescribe medications. Eczema is a skin condition that can be provoked by both internal and external factors. Below are some suggestions for helping the child avoid some eczema-aggravating situations.

■ Forget the Irish wool sweater look. Wool, fuzzy fabrics, and synthetic materials often aggravate eczema and produce merciless itching. Stuffed animals made of fuzzy materials may have to go. Choose loose cotton clothes for kids with this skin condition.

■ Avoid temperature extremes for your child. Make sure she doesn't go from a cool swimming pool into a hot shower. This may trigger the itching response. Since dry skin is associated with eczema, the use of a humidifier to keep skin moist in winter months is recommended.

■ Some dermatologists feel that diet plays a role in eczema, while others feel it has no effect. If you suspect a food makes your child's rash worse, avoid that food for a few weeks to see if the condition improves.

■ If your child is sensitive to ordinary soap, try a soap substitute such as Lowila Cake, or Cetaphil, a cleansing lotion. Avoid greasy ointments, such as Vaseline, that can block sweating. Rinse clothes twice with warm water to get rid of residue detergents.

Help your child through bouts of this difficult skin affliction by reminding him he will probably outgrow it. Additional stress may lead to more itching. Keep the youngster aware that scratching and picking will make the inflammation worse and may even cause infection and scarring, as mentioned above. Dr. Dvorine tells his patients to "develop a philosophy of treating eczema when it is there, forgetting about it when it goes away, and treating it again quickly when it returns."

■ Impetigo

One of the most common problems among children—and one of the ugliest—is impetigo contagioso, an easily spread skin infection caused by either a staphylococcus or streptococcus bacteria. Impetigo often starts at the site of a cut, bruise, insect bite, or even chicken pox. A reddish streak on the skin is quickly followed by the development of thick, yellowish crusts.

Impetigo doesn't normally scar, but an unevenness of the skin tone in the affected areas can remain for years after a bad case. The key to success in arresting this fast-spreading infection is immediate medical attention. My son's impetigo was mistaken for an allergic rash by a doctor when he was 2 years old, and overnight a small reddish area blossomed into a crusty swollen area covering half his cheek. If the impetigo progresses, children can develop fevers, swollen glands, and infections of internal organs.

Your doctor will advise you on the proper treatment for impetigo. Remember to keep your child's hands and fingernails clean with an antibacterial soap, since impetigo is easily spread with contact. Ask your child to leave the sores alone. Towels and other personal items can spread the infection, so wash these items after each use.

Birthmarks

Most children have some kind of birthmark. It may be the common mole, Mongolian spots (almost 90 percent of blacks, Orientals, and American Indians are born with these blue-black marks on their backs), strawberry marks, or any of the various birthmarks, or "nevi," as they are called in the medical world. Birthmarks are an excess of tissue in some part of the skin, caused by a small error in prenatal development. The concentration of these differentiated cells makes them visible.

Luckily, birthmarks almost never represent a medical problem, and many fade significantly by age 8. Even so, a child's birthmark is often upsetting to parents. Naturally, if the birthmark is disfiguring—an extensive port-wine stain on the face, or a large hemangioma (a raised birthmark) on the neck or ear—the parents should consult a dermatologist soon after birth. In rare cases, certain types of large birthmarks, usually hemangiomas, must be quickly repaired with surgery or other medical treatment, especially if they get in the way of eating, breathing, or hearing. But what about the other, more common birthmarks? Are there any new methods for removal? Or are they best left alone?

In the majority of cases, attempts to remove birthmarks leave scars more noticeable than the birthmarks themselves. However, new techniques are being refined at this time, and some are showing excellent results. What follows is a discussion of the most common birthmarks and a rundown on what can or cannot be done about them.

■ Mongolian Spots

Since these round or oval markings involve an excess of pigment cells, darker-skinned children are usually affected. As mentioned above, this birthmark is found on almost all blacks, Orientals, and American Indians. Only about 5 percent of Caucasian children have these blue-black or purplish splotches, and usually only those with a Mediterranean background. The spots are found on the lower back or buttocks, and only occasionally on the shoulders, arms, and legs. Treatment is never recommended, since they fade almost completely by adolescence.

■ "Salmon Patches" or "Angel Kisses"

The most common of all birthmarks. Over 50 percent of all infants will have a salmon patch, also called "stork bite," at the back of the neck! These light-red marks also appear on the upper eyelids and the forehead. Salmon patches on the eyelids usually fade by six months, but forehead patches may persist till age 5 or 6. These marks should be left alone. The salmon patch at the back of the neck never fades completely. Fortunately, patches in this location are easily disguised with hair.

■ Café-au-Lait Spots

"Coffee with milk" describes the color of these flat spots present at birth or later. Approximately 10 percent of the world population have anywhere from one to three spots. These birthmarks are usually medically insignificant unless they measure more than a half an inch at their greatest diameter, or number more than five. If this is the case, let your doctor know, because it could signify a rare medical condition called multiple neurofibromatosis. These marks are permanent, and removal is not recommended.

■ Strawberry Marks

Even though the doctor assured Jane, mother of a newborn girl born with a nickel-sized "strawberry mark," that the birthmark would eventually fade, the new mother was worried and upset. "Here is this perfect little girl," Jane confided gloomily to her husband. "Why does she have to have this ugly red bulbous mark on her back?" Chalk Jane's emotions up to postpartum blues and overreacting to a minor imperfection—minor when compared to the serious medical problems that can befall a newborn! But parents can and often do feel a sadness when a birthmark mars their child's otherwise perfect skin.

Also called a "hemangioma," the strawberry mark is a raised, reddish birthmark that really does resemble a strawberry. More common in premature babies, the strawberry is often seen on the back soon after birth, although it can occur anywhere on the body. Strawberry marks grow rapidly during the first year of life, then begin to involute and often fade completely in the next four or five years. Have patience during these years—by age 8, these birthmarks are usually gone. If the strawberry has not faded satisfactorily, laser techniques are a possibility. But this is a questionable option, since plastic surgeons have seen mixed results when these techniques are used on children.

The rarer "cavernous hemangioma" is a strawberry mark affecting deeper layers of the skin, often involving larger blood vessels, and in even rarer cases, presenting a critical medical problem. Surgery and lasers can help, but will probably not remove the mark entirely.

■ Port-Wine Stains

Perhaps the best-known bearer of a port-wine stain is the former Soviet leader Mikhail Gorbachev, who displays this reddish birthmark at the right top of his forehead. Like the strawberry mark and the salmon patch, the port-wine stain is a vascular nevus. This collection of dilated capillaries beneath the skin can be purple, blue, pink, or red, and is flat. Port-wine stains generally occur on the head, neck, arms, or hands, and appear on about three out of 1,000 children. An extensive port wine over the face may be a clue to a medical condition known as Sturge Weber Syndrome.

Nobel Prize winner Gorbachev seems to be unconcerned about his blemish, but what can be done for a child who has a disfiguring port-wine stain on an entire side of the face and suffers social and psychological repercussions? Until a few years ago, the only known treatment was use of argon lasers, which was only partially successful and often left disfiguring scars. In 1989, reports of great success using a "flash-pulsed tunable dye laser" on these birthmarks were published. This laser can be "tuned" to deliver different colors of light in very short pulses. The pulse is so brief that there is less chance for scarring. Results have been generally excellent, but not totally effective in all cases.

Many doctors recommend covering the mark with a makeup especially formulated for birthmarks or scars. There are several on the market. Dermablend and Lydia O'Leary Covermark are two excellent products. Write to Dermablend Corrective Cosmetics, Box 3008, Lakewood, NJ 08701, or call (908) 905-5200. Lydia O'Leary Covermark Cosmetics, Roberts Proprietaries, 1 Anderson Ave., Moonachie, NJ 07074. Call (800) 524-1120.

If you want more information on laser therapy, or if you need the name of an experienced plastic surgeon or dermatologist working with laser treatments for birthmarks, write to the American Society for Laser Medicine and Surgery, Inc., 813 Second Street, Suite 200, Wassau, WI 54401. Or phone (715) 845-9283. Parents can find support and additional information from the National Congenital Port Wine Foundation. The address is 125 East 63rd Street, New York, NY 10021. Call (212) 755-3820.

Moles

These tan, brown, or black permanent nevi are so common that we almost overlook them on ourselves and on our children. Most moles are harmless. Usually appearing at age one, moles tend to grow all during our lifetime, and by adulthood, the number of moles present on the average person is about thirty to forty. If your baby was born with a mole, or developed one soon after birth, bring this to the attention of your

ELEVEN-YEAR-OLD ALEXANDRA HAS A PERFECTLY PLACED "BEAUTY MARK," WHICH ENHANCES HER GOOD LOOKS. BEAUTY MARKS ARE ACTUALLY MOLES. TRADITIONALLY, THESE MARKS ON THE CHEEKS OR UPPER LIP HAVE BEEN REGARDED AS A SIGN OF GREAT BEAUTY.

physician, because congenital moles have a greater potential for becoming cancerous. Your doctor may recommend immediate removal or ask that you closely observe the mole for any changes and have it removed at a later date.

The concern here is that the mole might turn into a serious skin cancer called "melanoma," a tumor of pigment cells. Doctors report that melanoma is very unusual in childhood, but does occur. If any of the following changes in any of your child's moles are noted, see your doctor:

■ A mole begins growing rapidly in size.

■ The texture of the mole becomes raised or lumpy.

■ The color of the mole changes to blue or red.

■ The mole bleeds or becomes sore or itchy.

Many factors can cause changes in moles: certain medications such as cortisone; hormonal changes experienced in puberty or pregnancy; exposure to the sun. The last is the most dangerous. Research shows that exposure to the sun is, at least partially, a factor in malignant melanoma.

Parents should be aware that children who have many moles (eleven or more) are at greater risk for developing skin cancer than are those who have fewer. People who have between twenty-six and fifty moles have over four times greater risk than normal. Skin cancer is also far more common in fair-skinned people. If your child is fair-skinned, blue-eyed, and "moley," encourage him to cover up. A friend's 11-year-old son who is fair and "moley" was advised by his dermatologist to wear a sunblock with an SPF of 15 or higher every day from April to September and never go into the sun without a T-shirt—even while swimming! This advice may seem very rigorous, but dermatologists feel that skin cancer is easily prevented if we only guard against the sun.

If a mole looks suspicious or is raised and is located in a spot on the body where there is considerable friction (from collars or other clothes, or later, from shaving), your doctor may recommend removal. There is some medical controversy surrounding the removal of moles in high-friction areas. Ask your doctor about this. Methods for removing moles are simple, although children may not think so. A local anesthetic is usually administered. For raised nevi, the treatment of choice is "planing" the lesion with a scalpel so it is even with the skin's surface. Another method, called "electrodesiccation," injecting the skin with a needle that emits an electric current, actually chars the mole. It can then be scraped away.

■ Freckles

Movie and TV casting directors love freckles on children because they typify the "kid" look. Some children aren't as happy about them, but you can help them feel good about their freckles by referring to them as "special" and "cute," which indeed they are.

Blond, redheaded, and fair-skinned children are most likely to produce these clusters of pigment by age 5. Children are not born with them.

Will sunblock prevent freckles? No. Freckles are caused by an inherited tendency to have tanning pigment (melanin) clumped irregularly, rather than uniformly, throughout the skin. But freckles are a sure sign that skin should be covered by sunblock whenever exposed to the sun (see page 64). Sun exposure will cause freckles to become more pronounced, as the sun does stimulate pigment cells. Freckles tend to fade in the winter.

■ ■ ■ ■ ■ ■ ■ ■ ■

FRECKLES LOOK ADORABLE ON CHILDREN, BUT THEY ALSO INDICATE THAT THEIR SKIN NEEDS EXTRA PROTECTION FROM THE SUN.

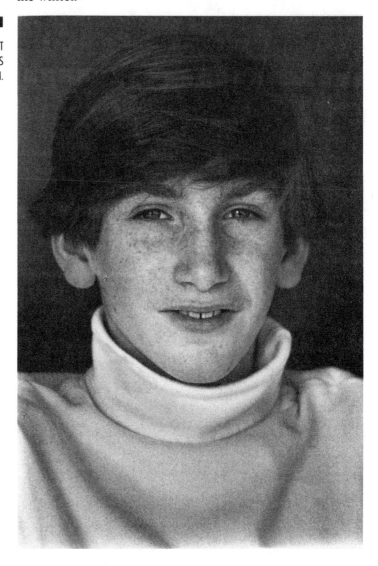

■■■■■■■■■■■■■■■■■■■■■■■■■■■■■■■■■

Miscellaneous Skin Problems

■ ## "Broken" Blood Vessels

These spidery red lines appearing on the legs are not really broken blood vessels but blood vessels that appear up close to the skin. Also called spider telangiectases, these red veins are permanent marks and can appear as early as age 7. Although the tendency to get them is largely hereditary, they can be aggravated by excess weight. When a child is heavy, there is more pressure on the venous return from the lower extremities. The combination of genetic predisposition and excess weight can sometimes leave your child with the considerable cosmetic problem of spider veins on the legs, making him or her feel uncomfortable when wearing shorts or a bathing suit.

Luckily, there are some effective remedies for these unsightly blood vessels. They involve some pain, so your child may want to wait till the teen years to pursue them. Your dermatologist will use an electric needle to cauterize the vein, which then dies and disappears. Another method that gets varied results involves injecting a saline solution into the vein. Sometimes a brownish circular spot at the site of the injection is traded for the spider vein. The dermatologist should do a patch test to see how your child's skin reacts. Laser therapy, the newest method for removing broken blood vessels, is still in the experimental stage. Helping your child control his or her weight will help prevent new spider veins from forming.

■ ## Warts

Kids may think that handling toads causes warts, but we know that a virus is the culprit. And because a virus is at fault, we also know that warts are contagious. If your child is a picker, his warts can spread and multiply, even from hands to the face.

Get treatment early to stop these "verruca vulgaris." Your doctor may prescribe a chemical or acid to wear down the skin and scale the wart off. Some of these wart removers are sold over the counter, but the prescribed ones are more effective. The doctor may also use cryosurgery, applying liquid nitrogen to remove the wart. Any wart on the face should be treated as soon as possible, since it can spread quickly.

CHAPTER THREE

Your Child's Teeth

What's New Is Enough to Make You Smile

M y kids don't have a single cavity. Why couldn't I have been born twenty years later?" laments Jeanne, a 42-year-old mother of three children ages 11 and under. "I was in the dentist's chair every two or three months when I was a child. Getting my cavities drilled is one of the worst memories of my childhood. Today I still have problems—and I'm looking at the major expense of having my fifth crown done and some periodontal work to boot. What's next, false teeth?"

Dental health has improved so dramatically since the 1940s that children today get only about one-fifth the cavities children got back then, when Jeanne was little. Our children are fortunate: half of kids age 10 and under have no cavities in their permanent teeth, according to a 1988 federal survey. As recently as the early 1970s, only 28 percent were cavity-free. Fluoride and "sealants" (thin coats of plastic film painted onto molars to prevent decay) are the champion treatments, accounting for the strong, cavity-resistant teeth of children today. High levels of dental care have made the United States the world leader in dental health today.

Obviously, genetics plays an important role in whether your children will have to suffer through the ordeal of getting cavities filled or will need orthodontic work. But preventive treatments such as fluoride and sealants, as well as informed nutrition, regular dental checkups, and good at-home care have given our kids an excellent dental prognosis, light-years ahead of our own.

■■■■■■■■■■■■■■■■■■■■■■■■■■■■■■■■■■■

Preventive Dentistry: Heroes of the Day—Fluoride and Sealants

■ Fluoride

What is this wonder substance called fluoride? It's a naturally occurring nutrient found in water and soil and a natural component of teeth. When it's added to our water or given as oral supplements while children's teeth are developing, the fluoride is incorporated into the tooth enamel, strengthening it permanently against acid attacks produced by oral bacteria. This is the main reason that 42-year-old Jeanne has lost out—

■■■■■■■■■

A CHILD'S SMILE IS ALL THE MORE CAPTIVATING WITH A FEW MISSING TEETH!

fluoride was not routinely added to water supplies in the 1940s. Only while teeth are developing—from birth to age 13—will fluoride in the water and fluoride supplements help as they enter the bloodstream and become part of the developing teeth. Even if fluoride has not been started before or shortly after birth, it can help children's teeth at any point before age 13. Fluoride, which is added topically through fluoride-containing mouth rinses, toothpastes, and fluoridated water, actually restores tiny spots of decay by remineralizing the tooth enamel. Most pedodontists recommend professional fluoride treatments for children, in which a gummy substance containing fluoride is swabbed on with Q-Tips or set into teeth using dental trays to provide fluoride topically. New studies show that the miraculous mineral may even help prevent osteoporosis by strengthening bones.

Although the cavity-fighting benefits of fluoride were discovered over fifty years ago, only a little over one-half of the United States today has fluoride at its optimal level in the water supply—0.7 to 1.2 parts per million. This level has been proven safe and beneficial. If your water is not fluoridated at these levels—and you can find out by calling your water company or calling the local health department—or if you have well water that has sub-optimal fluoride levels, talk to your dentist about getting fluoride supplements. These come in the form of tablets or drops. Schools can participate in these fluoride programs by adding fluoride to their independent water systems. If you are breast-feeding, you should know that fluoride is passed on in breast milk to your baby in only minimal amounts. Talk to your pediatrician to determine whether you'll need fluoride supplements for your infant.

In addition to getting fluoride through the water system or supplements, brushing teeth twice a day with a fluoride toothpaste is recommended by most pediatric dentists. Make sure the toothpaste carries the American Dental Association Seal of Acceptance. Fluoride mouth rinses are also good sources of fluoride, but only for children over 6. Mouth rinses should not be ingested, and kids under 6 may have difficulty controlling their swallowing instinct.

Be aware that too much fluoride in the water-supply system can cause a condition called "fluorosis," which, in its milder form, causes white spots on the teeth, or in its more severe form gives teeth a "mottled" or brown, varnishy look. Fluorosis among children can result in areas where the natural level of fluoride is too high.

Dentists across the United States are seeing increasing numbers of cases of mild fluorosis. Barbara Parks of the American Dental Association warns parents to take care they are not unwittingly giving their children too much fluoride. She warns that children under 6 may put fat stripes of fluoride toothpaste on their toothbrushes, then swallow the toothpaste because it tastes so good. This practice, in addition to getting fluoridated water and perhaps ingesting fluoride mouth rinses may add up to too much fluoride. Consult your dentist and pediatrician about how much fluoride your child is getting. Some communities have mixed amounts of fluoride in their water system—one side of a town street may be getting fluoridated water while the other side receives none from a different water system. If you are concerned about how much fluoride your family is getting, have your water tested.

Sealants

A particularly vulnerable area on teeth that even fluoride seems unable to provide protection for is the chewing surface of the back teeth, where 90 percent of all cavities in schoolchildren appear. (Amazingly, cavities *between* the teeth have almost disappeared among schoolchildren since fluoride has been added to water supplies.) "Sealing" these chewing surfaces with a plastic coating can now virtually eliminate the chances of cavity in this area. This procedure has been widely practiced as preventive dentistry since 1982, and our children have reaped the rewards!

All permanent molars should be sealed. Even though sealing doesn't work as well on baby teeth as on permanent molars because of a difference in the enamel, sealants can still be used on the baby teeth of children who have a high tooth-decay rate. Let your dentist know when your child's first permanent molar—the six-year molar—appears. It can come anytime between ages 5 and 7. Two months lapsed between the time my son's twelve-year molar arrived and his next dental appointment, and a cavity had already begun!

Had it been sealed immediately, his discomfort and our bill would have been much less. Make an appointment even as the molar is emerging.

The sealing process is simple. Your dentist washes the tooth, then applies a mild acid to roughen the tooth surface to help the plastic coating adhere. The dentist then paints the tooth with the sealant, the way one would apply nail polish. Finally, the sealant is hardened either chemically or with a light source. The seal may last up to five years, but sometimes needs to be replaced earlier. Have your dentist check your child's sealants at each checkup. These sealants may be applied all through the teenage years (when young adults are particularly cavity-prone because of frequent snacking) and even in the adult years. The *Journal of the American Dental Association* has deemed sealants the most important discovery in preventing tooth decay since fluoride!

Another bonus of this procedure: the ability to arrest borderline decay. Microscopic cavities may be prevented from developing into big ones if they are sealed over. The decay may simply stop if the tooth is sealed from contact with decay-causing bacteria. The dentist will check these sealed-over cavities periodically, and if the decay has been arrested, a filling will not be needed and the tooth structure will have been saved.

■■■■■■■■■■■■■■■■■■■■■■■■■■■■■■

At-Home Care—A Dental IQ Test for Parents

Providing your child with fluoride, sealing, regular visits to the dentist, and good at-home care gives your child an excellent start for great teeth throughout his childhood. But to test the full range of your dental IQ, try answering the following questions. Dr. Stephen Moss has helped me with the answers.

Q. *While my 3-year-old daughter has never been to the dentist, my neighbor is taking her 6-month-old baby for his first dental appointment. I know we do everything earlier these days, but 6 months old? Assuming there are no problems, what is the best age to take children to the dentist?*

Dental Hygiene for Kids

All the advances in pediatric dentistry won't count a hoot without that essential effort on parents' and children's part: good, old-fashioned at-home care of teeth. Until a child is 7 or 8, parents and caretakers must supervise and assist the child in brushing and flossing. At-home care for babies is described on page 95. By age 2, your child can be playing with and attempting to use a toothbrush, and by age 4 or 5, she may even be brushing her teeth. Because children don't really have the manual dexterity to brush and floss teeth properly until age 7 or 8, we must continue to assist them. Encourage your child to brush when she's interested, and then follow up yourself, brushing her teeth and making sure food particles are removed. Many dentists suggest putting your young child's head in your lap to brush his teeth and to see what's going on in his mouth. Try laying him down on a couch or bed with a good light source nearby if he won't lie still in your lap. Brushing in the bathroom often makes for poor visibility and inefficient brushing.

Brushing. Hold a child-sized toothbrush—soft-bristled and tufted—at a forty-five-degree angle and brush in circular motions to get teeth clean. Aim the brush toward the gums, paying particular attention to the gum line, where bacteria gather. Don't neglect the molars and the front and back teeth. Electric toothbrushes are fine for older children as long as they are reaching all the surfaces of the teeth. Only kids with braces should use Water Piks. They are inappropriate for most children.

It's best to use one toothbrush in the morning and a different one at bedtime so each brush will have twenty-four hours to dry. The possibility of the toothbrush harboring bacteria is cut down when it has sufficient time to dry. Replace these toothbrushes every three or four months.

A nonabrasive, fluoridated toothpaste is recommended to build fluoride topically. This fluoride is different from that in your water and has the effect of building fluoride from the "outside."

Flossing. Flossing is advised for all children—especially if your young child has close-set teeth—and many children's back teeth emerge closely set as early as 18 months. Flossing a child's teeth takes a little practice. Using a generous amount of floss, wrap the ends around your middle fingers and hold the floss tightly. Gently pass the floss through the touching teeth, taking care not to injure the gums by snapping the floss down. Floss your child's teeth the way you'd do your own, moving the floss carefully along the surface of each tooth, all the way down to and under the gum line. Scrape back and forth to loosen any food or plaque. Holding the floss against one tooth, bring floss from the gum line to the biting surface. Or pull the floss through to remove it. Continue this process anywhere teeth are touching, and do it twice a day. By the time a child is 7 or 8 or older—and you and your dentist must determine each child's ability to care for his teeth alone—he may take responsibility for flossing on his own. If your child is cavity-free and is not suffering from gum disease and you find flossing your child's teeth difficult, you and your dentist might decide to wait until the child is older to have him floss routinely. It is wisest, however, to let your child learn the flossing routine as early as possible. It will become an easy and valuable habit once he or she reaches adolescence.

Rinsing. Complete your child's dental hygiene by having her use a fluoride mouth rinse following brushing at bedtime *if* she is over 6 years old. (See page 90.) Mouth rinses that claim to remove plaque are not appropriate or necessary for children, since calculus, or plaque, does not harden rapidly. (Adults have a different pH balance in the mouth, which causes plaque to harden rapidly.)

How Well Are They Brushing? If you are worried that you or your child are missing spots and not brushing properly, ask your dentist for some "disclosing" tablets. When your child has finished brushing, have her chew these colored tablets to reveal plaque you or she may have missed in brushing or flossing.

■ ■ ■ ■ ■ ■ ■ ■ ■

BEING ABLE TO CARE FOR ONESELF IS ESPECIALLY
IMPORTANT FOR HANDICAPPED CHILDREN. NINE-
YEAR-OLD ASHLEY, WHO HAS CEREBRAL PALSY,
HAS BEEN ENCOURAGED BY HER PARENTS TO
BRUSH HER OWN TEETH. AFTER BRUSHING, THEY
MUST BE CHECKED FOR THOROUGHNESS.

A. While some pediatric dentists urge parents to bring children in as early as 6 months of age, the American Academy of Pediatrics states that children can wait until age 3,
when all 20 baby teeth are present. The best age *not* to
bring your child for his first visit is when that first cavity
begins. Disabled children should most definitely see
their dentist early on, since their dental health is especially important to their all-over health.

Dr. Moss, a pediatric dentist, feels that an early visit
to the dentist is important. Why? "This gives the dentist
a chance to discuss early nutrition habits so we can prevent cavities," he says. "We also try to prevent malocclusions and the need for braces later on by checking bottle
and pacifier habits. Is the bottle being used to keep the
baby quiet? What kind of nipples are being used on
the bottles and the pacifier? And what kind of position is
the baby in when breast-feeding? Malocclusions can result from early imbalances of the mouth musculature."

Your first visit with the dentist is an important one.
Be sure to discuss these additional topics: teething; fluoride intake; how to clean the baby's teeth as they erupt;
and what to do if your child falls and injures a tooth. (See
page 99.)

Q. *I've read that parents should be cleaning their babies' gums even before their teeth come through. Is this really necessary?*

A. Opening a baby's mouth and cleaning gums and teeth is not a simple task, especially when dealing with an active, feisty little one. The late Virginia Pomeranz, a pediatrician and coauthor of two books on children's health, took issue with pediatric dentists who advocate this early cleaning. "Parents can't open their babies' mouths long enough to give me a count of their teeth," she told me. "How can they be expected to clean their teeth every day?"

But it might be worth the effort. Dr. Moss believes that very early training can help eliminate parent-baby teeth-cleaning struggles later on. "Wiping gums with a piece of wet gauze once a day after feeding will get her accustomed to a daily cleaning—and will help your baby's teething as well," he says. "Later, when teeth start to erupt, you can apply a small amount of fluoride toothpaste—about the size of a split pea—on the wet gauze and gently rub gums and polish emerging teeth."

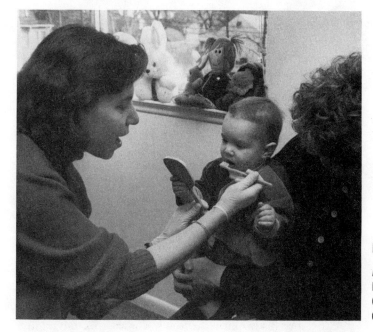

MANY PEDODONTISTS ASK TO SEE A CHILD BE-
FORE HIS FIRST BIRTHDAY. HERE, EIGHT-MONTH-
OLD DAVID AND HIS MOM ARE SHOWN HOW TO
CARE FOR HIS NEW PEARLY WHITES.

Q. *What can I tell my 2-year-old, Ben, to prepare him for his visit to the dentist?*

A. Let Ben know that this visit will be fun, and that the dentist is a friendly person who will help keep his teeth healthy. "Simply tell him the facts," says Dr. Moss. "He'll be getting his teeth cleaned and the doctor will be checking his teeth and gums." To allay any fear of the unknown, the dentist will probably employ the "tell-show-do" method before putting instruments in the child's mouth: telling him what will happen, showing him the instruments and technique, and then doing it. The careful handling of children, by the way, is a specialty of pediatric dentists, and a compelling reason to choose a pediatric dentist over a regular dentist. Their expertise in preventive dentistry also makes pediatric dentists a natural choice.

Older children can also be anxious about dental visits—as can adults! If you sense your child is apprehensive, you and she should talk to your dentist. Simply talking about the problem will go a long way in quieting dental fears.

Q. *Obviously, baby teeth are important for eating and for looking good before the second set come in. But why do I have to pay expensive dental bills for a 5-year-old's small cavity in a tooth that is supposed to fall out in a little while anyhow?*

A. Baby teeth, or "primary" teeth, are, as you mentioned, very necessary for chewing food and to present a pretty smile to the world. Baby teeth are just as important for learning to speak clearly and for maintaining or reserving a space in the jaw for the permanent or "secondary" teeth. If a baby tooth is lost too early through injury or decay (which your child runs the risk of), the teeth on either side may tip or drift into the empty space. Then, when permanent teeth come in, there may be inadequate space and the permanent tooth may be forced out of its proper position. Crowded teeth or a malocclusion might result. A dentist can replace a missing tooth with a "space maintainer"—a metal or plastic dental device that maintains the space until the tooth comes in. Your child's particular condition should be evaluated by a dentist. If a cavity has just started and the tooth is loose, your dentist may opt not to fill it. But only your dentist can make this decision. Make sure you help keep your child's primary teeth healthy for as long as possible to ensure proper transition to secondary teeth. And don't worry if your child's baby teeth are not perfect as they come in. Turned teeth and large gaps between teeth are not unusual. If teeth are still crooked after complete eruption, a dentist's advice must be sought. Many future orthodontic problems can be resolved by preventive or "interceptive" orthodontics.

Q. *My neighbor's 11-year-old daughter is actually being treated for periodontal problems her dentist discovered in an X-ray. I didn't know children could get gum disease. Is this common?*

A. Unfortunately, gum problems can occur at any age. Although usually associated with adults, children as young as 5 years old can show signs of periodontal disease. This disease, an infection of the gums and the underlying structures that support the teeth, is caused by plaque left around the collar of the gum. This plaque irritates the gums, causing them to swell and bleed. This first stage is called gingivitis. Left untreated, infection can spread down the gums, causing them to pull away from the tooth, forming pus and plaque-filled pockets. If your child's gums are swollen or bleed easily when brushed, let your dentist know immediately. In advanced cases, the bone that supports the tooth is ravaged and the tooth will fall out or must be pulled. Plaque should be removed every day with brushing and flossing to prevent the early stages of gum disease.

Because your neighbor's daughter is 11 years old, she is most likely suffering from a virulent form of gum disease called "juvenile periodontitis." This seems to affect girls more than boys, although all preadolescent and teenage children are at risk. It is estimated that a full 10 percent of American children may be suffering from this gum infection. Researchers differ on the origin of this disease, associating it with the hormonal flux of adolescence, poor oral hygiene, or heredity, usually from the

mother's side of the family. Unfortunately, juvenile periodontitis shows no outward signs such as bleeding or
swollen gums (differentiating it from typical periodontal
disease), but is detected only with an X-ray examination.
Brushing and flossing every day, and seeing a dentist for
two professional cleanings each year, will help your child's
teeth and gums stay healthy.

■■■■■■■■■■■■■■■■■■■■■■■■■■■■■■

Are X-rays Safe?

Many dentists like to take X-rays as soon as teeth have grown
in next to each other. An important diagnostic tool, X-rays
allow the dentist to see small cavities, especially between
teeth, before they become big cavities, and spot missing, and
extra, unerupted teeth, tumors, and early periodontal disease. Some 50 percent of all dental problems can be seen
with an X-ray only.

But are X-rays safe? Many parents are rightfully concerned about their safety. The danger of overexposure has
been well documented, and children are at special risk because they are still growing. A pediatric dental annal (see
bibliography for details) is somewhat reassuring, stating that
"The cancer risk to a patient from a dental radiographic
examination is estimated at one in one billion." Other data
suggest that there is less radiation from a dental X-ray than
being out in the sun all day (which is most definitely *not* good
for you, either!). Unfortunately, we have no conclusive findings concerning the harmful effects of X-rays.

Do the risks outweigh the benefits? According to the
American Society of Dentistry for Children, many important
groups, including the Bureau of Radiological Health of the
U.S. Health Service and the Council on Dental Research,
have stated that the benefits far outweigh the risks.

How can you be sure your child is getting the least
possible X-ray exposure? Certainly insist on having your
child's body covered with a lead apron during each X-ray.
According to the American Society of Dentistry for Children,
the apron "reduces the level of radiation reaching the reproductive organs to an amount equal to the background radia-

tion exposure we receive from our everyday environment." Ask your dentist if he uses high-speed radiographic film, which reduces exposure time, and modern equipment that filters scattered radiation and allows X-rays to beam on one area alone. Don't be shy! Ask your dentist to keep you up-to-date on the number of X-rays taken. If you switch dentists, request all your child's X-rays and pass them on to the new dentist to avoid new, unnecessary radiographs.

■■■■■■■■■■■■■■■■■■■■■■■■■■■■■■■

When a Tooth Is Chipped or Knocked Out, What Can You Do?

Your 9-year-old son comes through the front door with tears in his eyes and one of his beautiful front teeth in his hand, the result of a skateboard accident. What can you do?

Dr. Angelo Milazzo, a pediatric dentist who speaks to school and parent groups in Fairfield County, Connecticut, recommends the following: don't panic, and keep in mind that a permanent tooth might be saved—a baby tooth should not be reimplanted, as it may do damage to the emerging permanent tooth. First, check the child's mouth to make sure there isn't serious bleeding. Then take the tooth, handling it by the crown, or exterior end of the tooth. Avoid touching the root, because it contains tiny root fibers necessary for proper reimplantation. Gently wash the tooth off with cool water—do not scrub. Try to put the tooth back into its socket and hold it there or have him hold it there until you arrive at a hospital emergency room or dentist's office. Many parents may feel squeamish about reimplanting a tooth, but remember that the sooner the tooth goes back in, the greater the possibility that the tooth will survive.

"If the child won't let you put his tooth in," says Dr. Milazzo, "you have several options. One: Ask the child—if he is old enough—to place the tooth between his cheek and gum, thereby surrounding it with his own oral fluids until you reach medical help. This is the best environment to preserve the tooth, because letting it dry will make reattachment impossible. Two: If he's too young or won't cooperate in holding it in his mouth, place the tooth in a container of milk, or, if no milk is available, cool water." Dr. Milazzo says that if milk or water is not available, have your child spit into a cup or other container, even the palm of your hand, to surround his tooth with liquid. You can also pop it into your own mouth to preserve it—if, of course, you and your child are in good health.

Getting to a dentist or the nearest hospital emergency room within the first thirty minutes is critical. Ninety percent of tooth reimplantations are successful if done within that time. If you are hours away from medical help, though, don't give up hope, because some tooth reimplantations have worked even after the tooth has been outside for many hours. A dentist will place the tooth back into its socket and will splint it to its neighbors until it reattaches. He will give you advice on how to care for the tooth until it has reattached.

If the tooth is chipped or broken off, the fractured pieces are not usually salvageable. Your dentist will probably bond on new composite to match the color of the original tooth. One 11-year-old boy in our neighborhood bounced a wood croquet ball on the pavement only to have it come up and crack off the bottom half of one of his front teeth. He carefully protected it in his mouth on the way to the dentist only to find out that portions of teeth cannot be reattached. Only when the roots of a whole tooth are exposed are dental reimplantations successful.

According to studies, most dental injuries happen to children between ages 1 and 2 (when babies are learning to walk) and between ages 7 and 10 (when children are very active). Prevent dental injuries by keeping your floors clear of obstacles, installing baby gates at staircases, and, for older children, making sure they wear mouthguards and proper headgear for sports. The *Journal of the American Dental Association* reports that athletic mouthguards help prevent more than 200,000 dental sports injuries each year. Custom-made mouthguards fitted at the dentist's office are best, although ones purchased at sporting-goods stores are certainly better than none at all. Dr. Milazzo emphasizes that any boy or girl active in sports should wear a mouthguard, and parents should take responsibility in strictly enforcing this rule.

■■■■■■■■■■■■■■■■■■■■■■■■■■■■■■■■■

Nutrition and Diet: Feeding Your Kids Right Will Help Keep Them Smiling Bright for a Lifetime

Yet another awesome parental responsibility: what we're feeding our children *now* can spell the difference between healthy and unhealthy teeth and gums later when they become adults! According to dentist Dr. Dominick P. DePaola, early nutrition can have lifelong effects on the ability of teeth to resist cavities. "The pregnant mother provides the necessary nourishment when the baby teeth are forming *in utero*," says Dr. DePaola. "The need for nourishment continues after birth—from the development of baby teeth to the arrival of permanent teeth. When essential nutrients are deprived at certain points in a tooth's development, the effects can be harmful and irreversible." He notes that salivary glands are also formed in childhood and the lack of proper nutrients can cause these glands to produce less-than-normal salivary flow. This spells disaster for oral health, since salivary flow is the most important factor—aside from tooth structure—in preventing tooth decay. "Children need food from all four basic food groups—fruits and vegetables, breads and cereals, milk and dairy products, and meat, fish, and eggs," says Dr. DePaola. "These foods provide the essential nutrients of zinc, iron, protein, vitamin C, calcium, and phosphorus that are necessary for healthy teeth and gums."

Building and maintaining strong, healthy teeth through good nutrition is not our only culinary duty. While we all know that sugar causes cavities and that chewy, sticky sugars are the worst kind, it is also essential for parents and children to know that when, how often, and for how long food or snacks remain in their mouths is as important as what they eat. To understand why, let's take a look at how cavities begin.

■ How Teeth Decay

Plaque, that colorless layer of bacteria we all accumulate on our teeth, is the beginning of the tooth-decay process. Although we may brush and floss it away, plaque constantly forms anew. Bacteria in the plaque feed on the foods we eat, especially carbohydrates, which are sugars and starches, and convert them to acids. This acid then attacks tooth enamel. After repeated acid attacks, which occur when our children snack too frequently, for instance, the tooth enamel breaks down and cavities form.

■ Hidden Sugars

Even if your child hates candies and sodas (through some miracle), it is still virtually impossible to eliminate all cavity-causing sugars from her diet. Sugar comes in many forms, and while we may ban sugar-coated cereals from the house, sugar appears in the milk (lactose) and the bananas (fructose) that she eats on her cornflakes (which also contain sugar). Sucrose, the white, refined sugar in the sugar bowl, is present in most processed foods, so that avoiding enamel-damaging sucrose is very difficult. Kiddie food favorites such as peanut butter, french fries, ketchup, chewy bread, and luncheon meats are full of hidden sucrose.

Starches as well as sugars contribute to tooth decay. Foods containing large amounts of cooked starch, such as cakes, pies, and cookies, are setting up those baby and permanent teeth for cavities. Glazed doughnuts and birthday cake give double whammies, since the texture of these cooked starches allows them to stick to the teeth longer while sugars and starches create acid.

■■■■■■■■■■■■■■■■■■■■■■■■■■■■■■■■

Teaching Our Children Good Snacking Habits: *When* Kids Eat Is as Important as *What* Kids Eat

Make it a habit to confine starchy or sugary foods to meal-times, preferably at the *end* of a meal. The reason for this is that saliva production is greatest during a large meal and especially at the end of a meal. Saliva contains bicarbonate, which neutralizes destructive acids, remineralizing teeth and washing away food from the mouth. At snack time, give your child healthy foods that don't adhere to teeth—foods such as milk, crackers, cheese, fruit, yogurt, and, for older children, popcorn, nuts, and raw vegetables. Although it's not always convenient, brushing after each meal will give even more protection.

What to Eat for the Healthiest Teeth Possible

What children should and shouldn't eat is obviously just as crucial as when they eat. Cakes and doughnuts have been mentioned as particularly destructive—but would you believe that raisins are just as bad? A study reported in the *Journal of the American Dental Association* showed that because raisins adhere to the teeth and have a high percentage of sugars and other fermentable carbohydrates, they cause more cavities in laboratory animals than ten other snack foods, including fudge bars, granola bars, and chocolate-covered cookies with caramel!

Sadly enough, other dried fruits such as dates, figs, and bananas are just as dangerous as caramels and gummy candies, because they stick to the teeth and allow acid attacks to continue for hours. Lollipops and other sucking-type candies that remain in the mouth for long periods are also destructive. And *how* a child drinks a sugared soft drink is more important than the *quantity* of soda drunk. Sipping one sugared soft drink for hours, constantly subjecting teeth to acid attack, is worse than having two sodas with a meal.

What foods are *good* for your children's teeth? Any calcium-rich foods. Children and adolescents need extra calcium to build and maintain strong and healthy teeth. Dairy products are, of course, rich in calcium, as are fruits and vegetables, especially kale, spinach, and collard greens. Canned salmon and sardines are also high in calcium.

More good news about dairy products: some of them actually *protect* teeth from decaying by inhibiting the acid production that causes decay. Research has shown that several cheeses, because of their types of protein and fats, calcium, and phosphorus are cavity-preventing. Swiss cheese and Monterey Jack, as well as aged cheddar, seem to protect teeth. Another study has identified nine other plaque-attackers, including mozzarella, Romano, Muenster, Stilton, Roquefort, Port Salut, Tilsit, Edam, and Gouda. These cheeses are also saliva-increasers, as are most dairy products. If a child must have a sweet snack, washing it down with milk can help neutralize sugar-causing acids.

A final word about snacks and dental health: be aware of the kinds of snacks your child is getting at school or day care, too. Many day-care programs and nursery schools have instituted no-sugar snack policies. Peggy Marble, director of Christ Church Day School in New York City, which has banned sugar since 1981, reports, "The only time I had trouble with parents was on their child's birthday. Parents who arrived with frosted cupcakes were told they had to find an alternative. Even the teachers had to learn that cooking projects could not center around sugary treats such as cookies. We now make more entrée-type foods, such as tacos, and spaghetti and meatballs." If your school or day-care facility allows sweets at snack time, speak to the school and other parents to gather support for replacing them with healthy snacks. Although celery sticks with cream cheese are messier and more time-consuming to prepare than store-bought cookies, weigh the benefits of each and get active. If enough concerned parents speak out, the school or day-care center will certainly change policies.

■ Snacks for Adorable Smiles

Milk

Cheese (especially Swiss, aged cheddar, Monterey Jack)

Plain yogurt

Pizza

Hard-boiled eggs

Nuts

Popcorn

Raw vegetables (carrot sticks, cauliflower, broccoli)

Leftover meat, seafood

Fruits

■ Teethbusters

Sugar-sweetened gum

Honey

Dried fruit (especially raisins)

Sugar-sweetened soda

Sugar-sweetened cereals

French fries

Candy (especially taffy, caramels, hard candies, mints)

■■■■■■■■■■■■■■■■■■■■■■■■■■■■■■■■■■

Medical Alert: "Nursing-bottle Mouth"

"The only way I can get any sleep is to put a bottle of juice in the crib with Tim," sighed Lynne, mother of a 3-month-old baby and 2-year-old Tim. "It's a matter of survival."

Despite Lynne's desperate state, her dentist convinced her that allowing Tim to suck on a bottle of juice for prolonged periods, especially overnight, would put him at great risk for "nursing-bottle mouth." This condition is caused by frequent and prolonged exposure of children's teeth to sugar-containing liquids. The child's front teeth are especially at risk, but all teeth can decay. If teeth are very decayed, hospitalization may be necessary to repair the damage and unsightly metal or other caps may be the only solution for replacing damaged teeth.

How does this tooth decay happen? Juice or milk pools in the mouth around teeth during feedings or while the baby sleeps, and the sugars in them feed the bacteria in plaque, which then produce acids. This acid is allowed to attack teeth for prolonged periods, during which time enamel can very quickly break down. Unfortunately, the flow of saliva slows during sleep, so sugar doesn't get diluted and washed away. White spots on the teeth, then yellow or brown, are the first signs of this decay. Examine your children's teeth regularly, because if decay is found early enough, your dentist can prevent further decay.

The following rules prevent nursing-bottle mouth:

■ Avoid bottles of sugar-containing liquid or other food at nap and bedtime, and especially during the night.

■ Replace it with a bottle of cool water, if necessary.

■ Don't use the bottle as a pacifier while the child is walking around during the day.

■ Offer juice in a cup, not in a bottle.

■ Avoid too-frequent breast-feeding, and allowing the breast to be used as a pacifier. Refrain from letting the baby sleep at the breast.

■ Never dip pacifier in honey, then allow the child to suck on it.

■■■■■■■■■■■■■■■■■■■■■■■■■■■■■■■■■■■

Aesthetic Dentistry for Children: "Give Me Your Best Smile"

Do you have a child whose smile is marred by a stained, chipped, or broken tooth? Does she feel uncomfortable about smiling because of a huge gap in her front teeth or teeth that are crooked or malformed? Good news: dentistry offers new and exciting restorations for virtually any problem smile and virtually all ages. And because dental cosmetic problems are more likely than not associated with dental-health problems, including malocclusions and poor ability to bite and chew, your investment of time and money are well worthwhile.

Just as important as these dental-health considerations are the emotional and psychological ones. One 80-year-old great grandmother from Michigan still hides her teeth with her tongue and places her hand over her mouth when she laughs, a leftover habit from embarrassment when showing a chipped tooth she had all during her childhood. The tooth was repaired when she was age 20, but the embarrassment has remained all her life! Even today, many people in our society feel children can suffer with cosmetic problems—because they are just children. In fact, cosmetic problems are harder on children than adults, since classmates and other kids don't have the social inhibitions adults have. The results—teasing and cruel name-calling—can devastate and lower the self-image of a young child. Restorative dental work is not always expensive and is available in many clinics around the country. The reward is a child who can, without fear and embarrassment, smile and laugh spontaneously.

What modern techniques can be used on children? Dr. David Hendell, a Manhattan dentist specializing in aesthetic dentistry, says, "Most restorative processes used on adults can be applied to children as well. Baby teeth are not as receptive to some adult techniques, but they can be worked on—though with less success than permanent teeth." Other procedures are not indicated for children because they are irreversible and don't make allowances for growing teeth. What are the wonder techniques that will work for kids? Let's take a look at the most successful methods for repairing children's smiles today.

Bonding

Developed in the 1950s, bonding has been called a revolution in dental care. In one relatively inexpensive visit, a child's cracked or darkened tooth can be restored to its original beauty with no pain! This is truly a welcome change from the past, when cracked or injured teeth might have required a crown or "cap." Although crowns are stronger and have a long life span, they require filing down the tooth, thereby forever losing part of the permanent structure. Fitting the crown presents a problem if the child's tooth is still growing. In contrast, bonding works beautifully for children, since it is a reversible process that can be changed at any time to accommodate growth. Because of this and because it requires no anesthesia or drilling, bonding has been a godsend for pediatric dentistry. Dr. Milazzo reports that 50 percent of his work each day involves bonding.

How does it work? After the tooth is etched with an acid (to make the enamel more porous and allow the new bonding material to adhere, much like the sealing process), a tooth-colored plastic, or "composite resin," is painted onto the front surface. It is then hardened under a "visible curing" light. The final step is shaping and polishing the repaired tooth. Since bonding involves some aesthetic judgments, such as matching tooth color and shaping the tooth, it is best to find a dentist who has had considerable experience.

Bonding has very few drawbacks, but your dentist will have to check bonded areas regularly. Bonding can stain, chip, or nick more easily than crowns, and its life span is only four to six years. (But, in the case of young children, this is fine. Primary teeth will be falling out anyway.) Bonding on permanent teeth should be checked after three years. All these factors should be weighed when your dentist decides how to repair your child's teeth.

What can bonding repair? Read on.

■ *Chipped teeth*. Chipped or broken primary and secondary teeth are very successfully repaired by the bonding process. Dentists report that they are constantly repairing broken teeth in children. Bicycle falls, skateboard accidents, sports played without mouthguards, schoolyard falls, and fistfights account for thousands of cases each year. Bonding material is filled into the spots left open by the chip.

■ *Stained teeth*. In a bonding process, composite resins can be painted on teeth stained by fluorosis (mentioned on page 90) or by tetracycline. Although much has been written about the teeth-staining side effects of tetracycline, once in a while this antibiotic is prescribed for young children. The result is teeth stained in colors ranging from green to gray to black and purple. Bonding or creating porcelain laminates for these teeth can often transform a child's smile. "What I do," says one California dentist specializing in aesthetic dentistry, "becomes enormously satisfying when I see the look on the face of an 11-year-old girl seeing herself in a mirror with beautiful white teeth for the first time ever. It is very emotional for me and her!"

This painting technique can also whiten teeth left darkened by injury. Since bonding is a stopgap measure, it is a perfect cosmetic solution to an injured tooth that could die, requiring root canal at a later date. Root canal sometimes leaves a tooth darkened, too, if blood fills the tooth during the procedure. Bonding can reverse the unsightly look of these dark teeth. Bonding is also used on teeth that have grown in with pocked or stained enamel.

■ *Gaps between teeth*. Some children have unattractive smiles because their teeth are underdeveloped or too widely spaced for proper occlusion. Bonding can be used to fill in the spaces.

■ *Decayed teeth*. Why have your children get metal fillings when tooth-colored fillings made of composite resins are much more attractive? An added plus: teeth don't have to be drilled as deeply for composite fillings as they do for silver fillings. A minus is the life span of these "invisible" fillings and their poorer performance in the back molars. Metal fillings are slightly longer-lasting.

Mercury in these amalgams is a source of controversy. Some critics claim that toxic mercury vapors are being released during chewing and could cause ailments such as multiple sclerosis, headaches, memory loss, and colitis. The American Dental Association has stated that the level of mercury released from these fillings is harmless to most people. But some people have claimed relief from various physical ailments when fillings have been removed. The debate continues.

Discuss the option of tooth-colored fillings—especially where it shows. I have asked my children's dentist to use composite filling for all my children's cavities. Who needs to be a metal-mouth in the 1990s?

■■■■■■■■■■■■■■■■■■■■■■■■■■■■■■■■■

Bleaching

If teeth are stained or discolored from tetracycline, excess fluoride, or injury, bleaching has been used as a cosmetic answer—but for older children only and with less frequency today. Baby teeth are much too sensitive for this procedure, which involves painting teeth with a chemical oxidizing agent, then exposing them to heat or light, which activates the bleaching power. No anesthetic is needed. If the older child's teeth are sensitive to temperature extremes, however, he would not be a candidate for bleaching. Bleaching is cumulative, and three to ten sessions are necessary to lighten the teeth. The whitening effects may be permanent.

Bleaching remains somewhat controversial since its results are mixed. Get several opinions before resorting to this cosmetic technique.

■■■■■■■■■■■■■■■■■■■■■■■■■■■■■■■■■■

Porcelain Laminates

For badly chipped or discolored teeth in older children, the laminate veneer is an alternative to bleaching or bonding. The tooth is filed down slightly, then a thin layer of porcelain is bonded to the outside surface of the tooth. The result is like a porcelain half-crown and is usually very beautiful! Caution must be exercised when choosing a porcelain laminate, since once the veneer is applied, it cannot be reversed. On the plus side, the veneers have more strength and better color stability than that obtained through simple bonding. Since this procedure is quite new, the life span of veneers is unknown at this point.

■■■■■■■■■■■■■■■■■■■■■■■■■■■■■■■■■■

Crowns

Your pedodontist may decide that a crown is the only solution for a child's tooth that is badly decayed or injured. The crown is usually made of porcelain or porcelain and metal and is cemented over a filed-down tooth, as mentioned above. This is another irreversible procedure. Crowns can last fifteen years or more.

Make sure you discuss any cosmetic dental procedure in depth with your child's dentist. If the dentist chooses a procedure that is irreversible, you may want to seek a second opinion, especially if the procedure is elective. Dentists often differ in their approaches to a problem. One West Virginian mother took her two-year-old son to a specialist to fix his broken canine tooth. When the dentist applied a metal crown, she never thought to question his decision. By the time her son reached the first grade, he had become shy about smiling. Classmates had started teasing him about his "silver tooth." "I had no idea I could have had Noah's crown veneered with a tooth-colored face," says this mother. "The dentist never even mentioned it to me. I know it would have cost more and involved more visits, but I could have avoided Noah's being teased if the dentist had only given me the choice." The dentist was perhaps more convinced of the metal's durability and concerned about holding costs down, but he should have explained the alternatives to this parent. Be sure to question your dentist about all the latest techniques available for restoring your children's teeth for the most attractive smile possible. If you feel your dentist's know-how or equipment is out of date—and they can be—move on!

■■■■■■■■■■■■■■■■■■■■■■■■■■■■■■■■■■■■

Orthodontia

Applying braces to misaligned or maloccluded teeth is the specialty of orthodontists. A malocclusion may be inherited, or crooked teeth may result from bad dental habits such as when children use their mouths instead of their noses to breathe (mouth breathing), thrust their tongues against their teeth or bite their lips (lip biting), or suck their thumbs. Thumb sucking is not harmful among babies and only becomes a problem at age 3 or 4.

■■■■■■■■■

NINETY-SEVEN PERCENT OF ALL BABIES AND YOUNG CHILDREN SUCK THEIR THUMBS. AFTER THE AGE OF 3 OR 4, THUMBSUCKING MAY INTERFERE WITH SPEECH PATTERNS AND TEETH POSITIONING. ASK YOUR DENTIST FOR HELP IN GETTING YOUR CHILD TO STOP.

A wonderful book for children who are having trouble stopping thumb sucking is *David Decides About Thumbsucking*, by Susan Heitler (Denver: Reading Matters, 1985).

Missing teeth due to injury, dental disease, or premature loss can also mean orthodontic work. Orthodontists are also responsible for diagnosing, preventing, and treating facial irregularities, such as receding chins or jaws that jut to one side or the other. Severe jaw misalignments, known as "temporomandibular disorder," which often involve malocclusion and muscular disorders in the jaw joint, are treated by a specialist known as a maxillofacial surgeon.

Dr. Terry McDonald, chairman of the Council of Orthodontists and a practicing orthodontist in Salem, Oregon, strongly advises that a child have her first orthodontic examination at age 7. While your family dentist will probably be watching for early signs of malocclusion, Dr. McDonald believes the parent should take an active role in asking him about the child's bite from time to time. Not all dentists are sufficiently aware of the very early need for orthodontic attention, and the Council of Orthodontists is now conducting a campaign to inform dentists and the public about this. Dr. McDonald says, "I can't emphasize strongly enough that children need attention paid to their orthodontic structure while the child is *still* growing. It can make an enormous difference in our ability to correct 'buckteeth,' a receding chin, and other problems. Orthodontia is a dynamic science, and we should have the opportunity to make changes while the child's facial structure is still forming."

Correcting adult bones and teeth can cost much more—in time and money—and may not always be successful. My own experience is telling: my son would not have had to wear braces if a relatively inexpensive mouth appliance had been used for his cross-bite at age 7. But my former dentist did not prescribe this simple orthodontic measure. By age 11 he required three years and $4,000 worth of braces. True, these appliances are not always a hundred percent effective and braces may still be needed, but we certainly would have given it a whirl!

Dr. McDonald has witnessed dramatic personality changes after orthodontia. Unhappy children or teenagers with poor self-esteem have turned into kids who can smile

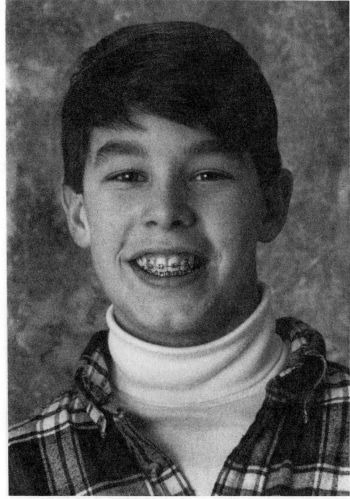

and present themselves with confidence. "The sooner we
start this process, the better," says Dr. McDonald. "At age 7
or 8, the bones *and* the self-image are still forming. If need
be, we can improve both." Dr. McDonald works with school
administrators who are very concerned with helping children
feel good about themselves. He understands that the child or
teenager who has a positive self-image is less likely to get
involved in drugs and alcohol. "There are many factors con-
tributing to how a child views himself," says Dr. McDonald.
"But sometimes simply correcting an odd smile or lifting a
receding chin can make the difference between a happy and
an unhappy child."

Aside from an improved self-image, what else can orthodontic treatment do for your child's teeth? Orthodonture can:

■ Help keep teeth healthy. A poorly aligned bite can cause teeth to dig into gums, damaging them, often resulting in periodontal disease.

■ Make teeth easier to clean.

■ Make chewing easier. Foods that are difficult to chew and were avoided in the past can now be added to the child's diet.

■ Help relieve tension in the jaw joints. Children who have misaligned teeth often end up chewing harder and longer.

Although 95 percent of the braces applied today are the standard stainless type (now cemented onto—instead of "banded" onto—the tooth surface), there are other types of braces available. "Invisible" braces with tooth-colored plastic brackets, and "lingual" braces that are attached to the tongue side of the teeth so they can't be seen, are two new alternatives. These braces are popular with adults but usually not suitable for children. Lingual braces take longer (braces pull in rather than push), may cause tongue irritation, and cost more because of more frequent visits for adjustments. Also, plastic-bracket "invisible" braces may stain and break more easily.

■■■■■■■■■■■■■■■■■■■■■■■■■■■■■■■■

The Future of Dentistry

Our children's dental destiny: just what is on the horizon? The most exciting news: by the year 2000, a vaccine against dental decay may be available. Amazing but true. Dr. Stephen Moss helped me report here on the other new treatments for our dental future:

■ A liquid that eats away tooth decay, already in use around the country. No drill, no anesthesia needed. Called the Caridex Caries Removal System, it has received conditional approval from the Food and Drug Administration. It won't replace all drilling, but can be used for certain types of decay.

■ Fluoride-releasing pellets attached to teeth. Low levels of fluoride will be released round the clock to harden the enamel and assure maximum protection for children's teeth.

■ Remineralizing solutions. These solutions will actually replace the tooth minerals lost through initial tooth decay.

■ "Cloned" tooth enamel, identical to the original. A perfect match!

■ Lasers to replace the dental drill. Lasers can vaporize the decay, then help seal tissues. They will be particularly helpful in root canal work. This technique will eliminate discomfort and speed healing.

■ Braces which work electronically to reposition teeth, requiring less than half the time needed for today's braces.

■ Less orthodontic work necessary in general. As pediatric dentists learn more about appliances and facial exercises, muscular imbalances and malocclusions may be able to be corrected without costly, time-consuming braces.

■ A smile forecast projected onto a TV screen, assisted by a computer, to show how cosmetic dentistry can work its wonders on your child. Also, a tiny video camera can show dentist and patient where cavities are on a TV screen and how they are repaired (if patients care to watch!).

The future in dentistry is bright. With proper care and with the awareness this chapter has hopefully provided, your child has the opportunity to have the healthiest, prettiest smile ever!

CHAPTER FOUR

Diet and Nutrition for the Growing Child

A
re you worried about:

- ■ Too much fat in your child's diet?

- ■ Providing your child with a well-balanced diet in a fast-food world?

- ■ Your children getting enough vitamins and minerals when they seem to hate vegetables?

- ■ Hidden salt and sugar in processed food?

Many parents I have talked to have these and similar concerns. These are people who are nutritionally informed yet often feel powerless in getting their children to eat a well-balanced diet. A serious problem? Yes, because a child's nutrition affects his health and looks not only now, but also in the future—as a teenager and as an adult. Factors working against providing your children with the most healthful diet and best eating patterns possible are numerous and complex.

"I know that our dinner table should be laden with foods that are whole-grain, high-fiber, low-fat, low-salt, and fresh, fresh, fresh," says Donna, a working mother of three children under the age of six. "But both my husband and I are gone from 7 A.M. to 5 P.M. when the baby-sitter leaves. I simply can't make fresh meals each night. Half the time it's frozen, processed, microwavable food that I confess has saved my life."

Donna's lack of time is not the only factor undermining her best efforts to feed her children wisely. Busy parents must also contend with the easiness of fast-food restaurants. Their advertising glamorizes them. Kids love them! And despite some positive efforts to provide some new "lean" choices on fast-food restaurant menus, most foods in these places are chock full of salts and sugars, as are many of the processed foods bought at stores.

Helping your children eat the foods that are best for them all throughout childhood is an enormous responsibility. The "Dietary Guidelines for Americans," published by the U.S. Department of Agriculture and the Department of

■ ■ ■ ■ ■ ■ ■ ■ ■

PARENTS ARE ABLE TO PASS ON GOOD NUTRITION TIPS WHEN CHILDREN HELP PREPARE DINNER. HERE, FRANCESCA'S SALAD DRESSING IS OFFERED UP FOR DAD'S TASTE TEST.

Health and Human Services (1985), outlines general rules that apply to children as well as adults:

■ Eat a variety of foods

■ Maintain desirable weight

■ Avoid too much fat, saturated fat, and cholesterol

■ Eat foods with adequate starch and fiber

■ Avoid too much sugar

■ Avoid too much sodium

■■■■■■■■■■■■■■■■■■■■■■■■■■■■■■■■

Do Children's Nutritional Needs Differ from Adults'?

"Not very much!" say the experts. The Recommended Dietary Daily Allowance chart published by the Food and Nutrition Board of the National Academy of Sciences reveals that nutrients for children and those for adults differ by a very small margin. Babies, of course, have radically different nutritional needs; they require more iron, more fat, and more protein per pound than either a child or an adult. "But after age 2, children can eat what their parents eat," says Dr. William Lattanzi, an expert in pediatric nutrition and clinical professor of pediatrics at Yale University. "There are no special requirements for growing children other than eating from the four basic food groups (see pages 123–24) with enough protein and calories for proper growth." If a child disdains one or more of the food groups, Dr. Lattanzi recommends adding more milk to cover their absence. "Milk really is an almost perfect food," he says.

Citing the lack of hard data in the field of nutrition to create an "ideal diet" for children, Dr. Lattanzi comments, "My message to parents is to 'relax' and don't worry if your child skips breakfast, or even a whole day of eating. If children generally eat a varied, well-balanced diet, and avoid food fetishes and fad diets, they will get all the nutrients they need to grow healthy and strong."

The 1988 "Surgeon General's Report on Nutrition and

Health" reiterates these suggestions and adds the recommendation that children (along with women of childbearing age and adolescent girls) should eat foods rich in iron as well as adequate amounts of calcium-rich foods.

■■■■■■■■■■■■■■■■■■■■■■■■■■■■■■■■

What About Extra Vitamins and Minerals During Childhood?

Children ages 2 to 12 have less need for extra vitamins and minerals than during other periods of rapid growth, such as babyhood, adolescence, and pregnancy. While babies up to age 2 do require vitamin supplements, older children do not. Even as your kids are growing, their nutritional needs are easily met with a varied and well-rounded diet. If a child absolutely refuses to eat any foods from one or more of the food groups listed on pages 123–24, talk to your pediatrician about prescribing a vitamin supplement. One way to help keep your doctor informed about your child's nutrition is to keep a diary of meals for a week or two. Show this record to your doctor or a registered dietician to help him understand whether the child's diet is adequate.

■■■■■■■■■

GRANDMOTHERS ARE FAMOUS FOR FEEDING CHILDREN DELICIOUS, BUT NOT ALWAYS NUTRITIOUS, SWEET TREATS SUCH AS COOKIES, CAKES, CANDIES, AND ICE CREAM. AS A GRANDMOTHER OF SEVENTEEN, THIS GRANDMA KNOWS THAT OFFERING A HEALTHY SNACK SUCH AS FRUIT IS BEST.

■■■■■■■■■■■■■■■■■■■■■■■■■■■■■■■

What Your Child Needs Each Day

To make sure your child gets the variety and balance she or he needs to stay healthy and grow strong, foods should be eaten from the basic food groups in amounts corresponding to the ranking in the "pyramid" food system (page 125). Calorie needs range from 1,500 to 2,800 each day (smaller children need less, while bigger, older children obviously need more). An average is 2,200 calories. Make an effort to eliminate junk food—candies, cookies, chips, soda, most baked products—from their food choices. They get enough of this type of food outside your house. Emphasize healthy, high-fiber foods such as vegetables, fruits, and whole-grain cereals.

The new nutritional thinking emphasizes how *often* we should eat which foods from each food group. For example, grilled fish, sirloin steak, and hot dogs are in the meat group, but fish is recommended to be eaten anytime, sirloin steak sometimes, and hot dogs should be confined to a once-in-a-while treat. From the milk group, skim milk can be enjoyed anytime, frozen low-fat yogurt sometimes, and ice cream should be eaten only occasionally.

Be aware of the kind of example you're setting, too. Don't expect kids to eat what you ask them to when you're eating differently. Kids learn by imitation. Set the example by eating nutritious foods and keeping junk food to a minimum.

How can you translate general advice on nutrition into what you put on your child's plate? The following guidelines have been compiled from three sources: *Health, Safety, and Nutrition for the Young Child* by Lynn Marotz, Jeanettia Rush, and Marie Cross; Dr. William Lattanzi; and the "Nutrition Action Healthletter," June, 1990. Serving sizes are approximate; little children should not be expected to eat a full serving. One nutrition expert suggests that for each year of the child's age, give one tablespoon of food from each food group. An 8-year-old might need 8 tablespoons of yogurt, or $1/2$ cup as a serving size.

Grain Group

(High in iron, thiamin, niacin, riboflavin, and complex carbohydrates)

(A younger child's serving size is 1/2 of an adult's; an older child's is equal to 1 adult serving.)

Four or more servings of:

■ Enriched whole-grain bread (1 slice = 1 serving)—anytime

■ Pasta (1/2 cup = 1 serving)—anytime

■ Rice (1/2 cup = 1 serving)—anytime

■ Dry, unsweetened, ready-to-eat cereal (1 cup = 1 serving)—anytime

■ Cooked cereal (1/2 cup = 1 serving)—anytime

■ Crackers (3 = 1 serving)—sometimes

Fruit and Vegetable Group

(High in vitamin A, vitamin C, and fiber)

(Serving size for young children is 1/2 raw fruit. Serving size for an older child is 1 raw fruit. All fresh fruits and most vegetables may be eaten anytime.)

Four or more servings of:

■ Fruit or fruit juice (especially those high in vitamin C such as oranges, strawberries, and grapefruit).

■ Vegetables or vegetable juices (especially those green, leafy, or deep-orange vegetables rich in vitamin A such as spinach, broccoli, carrots, and sweet potatoes).

Dairy Group

(High in calcium, protein, and riboflavin)

■ 3 cups milk or equivalent from group. One cup equals:
1 1/2 ounces American or cheddar cheese—seldom
1 3/4 cup of frozen low-fat yogurt—sometimes
1 cup nonfat yogurt (8 ounces)—anytime

Meat Group

(High in protein, thiamin, niacin, and iron)

(Servings for small children will be only 1 ounce, while an active 12-year-old's serving size might be 3 to 6 ounces.)

Two or more servings of:

- Lean ground beef (seldom)
- Lamb (sometimes)
- Pork tenderloin (anytime)
- Chicken breast with skin (sometimes)
- Broiled fish (anytime)
- Bologna (seldom)

Other foods high in protein are:

- Eggs (1 egg = 1 ounce meat) (seldom)
- Legumes such as beans and dry peas (anytime)
- Nuts (sometimes)

Other Foods

(to be used sparingly)

- Salt
- Sugar
- Oils

Water

(2 to 8 glasses a day, depending on age)

Don't be worried if your child skips a meal or two or refuses healthy foods that you want him to eat, as mentioned earlier. Keep offering new and old choices. If your child hates vegetables, offer more fruits or try burying vegetables in dishes such as meat loaf. The dinner table can become a battleground for your child at various stages of his childhood. Toddlerhood and preadolescence are fertile periods for power struggles with you, and food is a powerful bargaining tool. Accept your children's food preferences, but don't allow him to eat non-nutritious foods in their place.

Pyramid or Pie?
The USDA's Pickle

While the United States Department of Agriculture is responsible for promoting the meat and dairy industries, it is also responsible for educating the public about nutrition—a perfect scenario for a conflict of interest. When, in the spring of 1991, as the USDA prepared to publish its new pamphlet, the "USDA's Eating Right Pyramid" (see below), *The Washington Post* ran an article on it and the meat and dairy industries complained so vehemently that publication was halted. Why? The new pyramid food configuration, which would replace the old "pie" shape or "food wheel" for food grouping, while giving the same serving recommendation, places milk and meat groups in the seemingly unflattering position in a narrow band right below the notorious fats and sweets group. "We wanted to avoid a good-food, bad-food ranking and a de-emphasis of meat," a spokesperson for the National Cattlemen's Association told *The New York Times*. The pyramid, which is easy for children to understand, was finally published in 1992.

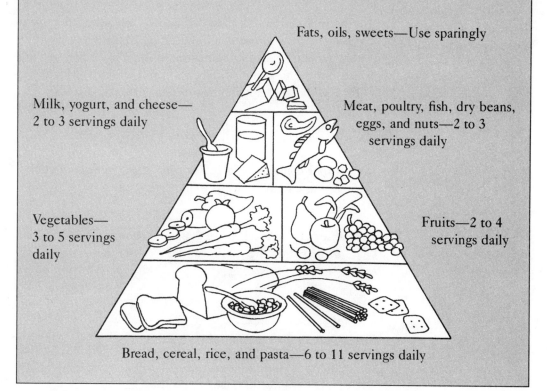

Fats, oils, sweets—Use sparingly

Milk, yogurt, and cheese— 2 to 3 servings daily

Meat, poultry, fish, dry beans, eggs, and nuts—2 to 3 servings daily

Vegetables— 3 to 5 servings daily

Fruits—2 to 4 servings daily

Bread, cereal, rice, and pasta—6 to 11 servings daily

■■■■■■■■■■■■■■■■■■■■■■■■■■■■■■■■■■■

Nutrition Risk IQ Test: How Much Do You Know About Salt, Sugar, Saturated Fats, and Cholesterol in Your Child's Diet?

There's been a lot written about fats, sugars, and salt in our diet. Do excessive amounts of them have the same negative effect on children as they do on adults? If they do, it certainly is hard to control intake, because food manufacturers are still not required to state exact amounts of ingredients on their labels. Although we know they are listed in order of greatest percentage, the largest amounts first, we still have no idea if the listed salt, sugar, or fats are 25 or 75 percent! In a 1988 *Parents* magazine poll, 90 percent of those questioned said they would like to see the present federal labeling law changed to assure greater accuracy. At least we now have uniform definitions of "lite," "low-fat," and other advertised claims, thanks to the Food and Drug Administration's 1991 announcement of new standards of definitions and serving sizes for the food industry, to be in full effect by May 1993. Try your hand at nutrition know-how and take this test:

■ Mark "True" or "False" after each statement.

1. A diet containing more salt than the minimum required during childhood leads to hypertension.
   True_____ False_____

2. After a child reaches age 2, parents should cut down on fat in the child's diet to prevent heart disease.
   True_____ False_____

3. Olive oil actually helps lower cholesterol.
   True_____ False_____

4. If you present your baby with every type of food, he will choose a well-rounded meal in proper combinations for excellent growth. True_____ False_____

■ Answers:

1. False, or not necessarily so. At this point, medical research cannot definitely relate excess salt to hypertension, although many factors (and some studies) seem to
link the two. Doctors do, of course, ask adult patients
with hypertension to reduce salt intake in order to reduce
fluid retention and allow blood vessels to contract or narrow more easily. The 1988 *Pediatric Nutrition Handbook*
states, "There is no conclusive evidence that high-sodium
intakes during infancy and childhood are detrimental to
the health of even the one fifth of children likely to develop hypertension as adults. But high-sodium intakes
are unnecessary, and parents and children should have the
opportunity to avoid unapparent sources of sodium in the
food supply."

    Remember that taking salt off the table and not adding salt to your cooking is only part of helping restrict salt
intake. Processed foods and fast foods contain lots of salt.
Try to serve fresh, unprocessed foods and you'll be better
able to control your family's salt intake.

2. True or false, depending on whether you listen to the
American Heart Association (true) or the American Academy of Pediatrics (false). According to the former, kids
should cut down on fats and cholesterol because of evidence that shows that fatty buildup in the arteries can
begin in childhood. The American Academy of Pediatrics
counters that more fats are possibly needed during childhood than adulthood because we don't know enough
about the development of the brain to unduly restrict fat
intake. It is thought that lipids, the main structural components of living cells, are still being deposited in the
brain during childhood. Fats are the source of these lipids.
Fat is also needed for fuel in body development and energy. Babies, before age 2, have the greatest need of fats
for optimum development; indeed, human breast milk is
50 percent fat!

    The typical American fare is high in fat, usually
making up 40 percent of the total amount of calories. The
American Heart Association would like to reduce that
amount to 30 percent, while the American Academy of

Pediatrics suggests that kids up to age 5 keep it at 30 to 40 percent. Children with a family history of atherosclerosis should be screened and those with elevated cholesterol levels (especially obese children) should be monitored, carefully watching their intake of saturated fats, or fats such as butter that solidify at room temperature.

3. True. Recent research has shown that the monounsaturated fat in olive oil and canola oil (primarily rapeseed oil) are helpful in lowering cholesterol. This is why the Mediterranean diet has consistently proven to be low in cholesterol. But be careful: this doesn't give one license to go crazy with olive oil. Fats still should not exceed 30 to 40 percent of your family's total diet, depending on the age of family members.

Here are some tips to help you and your family cut down on fats.

■ Train yourself to measure out fat when using it for cooking. You can gradually lessen the amount of oil in your cooking from many tablespoons to just one teaspoon with careful measuring. Don't toss a chunk of butter into the pan next time you sauté your sole. Butter is high in saturated animal fats. Just a teaspoon or two of margarine is enough to cook and add flavor. Better yet, use a vegetable-oil spray or a nonstick pan with broth. Best of all is to bake, broil, or grill meats and fish.

■ Chinese woks are great for keeping oil consumption down, and most kids seem to love stir-fried foods. My children actually eat the vegetables, too.

■ Those oily salad dressings can undo a lot of your fat-cutting efforts. Use an unsaturated oil, such as olive oil, in two parts to one part vinegar. Don't drench the salad. Train your family to use as little dressing as possible. Children will get used to tasting mostly fresh vegetables with a minimum of dressing.

■ When dining out, ask the chef to broil, bake, or grill instead of frying. Sauces can be served on the side. A 1987 Gallup poll survey reported that three out of four restaurants will cooperate with these requests. One out of three

restaurants polled stock low-fat milk and reduced-calorie salad dressings as well.

4. False. Pediatricians have been repeating this theory for years, but unfortunately it is wrong. It evolved from a study conducted in the 1920s and 1930s by pediatrician Clara Davis. Dr. Davis's infants and children did choose a varied and healthful diet in proper amounts. But what was not recorded was the fact that sugars, syrups, and sweetened foods were not included among their choices! I heard about this study when my children were young and tried it myself. I laid out all the food groups, including the dessert that Dr. Davis forgot, and was shocked, therefore, to see them go for the dessert first, every time! Now I know why. Studies have shown that babies almost always prefer sugared water over plain water and pudding and cake over strained vegetables and meat. No wonder my kids chose the cookies over carrots and chicken!

Try to curb your child's natural desire for sweets by not serving too many at home. Sugars are "empty calories," of no nutritional value, and often kill the appetite for better foods. Food manufacturers hide sugars in everything—from ketchup to "unsweetened cereals"— because they know we love sugar! Check labels for added sugars and eliminate when possible.

CHILDHOOD MEMORIES ARE OFTEN CREATED AROUND SPECIAL OCCASIONS WHERE WONDERFUL FOODS ARE FEATURED. AT THIS MOTHER-DAUGHTER TEA, CHILDREN COULD SAMPLE OLD-FASHIONED DELIGHTS SUCH AS PETIT-FOURS WITH MARZIPAN FILLINGS.

CHAPTER FIVE

Body Image

Too Fat?
Too Thin?
Too Tall?
Too Short?

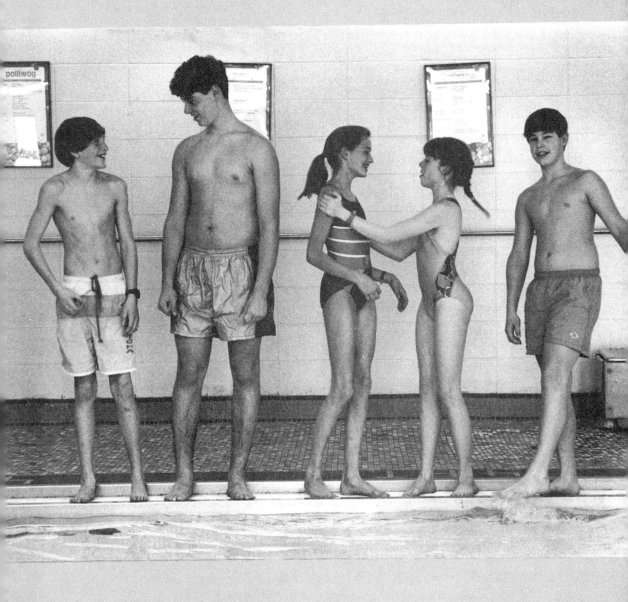

Old hurts die hard. My friend, Cindy, now in her forties having reached 5'8" by the seventh grade, remembers the taunts she received at a shatteringly sensitive time in life, especially at the hands of one boy who would not only tease, but also shove. Her parents reassured her that this boy, by teasing and striking out, probably had his own problems: he was insecure; or possibly felt threatened because he himself hadn't yet reached 5'3". Or maybe he was even attracted to her. Revenge was indeed sweet years later as a senior in high school, when they had both reached 5'10" and she was able to turn down his many requests to go out. When her twenty-fifth high school reunion rolled around, although Cindy was divorced, and he the same, she again took great delight in spurning his request to get together. She feels that perhaps by their fiftieth reunion she may be able to forgive him.

Do we ever get over the preoccupation with how we are physically less than perfect or perfectly average? And what is it about human nature that doesn't let us—especially us females—ever feel satisfied with our bodies and looks when we know our personalities, our kindnesses, good works, our love, intelligence, and creativity are much more important? The answer probably lies in childhood and adolescence.

A study in which adult women were asked to recall comments on their looks made between the ages of 8 and 16 showed just how damaging teasing is. J. Kevin Thompson, Ph.D., associate professor of psychology, told *Redbook* magazine, "We found that childhood teasing—no matter who made the remarks—was associated with adult anxiety, depression, eating disturbances and body image problems. A single teasing remark can cause a very negative self-image that frequently lasts even after whatever feature prompted that remark is outgrown."

Teasing remarks by parents were found to be especially damaging. We parents must be particularly careful not to "label" our children. Unfortunately, for all the positive efforts we make for our children, it's often the one or two mistakes, usually committed in anger, that become branded in children's memory cells forever! (Counting to ten and taking deep breaths before saying something regrettable go a long way in defusing anger.)

■ ■ ■ ■ ■ ■ ■ ■ ■

THESE 12- AND 13-YEAR-OLDS ARE AT AN AGE WHEN BODY BUILDS AND HEIGHTS VARY ENORMOUSLY. THESE DIFFERENCES AMONG PREADOLESCENTS—ESPECIALLY WHEN THEY CLASSIFY THEMSELVES AS TOO TALL, SHORT, THIN, OR FAT—ARE OFTEN CAUSES FOR SELF-DOUBT AND INSECURITY.

Words That Hurt

"Sticks and stones may break my bones but names will never hurt me." Perhaps this ditty arose to help kids through the social battlegrounds of childhood, but names *can* hurt forever. The TV public awareness commercials that warn parents against belittling children with insults—"You'll never amount to anything"—or calling them names like "dumb" or "stupid," have alerted us to the powerful psychological impact of negative words. Such verbal assaults are certainly one form of child abuse. One of the most valuable pieces of childrearing advice I ever heard came from Fred Rogers of "Mister Roger's Neighborhood." He warned parents never to say "You're a bad boy" or "You're a bad girl," but to separate the child's behavior from the child. The behavior or action may be inappropriate, of course, and the child must be accountable. But the child must also know he or she is basically good in order to form a positive self-image.

One way to let children know what they can and cannot do is to tell them how their behavior affects you. Dorothy Corkille Briggs in *Your Child's Self-Esteem* suggests ". . . simply telling youngsters *your* personal reactions toward their behavior." She urges parents to replace a remark such as "You're lazy," with a statement such as, "I'm worried about your grades." Or instead of saying, "You're a bad boy," let the child know, "It hurts little Mike when he's pinched. I don't like to see him hurt." Children who feel that at their center is a good self are better able to build a sense of self-control and to face the rest of the world with confidence.

When Does Body Image Develop?

I recently watched a group of 8-year-old girls excitedly examining a poster featuring the teenage stars of a popular TV show. With great detail, they determined which character had the best body, remarking on thickness of thighs, tightness of tummies, etc. They then began remarking how fat their own thighs or tummies were—who had good legs, who was "so fat." I tried to point out the show's characters' other qualities such as the compassion of one, the sense of humor of another, the high achievements of yet another and how their own positive personality traits were more important than a protruding tummy or big calves. But I knew then that I had lost them. Body image is a very important commodity in our culture and TV, rock videos, and advertising will never let them forget it. Eve had already bitten the apple in the Garden of Eden: these 8-year-olds had lost their freedom from self-consciousness, and this loss of innocence is happening earlier than ever before.

Dr. Mary Lee Ruff, a Virginia pediatrician, believes that not only are our own popular culture and the advertising media to blame for dissatisfaction with our bodies, but that parents must also be held accountable. "When a 6-year-old girl comes in and tells me she's getting too fat, I know she is mimicking her parents, usually the mother, who complains about how fat she is, what diet she is on, and how she could look much better," she says. "Children's body image comes from their parents first."

As preschoolers, children seem able to ignore or at least quickly forget the insults and blunt remarks about their looks and bodies by their peers. Steve Sternberg, director of the University of Michigan Children's Center told *Child* magazine, "Three- to five-year-olds tease each other about everything—not in an acrimonious sense, but in a discovery sense." He adds, "Luckily preschoolers don't internalize the teasing."

But by kindergarten, the teasing and heckling a child receives for being different begins to play a role in the way she perceives herself. This may lead kids to have self-doubts and even dislike themselves at this early age. By the second or third grade, they are also becoming increasingly aware of their own sex as well as the opposite one. Parents' discussions of their upcoming puberty make children all the more self-conscious about their changing bodies. By sixth or seventh grade, children may develop psychological defenses. In extreme cases they may react to negative discernment of their looks by isolating themselves or becoming the class jokester.

Some children seem to find strength in their unique appearance or physical problems and go on to achieve great success: there is the diminutive actor whose height handicap helped him develop his quick wit; the diet specialist who was obese as a child; the Olympic runner who was a bed-wetter as a child (he'd run home to try to beat the school bus, because his mother would hang out his wet sheets to embarrass and "cure" him of his disorder).

But for every success story there are many more cases of psychological hurt and damage as a result of a poor self-image. Adults often unwittingly confirm these poor body images in the child. One study showed that attractive children were thought of as better socialized, more competent, and more accomplished by their schoolteachers. It revealed that this high regard teachers held for attractive children translated into high achievement—a self-fulfilling prophecy.

And the reverse was true as well. The same study showed that children who have what we perceive as unattractive features may fulfill the prophecy by becoming aggressive, disruptive, and unhappy.

You cannot control all the messages your child receives from society, but your influence is still key during these younger years. Take the lead in letting your child know it's OK for kids to look and be different—a little more this way, a little less that—tall, short, thin, fat, black, white, Muslim or Methodist. Accepting themselves and others in childhood will go a long way toward preventing the sad blight of bigotry and prejudice in adulthood.

■■■■■■■■■■■■■■■■■■■■■■■■■■■■■■■■

Growth Patterns—How Do They Grow?

Every child's growth pattern is slightly different, predetermined by his own unique blueprint, a result of each of his parents' genetic contributions. But some general patterns can be seen emerging as they grow.

Babies have the highest proportion of body fat at one year (30 percent). Fat percentage slowly declines until age 6 or 7 when fat again reaches 30 percent. Children continue to slowly plump up until right before puberty. Girls continue to gain fat during adolescence while boys tend to become thinner.

After age 4, most children begin to appear slimmer because of the location of their body fat. Until 6 or 7, little girls tend to have protruding tummies, and clothing manufacturers account for this anomaly in their sizing. The American Academy of Pediatrics states, "As a youngster's entire body size increases the amount of body fat stays relatively stable, giving her a thinner look. Also, during this stage of life, a child's legs are longer in proportion to the remainder of her body than they had been before" (*Caring for Your Baby and Young Child*).

Growth may be steady or it may happen in spurts, with an increase in height of a little over 2 inches and 6.5 pounds a year. Some children grow during particular seasons of the

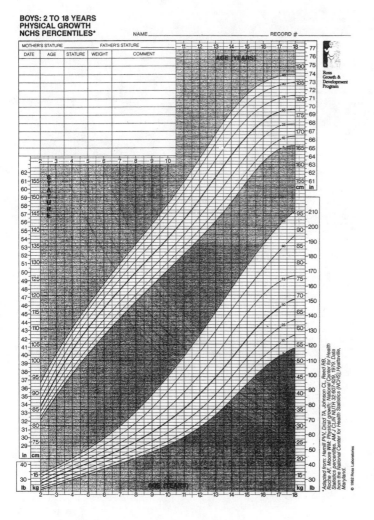

BOYS: 2 TO 18 YEARS
PHYSICAL GROWTH
NCHS PERCENTILES*

year, with little growth during the other seasons. Remember that each child grows in his own way, depending on genetic and environmental factors such as nutrition, exercise (exercise among children increases bone density and bone strength, according to one recent study), as well as how close he is to puberty.

◼ Prepubertal Changes

As you watch your 9-year-old kick a soccer ball down the field, you notice that she is gaining muscle mass and her motor skills are improving. Your sons are able to play sports

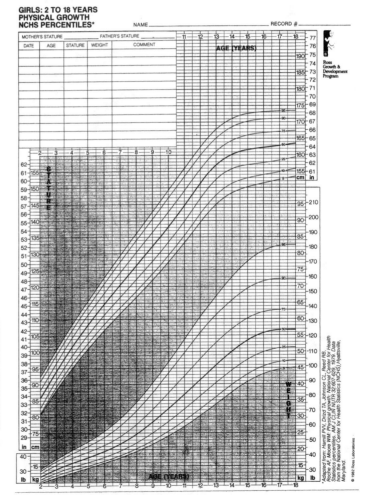

PROTRUDING TUMMIES ARE TYPICAL ON LITTLE GIRLS UNTIL AGE 6 OR 7.

with an astonishing increase in coordination and facility. The 10-year-old's movements and coordination are strikingly different from a 6-year-old's.

You may see signs of puberty in your child as early as 8 years old. Boys begin changes one to two years later than girls. But the age of onset of puberty varies greatly for both sexes— girls today enter puberty between ages 8 and 13, and boys begin between 9 and 14. The onset of puberty can make children extremely self-conscious. A boy or girl who matures very early or very late may feel uncomfortable socially.

Until puberty, growth is similar for boys and girls, and heights and weights are generally equal. At puberty, heights and weights become wildly divergent. Girls first become taller, then are eventually surpassed by boys. Children do 25 percent of their growing during puberty.

YOUR DOCTOR WILL BE MONITORING YOUR CHILD'S GROWTH AND WEIGHT THROUGHOUT CHILDHOOD. IF A CHILD'S HEIGHT OR WEIGHT FALLS BELOW THE 5TH OR ABOVE THE 100TH PERCENTILE OF NATIONAL AVERAGE, AND YOU AND YOUR SPOUSE ARE NOT EXCEPTIONALLY SHORT, TALL, THIN, OR HEAVY, YOUR DOCTOR MAY DECIDE TO INVESTIGATE HIS OR HER HEALTH. HERE MOLLY FINDS OUT SHE'S GROWN 2 INCHES SINCE LAST YEAR.

■ Too Short?

Your pediatrician will be tracking your child's growth pattern, but if you have any concern about a child who is too tall or too short, bring it to his attention. Although there are height variations—with a 4 to 5 inch spread among elementary school children—a small number of children may have a growth disorder, a result of thyroid or growth hormone deficiency. This condition is usually treated with hormones. Other causes of slow growth could be malfunction of the liver, kidney, or bowels.

But what about the healthy child with normal hormonal output who is under the fifth percentile, whose parents are short and, in all likelihood, will also be short?

At age 11, Marco Ortiti was 4′1″ and weighed only 49 pounds. "Everybody at school calls me shrimp and stuff like that," Marco told a *New York Times* reporter. "I feel like a loser. I feel like I'm nothing," he said. He dreamed of the day he would walk into school taller than the other children.

Marco and his parents had decided to try an experimental treatment for "cosmetically" short children. The *Times* reported that although Marco was able to produce sufficient quantities of human growth hormone, or HGH, on his own, he was receiving injections of synthetic HGH in the hopes of stimulating his growth. Without the hormones, his adult height was predicted to be 5'4". Controversy surrounds this hormone treatment, as it seems to make a child grow faster, but perhaps not ultimately much taller (1½ to 2 inches according to one study) than the predicted height. It may also have undesirable side effects.

Are these treatments worth an extra two inches, if indeed they are successful? One report documents the "heightism" that exists in our society: "College graduates more than 6'2" earn 12 percent more than their shorter classmates; of American presidents, only two have been shorter than the national average for the men of their time; short men find it harder to marry; growth-retarded children have more social problems in school."

Of all the treatments to improve children's looks, hormone treatment for small stature is the most radical and one of the most uncertain in outcome. It is also one of the most uncomfortable for the child, often requiring daily injections for 6 to 8 years and costing about $20,000 a year. Medical insurance usually pays for children who have a hormone deficiency, but not if the child's hormone output is normal.

In reality, diagnostic tests to determine whether a child's output of human growth hormone is sufficient are not completely reliable at this point. Some children who make some growth hormone may still benefit from growth hormone therapy, according to Dr. Myron Genel, professor of pediatrics at Yale University School of Medicine. He feels that a 6 month trial with hormone therapy may be helpful. "This is only for the extremely short child for whom the growth hormone testing is somewhat equivocal," says Dr. Genel.

Naturally, growth hormone therapy is not a procedure to be undertaken without research, expert consultation, and a number of medical opinions. In the end, most experts agree that treatment for short stature be avoided. One doctor suggests that the parents who subject their child to daily injections may be sending the message that they don't care for him the way he is. By helping our children understand that short stature is perfectly normal, we can perhaps start to help change our society's view of short people. Parents are urged to talk to their children about accepting the natural differences among children and among adults. This may also help them appreciate their own unique qualities and abilities.

■ Too Tall?

Endocrine disorders that make children abnormally tall are rare, but if a child is taller than the 100th percentile, and the parents' height is not unusually tall, a pediatrician would probably run tests, just as he or she would test a very short child with average or tall parents.

Some parents worry their daughters will grow too tall for social acceptance. In years past, many parents of preadolescent girls who were tall (like Cindy at the beginning of this chapter), consulted doctors to help arrest their daughters' growth.

Today, thank goodness, this is far less common, because standards have changed from the 1950s "pixie" or petite cheerleader look to the tall, fit ideal. Even for girls with height predictions of over 6', hormonal therapy is requested less now than any time since its introduction.

If parents want to know how tall their child will be, doctors can make a height prediction by X-raying the child's hands and wrists to check bone fusion. Although height prediction is relatively inaccurate (one doctor labeled it "about as accurate as the weather report"), it does give parents a rough idea of what to expect. Most predictions come with a 4-inch leeway—"give or take 2 inches." For a girl whose height prediction is 6 feet, or a boy whose prediction is 5 feet 8 inches, those two inches can be very significant.

Treatment to arrest a girl's growth is accomplished with hormone treatments that accelerate and "telescope" or compress the growth period that is associated with puberty so as to hasten the closure of the bones.

Dr. Myron Genel recommends conservatism when choosing hormonal treatment. "Our concern is that if hormones stimulate growth in a child," says Dr. Genel, "what else are they stimulating?" He has never observed any negative side effects from the use of natural estrogens for the treatment of tall girls, but notes that, in theory, there are risks involved.

For parents who feel being very tall would handicap their daughter, Dr. Genel recommends consulting with a growth disorder specialist. Children in this category would usually measure over the one hundredth percentile and have parents who are both extremely tall. Children should be evaluated as early as possible. "I can help a girl of 8 or 9 much more easily than a 12- or 13-year-old whose growth has already advanced significantly," says Dr. Genel. A child's maturity must also be evaluated: menstruation is not easy to handle at age 8 or 9. This treatment, though not as controversial as that for short stature, is one to be entered into with a great deal of research and thought.

For the tallest children—especially girls—who always get stuck in the back row at school, reassurance is the best therapy. They may not like being asked "How's the weather up there?" and may even slump to appear shorter. (See page 157 on posture.) Let your tall child know that her height will be an advantage as she gets older. Tell your tall boys and girls that one study mentioned in *The New York Times* revealed ". . . a correlation between intelligence and height in children from 6 to 17 years old, an effect that persisted even when other factors that influence I.Q. scores, such as family size, wealth, and birth order, were filtered out." Another recent report notes that tall people suffer less heart disease. "Tall girls are lucky these days," says Dr. Genel. "They're 'in.' Now if we could just get society to accept short men."

■■■■■■■■■■■■■■■■■■■■■■■■■■■■■■■■■■

When Children Are Overweight: A Common and Difficult Dilemma

Pamela was in tears. She was explaining to the pediatrician how her daughter, Robin, 10 years old, and obviously overweight, had returned from her first coed swim class at the pool so hurt and humiliated she could barely get the words out. "They called me 'the Blob' and 'tubby.' I'm never going back to that class again. I never want to even see those kids again—they're so mean!"

Pamela's hurt was as palpable as her daughter's. But Robin's weight problem was nothing new. The mother shook her head in frustration and told the doctor, "I've tried nagging, bribing, being nice, I've offered to send her to weight-loss camp, I've threatened, I've tried every possible angle, and nothing helps Robin watch her weight. Now she's getting so withdrawn I'm afraid for her emotional health. She's already getting stretch marks around her hips and thighs. What can I do?"

Pediatricians and parents alike share frustration in trying to help a heavy child slim down. Parents like Pamela often feel guilt, anger, and even embarrassment over the plight of having an overweight child. (One study showed that both children and parents preferred children in wheelchairs, those with disfigured faces, and kids with missing limbs over fat children.) The older child, hearing and seeing the "thin is in" message repeated over and over in TV and advertising, often begins measuring her self-worth by the amount she weighs in at each morning.

Today a whopping one in every five American children is obese (or 20 percent or more over their ideal weight), according to a 1988 national survey of 7,000 children. And there has been a 50 percent increase in obesity among 6- to 11-year-olds since the mid-1960s, according to another recent report. This means that a lot of American children aren't looking and feeling their best. Of all the cosmetic problems addressed in this book, heaviness during childhood is the most common one. It is also one of the most disheartening since it is so difficult to reverse. Obese children tend to grow into obese adults and, even if weight is lost, fat cells, which grow as a result of obesity, will remain there forever, "wanting" to be filled again. Maintaining ideal weight is that much harder for the person who was once overweight.

Kids who are obese may have long-range health repercussions, too. At higher risk for respiratory disorders, they are also prone to diabetes, orthopedic conditions, stretch marks, and even cardiovascular problems such as hypertension and excess serum cholesterol.

Why Me, Mommy?

In a family of four children, Ronny was the only heavy child. At age eight, Ronny had already graduated to the men's department, and even the "men's small" was getting tight. His brother and two sisters were of average height and weight, one was even quite lean, while Ronny hit 110 pounds standing 4'8" by his 9th birthday. Ronny's father was a little heavy, and his mother was average.

Is Your Child Overweight?

Some experts define the obese child as one whose weight is at or above the 85th percentile for all children his or her age. But numbers and charts give parents only a rough idea of what other children weigh at specified heights. Some children have heavier bone structures, and parents should be aware that each child is individual in body shape and biochemistry. Some lean, well-muscled children can weigh as much as an overweight child with flaccid body tone. Your doctor can help you assess your child's body type.

Never put your child on any kind of diet without first checking with your doctor. If your youngster is starting to look heavy, make an appointment with your pediatrician to have him or her help you determine whether your child really is overweight. The charts on pages 137 and 138 can help you keep track of your child's weight and height (and how they stack up with other American children). Though you'll probably be seeing the pediatrician at least once a year after infancy, you may want to weigh and measure your child every three months, especially if you are worried about his or her weight.

To gauge degree of obesity more accurately, pediatricians use a device called a caliper to measure skin fold thickness on the underside of the upper arm. This "pinch test" gives a fairly accurate account of the percentage of body weight that is fat. Skin fold measurements in the upper 15 percent (or 85th percentile) are considered obese. Kids in the upper 5 percent (95th percentile) are classified as super-obese. Remember that there are periods in a child's life when a small accumulation of fat is normal, such as right before growth spurts. Girls may start plumping up two to three years before menstruation begins.

Your child's yearly checkup should include a discussion about whether the child is maintaining an approximate "ideal" weight. If he or she is getting heavy, discuss measures for weight control with your doctor and remember that obesity is easier to prevent than it is to change.

"Why am I the only one in the family who's fat?" Ronny asked his mother. Since Ronny was fed the same diet as his slender siblings at home, his mother had no answers—although she did notice that Ronny was the one who always clamored for seconds. And while the others rejected meals once in a while, Ronny always ate his three squares and never missed a snack. On the whole, though, since his diet was almost the same as the rest of the family's, Ronny's problems seemed to belie environmental origins. So why was he overweight?

"It's in the genes," says a widely cited study conducted in 1986 by Dr. Albert J. Stunkard, a psychiatrist and obesity specialist at the University of Pennsylvania School of Medicine. After studying 540 adopted children in Denmark, a U.S. and Danish team of researchers found that the degree of fatness of the children strongly resembled that of the *natural* parents. There was no correlation between the size of the adoptees and their adoptive parents. Ronny, indeed, may have had an obese ancestor, especially on his mother's side, according to the results of this study.

Dr. Stunkard's "biology is destiny" thesis is distressing news to families who have overweight children. But he also gives hope to these families. He told a *Newsweek* magazine reporter that overweight children can and should be targeted early. Extra efforts are needed for weight control for those children, including vigorous exercise programs. "Such persons can already be identified with some assurance," he says. "Eighty percent of the offspring of obese parents become obese."

It should be noted that not all researchers are in agreement with Dr. Stunkard. Dr. Stanley Garn, an anthropologist with the University of Michigan, disputes Stunkard's findings and says that his own research indicates that adopted children resemble their surrogate parents in fatness almost as much as other kids resemble their genetic parents.

Factors other than genetic predisposition do seem to play a role in obesity. Research shows a few: poor dietary habits, of course; social and economic environment (the poorer the family, the heavier the child tends to be); and some studies indicate that those children who gain weight rapidly during infancy are at greater risk for obesity later on. Black children are now becoming obese at a faster rate than whites. If you or a member of your family is obese, and your child shows any sign of plumpness, consult the next few sections of this chapter to help keep his weight under control.

■■■■■■■■■■■■■■■■■■■■■■■■■■■■■■■■■■

How Can We Help Our Children Lose Weight?

A simple question with no sure answers except for one: do not focus all your attention on your child's weight. In a *New York Times* column on childhood obesity, Lawrence Kuttner quotes psychologist Kathie Johnson; in trying to get a child to diet, she says, "There's a message that 'I don't love you the way you are. You'll have to change for me to love you.'" Kuttner remarks, "Paying attention to other assets like intelligence or social skills can make it much easier for a child to lose weight." Jane Brody, health editor for the *New York Times* reports that ". . . experts insist that parents should never tell children they are fat, never put them on diets, and never mention a child's weight unless the child brings it up first."

When well-meaning parents withhold food (especially fattening foods) from young overweight children (ages 2 to 6), the children may actually fear they won't get enough to eat. This results in constant snacking and overeating on the child's part, making the concerned parent all the more panicky and forceful about restricting the child's diet, ending in a dangerous cycle. Even as adults, we may react to what we feel is deprivation by overeating.

For older overweight children, the kitchen can become a battleground if parents focus on the child's ability to resist the "bad" foods and eat only "healthy" ones. Power struggles are set up as parents try to police their children's eating. For preadolescents especially, forbidden foods become all the more desirable. One friend who was a little overweight as a child recently told me that she remembers her well-meaning father refusing to buy her cotton candy at a circus and swearing to herself then that when she grew up she would buy herself enough cotton candy to fill a room. She is slim today, probably because she *knows* she can have as much cotton candy as she wants without anyone withholding it from her.

This is the premise of your approach to helping your child lose weight, and supporting it is a 1985 study conducted by two Duke University psychologists who found that the more parents restricted and oversaw their children's food intake at meals, the more weight the kids gained. Nagging actually does more harm than good. For your young child, nutritionist Ellyn Satter recommends offering three good meals each day with two healthy snacks and allowing him to eat as much as he wants during that time, giving him the power to satisfy his own hunger. Food should not be taken at other times. Feeling he is not being deprived of food at meal and snack times, and that he can eat as much as he wants, his desire to constantly eat will probably subside. For the older child, the recommendation is the same, making choosing the right foods his or her own responsibility.

This, of course, is not the entire answer to helping your overweight child, but it does set the tone for your approach.

Another way to help your child is to remind him that each of us has a different build and body type. We have to accept our bodies in the same way we accept the fact that our eyes are green or our hair is brown.

Support and Compassion

An overweight child is a child who has suffered. He or she needs extra love and affection as well as extra efforts to boost self-esteem. Emphasize your child's talents and the parts of her personality you appreciate. When the younger ones do something well, praise him or her and give him or her non-food rewards. Never tease, nag, or lose your temper at your child's failure at weight control. She knows when she is failing. When she has setbacks, gently remind her about good nutrition.

Give your overweight child lots of hugs and touching. She should feel that you love her exactly the way she is.

During pre-school and elementary school years, check with the adults—teachers, coaches, or camp counselors—who are in charge of your child to be sure the youngster is not being made uncomfortable by being teased. Remind these adults that they must take steps to stop any cruel name-calling that might be going on. One West Coast mother's overweight ten-year-old son was being made the target of snide remarks by an adult male tennis teacher. When she heard about this she called the instructor and let him know that she might expect this type of behavior from younger, thoughtless peer, but never from an adult teacher. He apologized, but it was too late. The boy was unwilling to go back to his tennis lessons and dropped out.

Making an overweight child feel good about himself is our responsibility. He did not choose his metabolism, his appetite, or society's obsession with slimness. Dr. William Lattanzi remarks, "Being overweight or even obese never causes death and is not usually a medical problem in childhood. But *not* eating can kill. Anorexia, bulimia, and other food disorders are often the result of food obsessions created by an over-concerned family." Try to accept your child as he is while working to create an environment of nutrition awareness.

MEDICAL ALERT
Adult Diets May Be Dangerous for Children

Any "fad" diets adults may resort to are out of the question for children. These diets—whether they are unusually high in protein, require pills, or rely heavily on one food such as grapefruit—can be very dangerous for a growing child. Calorie-restrictive diets which place kids on a 1000 to 1300 calorie regimen can also spell trouble for children, often causing dizziness, fatigue, and sluggishness. The child may actually end up malnourished, lacking the essential nutrients for good growth. Sexual maturation may be delayed due to calorie restriction.

■■■■■■■■■■■■■■■■■■■■■■■■■■■■■■■■■■■■

A Safe Solution: Arrest Your Child's Weight Gain and Wait for Him or Her to Grow

Getting an obese or overweight child to actually drop pounds is not only difficult, but may also begin the cycle of yo-yo dieting. The *Pediatric Nutrition Handbook*'s prognosis for weight loss among children is not hopeful: "Although some weight is lost at first, the long-term success rate for treatment of obesity is poor; and it remains to be seen whether efforts at prevention will be effective."

Dr. Leonard Krassner, a nutrition expert and medical chief at Choate/Rosemary Hall in Wallingford, CT, reports that 95 percent of all children who lose weight relapse. A child's motivation must be very high. "Diets are never successful unless a child wants to lose weight," says Dr. Krassner. "Trying to get an unwilling child to diet is like fighting City Hall." Any adult who has ever tried to lose weight cannot help but be sympathetic. But other experts express more hope. Indeed, we've all seen plump children who have grown up to be average weight adults. But the process becomes harder the longer the child remains overweight. A child who is obese in the early stages of middle years—from 5 to 7—will probably become thinner when he's grown. If obesity is present later—at 11 to 12—children have a 50 percent likelihood of being obese or overweight as an adult.

If children have such a difficult time *losing* the pounds, what is your option to help your child lose weight? The answer is growth. The one thing overweight children have going for them that overweight adults don't is that they are growing taller. If the child's weight gain is slowed or is arrested, his or her height will catch up and the child's body will be thinner as she or he grows.

Jane Brody summarizes a parent's best approach to an overweight child as ". . . the adoption of a wholesome approach to eating and exercising that comes from within the child and can be maintained for life, regardless of how much the child may ultimately weigh. Before adolescence, except for cases of extreme obesity, children should not be encouraged to lose weight. Rather, the goal should be to slow the rate of gain to allow them to grow into a more normal weight, gradually thinning as they get taller."

Brody's approach is not license to let kids go crazy with junk food, but rather to offer children healthful, nutritious foods of all categories, especially those low in fat and salt and high in fiber. No category of food should be denied. For example, when going out for fast food, Brody suggests, discuss choices such as ordering a plain burger rather than a cheeseburger, or chocolate milk instead of a shake. A small candy bar or ice cream can be dessert once a week. Two small cookies can serve as a snack twice a week. Encourage exercise, too.

Some parents and some doctors may find this approach too slow for children who are suffering negative social and psychological repercussions, but if parents do opt for a weight loss program, experts advise a slow, steady weight loss of one or two pounds per week, without severe caloric restriction.

Overweight children are often in need of outside help. Dr. Alvin Mauer, past chairman for the Council on Nutrition for the American Academy of Pediatrics says: "If a child is very overweight, your doctor should refer the family to a dietician who can assess the child's history, eating patterns, and home environment. He or she can set up guidelines for that particular child. Follow-up is needed and the entire effort requires a great deal of commitment."

To find the names of nutritionists near you, write to:
Consulting Nutritionists, Public Relations Director
2191 London Drive
Glendale Heights, IL 60319.

■ What About Weight-Loss Clinics or Camps?

"When Montana came home from weight-loss camp 12 pounds lighter," said Ginger, a 35-year-old mother, "I saw an 11-year-old girl so happy I thought she'd explode. We bought her new clothes for school—clothes she never could have worn before! I saw a new personality, too, one with more confidence and more self-assurance. It's been six months and she's put on four pounds but she's growing, too. It was Montana's idea to go in the first place, so I feel lucky. The change has been remarkable."

Being able to see other children at camp who had the same problem she had helped Montana enormously. But so did her new social status when she returned. In fact, her social acceptance at school has been so significant, reports Ginger, it has motivated her to maintain her new slender form.

A Weight Watchers Success Story

My name is Missy and I am eleven years old. I will be in the seventh grade this year. At the age of six I started to put on weight. I just kept on getting fatter and fatter. At first it didn't bother me, but then when I got into sixth grade some of the kids would call me names. Also, I tried out for the middle school basketball team, and I didn't make it. The girls that made it were slim. I wasn't!

I asked my Mom and Dad if I could join the Weight Watchers program. I knew the instructor was Mrs. Crowley, my second grade teacher. I knew she would be a big support to me. I started the Weight

Watchers program on April 10, 1991. I weighed in at 144½. Now

I weigh 108½ and I LOOK and FEEL GREAT!

Not all parents report successful weight maintenance when children leave the "false" environment of camp, where low calorie meals are carefully prepared and behavior modification classes help children lose weight. But many kids *are* able to break old habits and begin new, healthful ones learned at camp. Out patient weight-loss clinics for children can often be more successful than camps—especially in maintaining weight. Youngsters must return each night to their homes where most food problems start and where they must learn to deal with these problems. Any decision to attend a weight-loss camp or clinic should involve your child, of course. If children are forced to go, chances are the results will be poor and can even be detrimental.

Where can parents find information on weight-loss camps and clinics? Ask your doctor, dietician, or local hospital or medical school for names of camps or clinics, which include weight-loss camps for ages 7 through 29. Parents can write to:

American Camping Association
Bradford Woods
Martinsville, IN 46151
Tel. (317) 342-8456.

Weight Watcher Camps, in particular, have been successful in helping children ages 10 on up lose thousands of pounds. For information write:

Weight Watcher Camps
183 Madison Avenue
New York, NY 10016
Tel. (800) 223-5600.

Wherever you look, check the credentials of the staff carefully. Look for camps with registered dieticians and exercise experts and ask the camp for names of several parents whose children have attended for further references. Programs should include behavior modification and stress image-building and improving self-confidence.

Tips for the Waist-Watching Household

When one child in the family is obese or overweight, the entire family must make some compromises to help him change his weight. Dr. Krassner of Choate Rosemary Hall says that when one child is overweight, his siblings must simply accept the fact that fattening foods be kept to a minimum in the house, the same way a diabetic's household responds to his disease by keeping cupboards free of sugars. This effort to eat healthy foods and eliminate junk food is actually a benefit for the whole family. Here are some hints that can help you lighten your larder and keep your child's weight in check:

■ Serve more chicken and fish in place of pork, beef, fatty sausages, and luncheon meats. De-emphasize meat by serving stir-frys and adding more vegetables to meals.

■ Go heavy on vegetables such as spinach, cabbage, zucchini, summer squash, etc., in place of starchier ones such as lima beans or corn. Kids usually prefer raw vegetables, so keep them handy for after-school snacks or before-dinner hungries.

■ Use low-fat dressings for salads. Try lemon juice (fresh is best) and vinegar with a small amount of olive oil in place of creamier dressings.

■ Choose lower-fat dairy products such as yogurt, low-fat or skim milk, and low-fat cottage cheese. Most cheeses are high in fat and salt and should be used only two to three times a week. Opt for low-fat cheeses, which are available at most grocery stores.

■ Buy breakfast cereals which are low in sugars and fats. Read labels carefully.

■ Choose breads with lower fat and higher fiber content such as whole wheat, rye, and other whole grain breads. These breads actually step up weight loss. A 1986 *Family Circle* magazine article on fiber reported, "Participants in an eight week experimental 'bread diet' ate 12 slices of bread a day, along with other foods; those who ate white bread lost an average of 13.7 pounds; those who ate whole wheat bread lost an average of 19.4 pounds." Read labels of cracker boxes carefully to check their fat content. Crispbread crackers, whole wheat matzohs, and flatbreads are usually fiber-rich and fat-lean.

■ Keep junk foods, sweets, and salty snacks out of the house.

■ Don't outlaw certain foods lest they become all the more desirable. It's fine to allow your child who's watching her weight to have a piece of cake at someone's birthday party. Before the party, coach her to eat just half of a large piece of cake and a little ice cream. In your house, allow your children something sweet from time to time. Muffins or puddings can be an occasional treat.

■ Remove the salt shaker from the table. Experiment with herbs and spices as flavorings.

■ Make pretty fruit desserts. Introduce children to the sweetness of plain baked apples sprinkled with cinnamon, and, on the side, yogurt sweetened with a little honey.

■ Plan menus in advance. This makes sticking to nutritious foods easier.

■ When you go out for fast food, choose lower calorie items. Many fast-food restaurants now feature "lean" food and salads and salad bars. Ask children to start the meal with a garden salad (with oil and vinegar or low-calorie dressing, which is usually available) followed by a plain hamburger and juice or milk. If the children are dying for french fries (and when aren't they?), split one or two orders among the family.

■ Watch your family's food patterns. Habits such as snacking while watching television or doing homework should be prohibited. All meals should be served in one of two places: the kitchen or the dining room. Try to eat at your regularly scheduled times. If your family tends to eat in response to stress, anger, sadness—or even joy—make a conscious effort to find other, non-food outlets and rewards.

■ Serve food from the kitchen stove, in smaller portions than you're used to. Serving meals family-style from a platter at the dinner table invites larger helpings and seconds.

■ Have water as a drink at lunch or dinner once in a while and offer it frequently during the day. Dilute juices (which are up to 20 calories an ounce) with water or seltzer. Keep your house soda-pop free. Kids drink enough soda outside the home.

■ Great for after-school snacks are foods such as air-popped popcorn, homemade frozen juice bars, and pieces of celery filled with peanut butter. Try weaning your children from sugar-rich commercial peanut butters to fresh-ground peanut butters sold in the health food sections of stores by mixing half-and-half in your own kitchen and then gradually switching to pure peanut butter.

■ Tote nutritious snacks to the movies, baseball games, etc. Carrots, apples, bread sticks, and popcorn are healthier, less caloric, and less expensive than soda and chips at the food stand.

■ When kids get older and have the freedom to spend their allowance on whatever they want, including candy bars and chips, it's time for a talk. Tell children that since they have all the freedom they want to choose what they will spend their allowance on, that candy and other junk food is simply counterproductive to good health. Put the responsibility in their hands (it's there anyway), but let them know you expect them to spend their money using good judgment.

MEDICAL ALERT
Are Diet Sodas Safe for Kids?

Most diet sodas now contain aspartame, a "nutritive" sweetener. (Check label to be sure.) Aspartame, marketed under the name of "NutraSweet" or "Equal," is actually metabolized as a protein by the body, since it is a combination of two amino acids (phenylalnine and aspartic acid, both protein building blocks).

Aspartame has never been proven to be a carcinogen, but some cases of allergic reactions have been recorded. These cases are now being studied. The Center for Disease Control has deemed aspartame safe since 1985. It has been shown, however, that high levels of phenylalnine have a toxic effect on the brain of the developing fetus. In light of this, pregnant and nursing women and, of course, babies, should not drink diet sodas and avoid aspartame and probably other artificial sweeteners, which are now flooding the food market. Children should also avoid making diet sodas a regular habit. While children who are watching calorie intake may have a diet soda once in a while, they should not depend on them to help control weight. Daily consumption is certainly unwise. Encourage your little waist watcher to substitute flavored sparkling waters or seltzer mixed with a little orange or apple juice.

■ Exercise: The Key to Weight Control

What is the most important adjunct of weight loss? The answer, of course, is a conscientious exercise program. Institute family after-dinner walks. Bike together, jog together, hike together, play tennis and swim together. Encourage kids to play organized sports—the more they get involved in local recreational programs, the better they will feel about themselves. (For more information about the importance of exercise to a child's physical well-being, see chapter 6.)

■■■■■■■■■■■■■■■■■■■■■■■■■■■■■■■

The Underweight Child

"I remember being embarrassed and not wanting to take off my shirt at the swim club," says Jeff, 45 years old, of his skinny physique when he was a child. "And sitting on a bony bottom in a hard chair at school for 40 minutes at a stretch was not just uncomfortable, it was painful. My son has always been skinny, too, but he seems never to have suffered like I did."

Perhaps it's the last few decades' emphasis on slimness that has changed the perception of the "too thin" child. It seems that the "skinny" child is as rare as the overweight child has become commonplace.

We know that it's not unusual to hear "Fatso" on the playground, but do any children today call each other "skinnybones" when "thin is in"? An informal survey at my children's schools revealed that very slender children are rarely teased anymore. I did identify one or two very slender children who did feel unhappy about their bony frames. Their parents, however, always assure them that they should be thankful they are not overweight.

Dr. Mary Lee Ruff reminds us that in previous decades, "thin" was considered unhealthy and sickly and efforts were made to fatten up skinny children. In past centuries, portly people were considered well-to-do. How times change!

Of course, in ages past, nutrition was often poor, and many children would have a "failure to thrive" or would grow poorly. Today, with the abundance and variety of food products available to children, slender children will get adequate

MEDICAL ALERT
Anorexia Nervosa and Bulimia

Experts feel that food disorders such as anorexia and bulimia are often the result of food obsessions created by an over-concerned family. Most victims of anorexia nervosa and bulimia are young girls, usually between the ages of 12 and 19, although occasionally a child as young as 8 succumbs to these medically dangerous emotional disorders. Children who are anorexics are often "model" children. They strive to do well in school and sports and generally try to please their parents. An exaggerated fear of obesity and a distorted body image often causes young girls to diet, sometimes to the point of harming themselves. Anorexics have a pathological desire to look thin and are literally starving themselves to death. Six to ten percent of all anorexics die from starvation. Bulimia victims binge on high-calorie food and then purge by inducing vomiting and/or taking laxatives; some also starve themselves. Bulimics are usually extroverted before their illness, but then become subdued as the obsession progresses.

A study conducted by Laurel Mellin, assistant professor of family medicine at the University of California, San Francisco, surveyed 492 San Francisco school girls from middle income families and found that while more than half of the girls considered themselves overweight, only 15 percent were actually above their ideal weight. Fifteen percent of the 9-year-olds and 81 percent of the 10-year-olds had put themselves on diets. We know that these early dieting patterns can eventually degenerate into eating disorders such as anorexia and bulimia.

Why are so many young girls dieting? It is believed that parents who are obsessed with their own weight may be influencing their children. Also, earlier sexual maturation patterns among this generation of girls, i.e., fuller hips and breasts, may leave some with the mistaken idea that they are fat.

Be alert to these symptoms, which could mark the start of an eating disorder:
- excessive dieting
- patterns of perfectionism and high achievement
- depression, social withdrawal, obsessive compulsiveness

If you suspect your child is showing early signs of anorexia nervosa or bulimia, write or call for more information:

ANAD-National Association of Anorexia Nervosa and Associated Disorders
P.O. Box 7
Highland Park, IL 60035
Tel (708) 831-3438

American Anorexia Bulimia Association, Inc.
133 Cedar Lane
Teaneck, NJ 07666
Tel (201) 836-1800

National Anorexia Aid Society, Inc. (NAAS)
P.O. Box 29461
Columbus, OH 43229

nutrition. One doctor told me that barring a medical or emotional condition or malnutrition, the "underweight" child does not exist.

If a child is below the 5th percentile in weight, which means that 95 percent of all children his age are heavier than he, there might be reason for some medical consideration. If this child's weight has always been at 5 percent, and the parents are thin or wiry, he or she is probably fine. Growth chart variations in the child's height or weight history (such as a sudden loss or gain of weight) are two important considerations. Some weight loss may be attributed to a new physical activity level, as when babies and toddlers finally learn to walk and run, or a sickness such as flu or chicken pox. Some children are simply growing so fast that the gain in height can't match the gain in weight and muscle.

■■■■■■■■■■■■■■■■■■■■■■■■■■■■■■■■■■■■

"Stand Up Straight!" Your Child's Posture and How You Can Help

What is your child saying when he suddenly starts shuffling around slump-shouldered, head lowered, stomach lax? (One of my sons hangs his head and slumps his shoulders so dramatically when he's upset, it's become a family joke.) We instinctively read this body language to mean that something is amiss—emotionally or physically. The child may be feeling sad or may be sick. It may also be that he is getting less exercise than before and needs to step up his fitness program—because the foundation for good posture in children is a fit, well-exercised body. A child who naturally stands straight and tall usually possesses good levels of muscle strength, flexibility, and endurance.

Poor posture must be pointed out and gently corrected because poor posture requires more contraction of antigravity muscle groups—especially in the upper back. If not corrected, the child's muscles can, in time, adapt to that position. This not only looks bad, communicating a negative attitude to others, but may also spell back and neck problems for the future.

Dr. Wendy Coren, a chiropractor and the mother of two pre-schoolers, advises that good posture be emphasized by parents as soon as a child can understand—even though slouching or other sloppy posture does not usually begin until age 9 or 10. Dr. Coren has a special interest in educating children about posture, back and body care. She visits nursery and elementary schools to teach good posture today to help prevent back and other problems years later.

When discussing posture with your child, ask him to

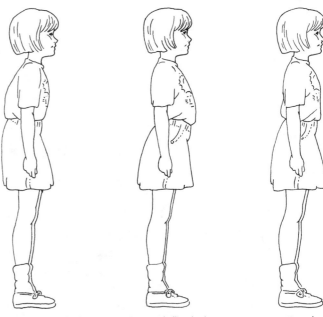

Humped or rounded back   Sway or hollow back   Normal

pretend he's hanging by a string, head held high, with shoulders level, tummy and buttocks pulled in. He doesn't have to adopt the stiffness of a wooden soldier, but simply be aware of the way he stands or sits. Dr. Coren has written the following poem for young children to help children remember to stand and move "tall" throughout their day:

So Shall You Be

Stand up tall
though today you are small.
Each day you'll grow
from head to toe
to be the someone you're meant to be.
Think of the twig that becomes a tree—
if it's watered and fed and plays in the sun,
it'll reach high in the sky before it's done.
If you treat your spine just as a tree
and bend and stretch most carefully,
then you'll grow tall and straight and strong,
and energy will flow where it belongs.
As you think so shall you be,
from little twig to mighty tree.

■ Posture-Busters

Children face many posture-busting hazards in school, according to Dr. Coren. "Flat-topped desks will cause unusual bending over and stress on the back. And heavy backpacks worn stylishly on one shoulder will result in contraction of the muscles on one side of the back and stretching on the other. These stressful postures may cause back, neck and other body problems which may not show up until a child is in her thirties or forties," says Dr. Coren. (I weighed my twelve-year-old son's backpack after talking to Dr. Coren and found out it weighed twenty-two pounds! He's now made special arrangements for extra time at the end of the school day to drop off books he doesn't need for homework.)

■ "Like Father, Like Son"

Before becoming alarmed about a child who consistently stands with rounded shoulders, head thrust forward, or bow-backed, you should know that there is no true standard of "good" posture that applies to all children. A common variation, especially among the two- to six-year-old set, is a protruding abdomen, a slight hollow in the back, and protruding shoulder blades. This body carriage usually resolves itself as the child grows, providing his nutrition and exercise are adequate.

Variations of erect postures can simply run in families, according to pediatric orthopedist Dr. Walter Huurman. "I have learned to look at both Mom and Dad before I go looking for medical problems," he says.

One of my own sons walks with feet slightly turned out and a spine so straight he almost leans backward—just like his Dad. I have noticed a likeness of postures in a Minnesota family I know. The father, the mother, and the eldest son all stand stoop-shouldered, while the two younger children stand straight. Lack of physical fitness is ruled out because all family members are athletic and in terrific shape. Has the eldest son begun to imitate his parents, while the others are too young to do the same, or do the youngest two simply have different centers of gravity?

Dr. Harrison Pierce, a pediatrician associated with Yale/New Haven Hospital believes most unusual postures such as

slumped shoulders are structural, i.e., determined by genetics. "Some people simply have smaller clavicles or promi-
nent thoraxes which make their bodies tilt forward," he says.
"Their bodies would not feel comfortable standing with
shoulders held back, hips forward." Chiropractor Wendy Coren feels that although there may be a genetic predisposition
to "bad" posture, early attention to some of the problems can
correct, or nearly correct them. A series of exercises may help
alter the course that nature wants to take. If you notice that
your child is falling into bad posture habits—even though
they may resemble yours—see your pediatrician or a chiropractor who is trained to work with children.

■ Standing Straight—Getting a Leg Up on Knock-Knees, Bowlegs, Toeing In, and Toeing Out

"When I see movies of myself as a toddler I realize my
legs were so bowed I think I could have passed a softball
through them without touching either side," says fifteen-
year-old Tory. Note that Tory is now a model with near-
perfect legs.

| Toeing in | Toeing out | Normal |

MEDICAL ALERT
Medical Conditions Underlying "Bad" Posture

Miss Kinley, Mara's fourth grade homeroom teacher, noticed that Mara seemed to increasingly favor one side of her desk as she worked. When she recommended that Mara be screened for possible skeletal problems, the results showed a slight scoliosis, which was subsequently treated with a brace.

Scoliosis (curvature of the spine), kyphosis (round back), and lordosis (hollow back) are skeletal problems your doctor will be checking for throughout childhood. In elementary school, school nurses screen as well (particularly after fifth grade, when these problems become more evident) by check-ing a child's spine as she is bent over from the waist. Even so, the affliction is often subtle. You, too, can keep an eye out for posture changes, as Mara's sharp-eyed homeroom teacher did, and report any odd alignment seen in your child's body to your doctor.

To detect major postural problems doctors and nurses use a "plumb line" test, in which they hold a string with a weighted bottom near the child's spine. You can take your own test by posing your child next to a door frame or any other vertical line in your house or apartment.

If your little one has bowlegs, knock-knees, or walks or stands in either a "duck" style (toes out) or "pigeon" style (toes in), chances are overwhelming that he or she will outgrow these very normal variations by puberty. Dr. Walter Huurman observes that a single child can adopt almost all of these various leg and foot positions as he grows. "Children normally start out bowlegged and toeing out when they begin to walk at about one to two years," says Dr. Huurman. "By three to five years of age they naturally become knock-kneed. Then, by the teen years, legs usually end up perfectly straight."

Toeing in is also common in the early stages of walking, and walking "pigeon toed" continues in 5 to 10 percent of children throughout childhood. It is considered a normal variation unless the problem originates at the hip joint, in which case braces and other aggressive measures might be used to correct the problem. Deformities of the knee and other foot problems may also be the genesis of toeing in.

Another type of toeing in starts at the femur, between the hip and the knee. This condition, of unknown cause, is called "femoral tortion," and it usually resolves itself spontaneously by age 8. Braces and shoe modifications are useless for this condition and would only make children uncomfortable. If, by age 8 or 9, your child still toes in with one or both feet, he should be seen by an orthopedist who specializes in treating children.

Any concern that you have about your youngster's knock-knees or duck walk being out of the normal range should be reported to your doctor. Certainly see an expert if your child has any of the following conditions: legs severely bowed (from rickets, caused by a genetic disorder, or—less likely today—a nutritional deficiency); one or both legs bent inward or "pronated"; or if your child has any of these conditions to a slight degree and it tends to run in the family.

■ If They Can Clap Them, They're Flat— Flat Feet

They don't possess much elegance, but flat feet are just as functional as delicately arched feet. (As a matter of fact, highly arched feet cause more medical concern than flat feet.) Fifteen percent of all adults have archless feet, and there are functional problems in only 1 or 2 percent. Medical attention is needed for flat feet that are stiff, painful, or very severe.

Flat feet got a bad name years ago and were actually reason for rejection from the military service during World War I. Thankfully, the "corrective" shoes doctors ordered even twenty years ago are rarely prescribed by pediatricians today. My husband Geoff is still upset about a dance he went to as a pre-teen where his most carefully guarded secret—corrective plates in his shoes for flat feet—was exposed. Each of the boys was asked to put one of his shoes in the center of the dance floor. The girls were to pick a shoe and then try to find the owner of the shoe to be her dance partner. With no amount of ceremony or tact, the girls quickly rejected the shoe with the metal plate. Geoff just about retired from social life for the year!

Although some doctors and chiropractors still prescribe corrective devices for leg and foot problems for children, most medical experts now feel that they are not useful—in addition to being expensive and potentially embarrassing. Orthotics, or foot molds worn in shoes, used to correct problems such as pronated feet, collapsed arches, or one leg that is shorter than the other (not uncommon in children or adults) can be helpful in a number of cases. Many athletes have found orthotics especially helpful, and if your child is worried about how he may appear to his friends, remind him that many famous football, basketball, track, and tennis stars are devoted orthotic wearers. If corrective devices are prescribed for your child, be sure to seek a second opinion before investing in them.

Growing Pains

Keep in mind that so-called growing pains may also be the source of leg discomfort. These pains in the joints or muscles occur among children ages 4 to 7—usually in the middle of the night. Medicine has still not determined their cause. Dr. Robert Weiss, an orthopedist specializing in sports medicine notes that some growing pains may originate from pronated ankles or feet that roll in. He points out that wearing orthotics while young may correct a foot problem, whereas adults with such problems must wear orthotics permanently. Treatment consists of heat, massage, and a non-aspirin pain medication. These leg discomforts should be reported to your physician, as they may be caused by ills or injuries other than growing pains.

Dr. Walter Huurman, an orthopedic surgeon, warns that the presence of any of the following three symptoms warrants a trip to the doctor's office: a limp the child has developed; a complaint of back pain; or a sudden onset of pain in the knees or legs. Make sure your child's shoes are not the cause of discomfort. (See chapter 7 for a discussion of footwear.)

■■■■■■■■■■■■■■■■■■■■■■■■■■■■■■■■■■■■■■

Improving on Nature—Plastic Surgery for Kids?

The child who has slightly exaggerated facial features—a large nose or protruding ears—and is teased, may pretend to ignore the taunts but often ends up bearing real emotional hurt. While some kids seem to be able to shake off the jibes or are able to successfully put down their enemy with witty comebacks, they are often psychologically affected. Like their overweight counterparts, children sometimes go into their teen years with a heightened sense that they are somehow ugly or unattractive.

While plastic surgery is obviously needed for birth defects such as hare lip and cleft palate or extra digits present at birth, the necessity for other cosmetic surgeries such as ear pinnings or "nose jobs" is more subjective. Of course, children under 12, the ages focused on in this book, are not capable of fully understanding whether plastic surgery is appropriate, so the decision rests largely with parents, medical experts, and concerned relatives and friends. Of course, the child should be involved to the degree possible, depending on his or her age. Children will certainly have let parents know if they've been teased or singled out for ridicule because of a problem feature or features.

By the time children are teenagers, they should become fully responsible for their decision to have cosmetic surgery. "The first thing I ask is whose idea it was to come see me," said Dr. Peter Bela Fodor, a Manhattan plastic and reconstructive surgeon, to Parent & Child columnist, Lawrence Kutner of *The New York Times*. "If it's simply the parents' idea, I won't do it. If it's the child's idea, I'm much more likely to consider it."

Parents of a young child should be careful not to opt for plastic surgery for their own satisfaction. A child's big nose or receding chin and the teasing resulting from it often strikes an emotional chord, reminding parents of their own insecurities. "Parents are so emotionally invested in their children's appearance," says Kutner, "that it is sometimes not simple to tell when a few reassuring words are enough and when changing a child's appearance is best. Sometimes, a parent's interest works against the child's."

Some of your child's body or facial irregularities distinguish him and cannot and should not be changed. But in a few cases the psychological benefits are great enough to warrant surgery. The questions and answers that follow include some more grown-up methods for improving on nature.

Q. *My three-year-old's ears could give Dumbo's a run for his money. He hasn't been teased by his classmates yet, but I worry about the future. Will sleeping on his side help train them to lie back? He prefers to sleep on his back now.*

A. Sleeping on his side may help a baby's protruding ears lie closer to his head *if* he has a natural fold behind his ears.

It sounds as though your son lacks this fold, since he is now 3 and his ears still stick out dramatically. Many children lack this fold, and while girls use long hair to cover protruding ears, boys have more difficulty hiding them.

There is an operation to correct protruding ears, if you feel it's necessary. By the time your boy is 8, (when the ear is almost fully developed), he can have an *oto-plasty*, or ear reconstruction. (Girls are usually advised to wait until their twenties since they can cover their pro-truding ears.) The surgeon makes an incision behind the ears and remodels the cartilage to pull the ears in. Ears will be bandaged for about a week and after that may be swollen and red for a month. This operation is not uncom-mon.

Incidentally, I have an adult friend with rather large ears who assures me that big ears indicate a great soul—Buddha had big ears. So did Clark Gable!

Q. *I can tell that my 3-year-old, Allegra, has inherited her dad's large and distinctive nose! It's cute on my husband but I think it really detracts from my daughter's otherwise adorable looks. I don't want her to spend her whole childhood looking like Pinoc-chio telling a lie! What is the earliest time I can have her undergo nose surgery?*

A. Not until the mid- or late teens, when cartilage and bone in the nose have stopped growing, can Allegra get a "nose job," or *rhinoplasty*. Sixteen or 17 is the age most plastic surgeons deem the end of the growth period of the face, although some plastic surgeons will operate as early as 14 years. Some experts claim the nose reaches its adult size by age 13 for girls and 15 for boys, but the chin does not com-plete its full growth until 18 in girls and 21 among boys. Chin augmentation surgery is never recommended earlier than these ages. Computer imaging is not always reliable and most plastic surgeons use photographic techniques to help show patients how they will look after the surgery.

Your daughter may "grow into" her nose—and you may find it less "large" than you thought it would be by the time Allegra is 8 or 9. Some families take great pride in large noses—as my friend's family has. Their father's nose dominated the gene pool and all eleven of the children (yes, eleven!) have proud proboscises that instantly identified them to their schoolteachers and community as members of this large family. Now that they are adult, three of the women have succumbed to society's standards and have opted for rhinoplasty. They do look gorgeous, but, wouldn't you know it, something's missing!

Don't worry about your daughter spending her childhood years not looking like what you feel is her best. You may be overly sensitive to Allegra's appearance, exaggerating the size of her nose in your mind. Concentrate on her health and happiness. She may choose to stay "natural" by the time she's fully grown.

Q. *What is the most common cosmetic surgery performed on children?*

A. The most common time for consultation with a plastic surgeon (or aesthetic or reconstructive surgeon) is after a traumatic injury such as a facial laceration, animal bite, or burn. Although a plastic surgeon is not always needed, the ultimate scars or deformities can usually be reduced significantly or be well camouflaged by a doctor skilled in surgery for aesthetic results. Many of these techniques have been borrowed from procedures such as face lifts or eye lifts. Parents should know that if they want a specialist, they usually must *ask* for a plastic surgeon in the hospital emergency room. (For more details, see the discussion of facial injuries in chapter 2.) The next most common reason is ear surgery. Congenital abnormalities such as hare lip and cleft palate repair, surgery for problems such as extra fingers in infancy, and for skin lesions such as birthmarks are the next most common plastic surgery procedures.

CHAPTER SIX

Exercise

Keeping Our Children Fit

A group of mothers sit on a beach in Long Island, watching their children play. One of the women, visiting from England, remarks, "American children are so round—and seem to tire more easily than our children." She explains that if they were on a beach in England or practically anywhere in Europe, most of the kids would look almost skinny compared with their American counterparts. And put them on a soccer field—they could run furiously for hours, she added.

The President's Council on Physical Fitness and Sports 1985 survey of 19,000 6- to 17-year-olds gives credence to the barbs of this British mother: 40 percent of American boys and 70 percent of American girls cannot do more than one pull-up. The performance of American children on the track is also poor: 33 percent of school-age boys and 50 percent of girls take more than ten minutes to run a mile. As long ago as 1953, a study conducted by Dr. Henry Kraus showed that the strength, flexibility, and endurance of an American child was significantly inferior to a comparable group of European children. Upset by this information, President Eisenhower decided to create the Council on Youth Fitness to make Americans aware of and improve the shape of children, teens, and adults in America.

Almost forty years later, not only does America's youth still look flabby next to their European counterparts, but they also lag way behind in athletic ability compared to America's *own* children ten and twenty years ago and compared to today's *adults*, 60 percent of whom now exercise regularly! Aside from the poor physical state of our children today, health experts have recorded an 18 to 27 percent increase in obesity among children ages 6 to 11 in the last twenty years (see Body Image chapter). Add to this the fact that 40 percent of children ages 5 to 8 have elevated blood pressure or elevated blood-cholesterol levels (according to studies reported on in *Time* magazine), and the result we are looking at is that our children will have more risks for heart disease than any generation ever before.

Why the decline of the American child's physique? "The main culprit, by far, is television," says Dr. Thomas Flynn, past committee chairman for sports medicine for the American Academy of Pediatrics. "The VCR and video

■ ■ ■ ■ ■ ■ ■ ■ ■

THE BEST WAY TO ENCOURAGE YOUR CHILDREN TO EXERCISE IS TO MAKE IT A FAMILY AFFAIR.

games haven't helped, either." Other sources point the finger at cars, buses, and the public transportation that save us the trouble of walking. York Onnen, director of program development at the President's Council on Physical Fitness, blames the cuts in physical-education programs in schools throughout the nation as another cause, citing that only 36 percent of all school-age children have gym daily and only 10 percent of all elementary schools in America require physical education at all. "When budgets must be cut," he says, "the first program to go is phys ed. School is precisely the place where lifelong fitness habits should be taught and incorporated into an overall education." School districts are admittedly pressed to fit in all the curriculum stressing academic basics, but some studies have shown that when fitness levels rise, academic achievement scores do the same.

All too often, sports and exercise must take place outside of school. Among families in which both parents go to work, transportation to organized sports can be difficult to arrange. Lessons and leagues for extracurricular sports such as ice hockey or tennis lessons are very expensive—not to mention the gear needed for these sports. And many children don't feel they are particularly good at sports. When coaches or parents set up an atmosphere of heavy competition in which "winning is all," and only the "stars" get to play, many children are understandably reluctant to sign up for the local sports leagues. Simple street play among kids has decreased as neighborhood streets have become increasingly dangerous. Ultimately, of course, watching TV is more comfortable than going outside to climb trees or play touch football on a chilly day.

■■■■■■■■■■■■■■■■■■■■■■■■■■■■■■■■

What Exercise Can Do for Your Children

Scientific studies of the effects of exercise have concentrated more on adults than children, but it is generally believed that children benefit from a fitness program in the same positive ways that adults do. These include "adult" concerns such as a trimmer body, stress reduction, and the wonderful "joie de

vivre" that comes from a good workout and maintaining a well-exercised body.

For a child to experience true fitness, he must do more than attend the toddler workout spa twice a week or, for an older child, play soccer three or four hours a week. True fitness is a total discipline involving a well-balanced diet, adequate amounts of sleep, and a positive mental attitude as well as workouts or sports programs. The earlier children make this commitment to fitness and good health, the greater the benefits.

Having said that, let's take a look at why physical exercise is so important for kids. Here are a few reasons:

■ Exercise helps keep your child's weight in check. If your child is overweight, cutting down on empty calories, in combination with exercise, will help make weight loss permanent. Calorie intake is probably even less important than the role that exercise plays in weight reduction among children, according to many experts. In his book *Your Child in Sports: A Complete Guide*, Lawrence Galton cites a study conducted by Dr. Jean Mayer and a team of researchers from Harvard Medical School. "When they compared food intake and activity schedules of obese and normal [school] girls," he writes, "they found that most of the obese girls actually ate less, not more than the normal girls, but spent two-thirds less time in physical activity." Another study showed that when a group of university students increased their exercise, they were able to increase their calorie intake from 3,000 to 6,000 a day and not gain weight! Exercise not only raises the metabolic rate with which the body burns calories, but continues to do so five or six hours after the exercise is over. Exercise also increases muscle mass and decreases fat percentage, leaving your child with a firmer, tauter body.

- Exercise increases muscle strength, tone, and flexibility. It keeps children's already supple joints even better able to move quickly without damage. Exercise also can increase muscle definition among older children.

- Exercise helps control fatigue. Because a physically fit child has more muscular capacity and more endurance than the sedentary child, daily physical efforts are less taxing. Children who exercise also feel more rested after a night's sleep. Two significant studies have shown that the more people exercise, the more deeply they sleep.

- Exercise strengthens the heart muscle itself. Studies show that children who exercise regularly have a slower heartbeat when they are playing vigorously. This means that the heart has increased capacity and can keep the body moving with fewer beats than that of a child who doesn't exercise regularly.

- Exercise helps keep the heart free of disease that can eventually cause heart attack or heart disease. Regular fitness workouts help mitigate risk factors that make adults prone to these diseases. The risk factors that can start in childhood are the following: high blood pressure; stress; an inactive lifestyle; obesity; diabetes; high levels of cholesterol and lipoproteins (materials in the blood that transport cholesterol). One survey of 360 elementary-school children in Michigan found that 98 percent of them had one or more risk factors for eventually developing heart disease. Finally, exercise actually bolsters the fight against heart disease. Regular exercise increases HDL, the "good" or protective cholesterol that reduces the risk of heart attacks and strokes.

■ Exercise helps relieve the mental and emotional tensions so many of our children are feeling in today's competitive and pressured atmosphere. A swim at the YMCA, a half hour of roller-skating, climbing on the jungle gym, each can result in your child feeling calmer. Why? Mood-elevating hormones called endorphins are released by the pituitary gland into the bloodstream during vigorous exercise. These neurohormones resemble the opiate morphine, and give the similar effects of "well-being." One study from the University of Southern California showed exercise to be more effective than tranquilizers for relieving anxiety.

■ Exercise may help increase learning potential. For centuries, teachers have believed that fitness enhances learning ability. "Mens sana in corpore sano" (a sound mind in a sound body) has been the watchword among educators since Plato's time. Studies are admittedly limited, but most of the research shows a positive relationship between fitness and academic achievement. One study on Canadian children who were taken out of their regular classes to exercise vigorously each day showed that these children did better on math and language tests than children in comparable schools. Their fitness levels rose as well!

■■■■■■■■■■■■■■■■■■■■■■■■■■■■■■■■■■■

Fitness Begins at Home

"I like to take my 4- and 6-year-old girls out to the park for at least two hours of play and sports each day of the weekend," says Bill, a very fit 40-year-old. "My wife takes them for family swims during the week, too. They even exercise to the Jane Fonda video along with her. I simply need to exercise a lot, and I figure they do, too."

Bill's daughters will probably grow up feeling that exercise and sports are a natural component of fit living and a full life, according to Dr. Thomas Flynn. As a pediatrician, a sports-medicine expert, and father of nine children, Dr. Flynn is well qualified when he says he believes that parents

CHECK A JUNGLE GYM FOR SAFETY BEFORE AL-
LOWING YOUR CHILDREN TO PLAY ON IT.

are the most important influence on a child's exercise habits when he grows up. "Parents are the best physical-education teachers a child can have," he says. "If Mom and Dad participate in sports and recreation with their children and on their own, this active lifestyle will shape how a child will live the rest of his life. The earlier a family begins exercising together, the better, but it's never too late to start."

Parents are not required to be triathletes or even necessarily so physically fit themselves. Most parents who exercise with their children simply enjoy being with their children and find the play and sports a solidifying bond. Of course, if you have organized your own fitness program, you will be setting an excellent example for your children, letting them know that exercise is a priority in your active life. On the other hand, if your lifestyle is sedentary, you can give the opposite message.

Organizing time for family fitness is not only not easy, it's tough. Many parents are running homes as single parents or have jobs that demand so much time and energy that exercise is often the last detail on their minds when they come home. Housework and errands often dominate weekends, and in light of the fact that there are so many other demands on the parent, fitness often becomes a luxury. Exercising as a family group can present other problems: depending on the ages of the children, fitness levels vary dramatically so that fitness is not always promoted equally for each member of the family. A 2-year-old's need for attention in a swimming pool will not allow Mom to do her laps (but if both parents are around, they could take turns). Or the 12-year-old brother might get frustrated that the 6-year-old sister is not keeping up the jogging pace. Despite the drawbacks, however, fitness as a family project gives your child the best possible start in adopting good exercise habits for life.

■■■■■■■■■■■■■■■■■■■■■■■■■■■■■■■■■■■■

The Family Conference

A good beginning for any fitness program is a family conference. Find out how the different members feel about their own levels of fitness (if they are old enough) and what they feel can be done to improve their conditions. Review the sports or activities they are already involved in. If your 10-year-old son is playing two hours of ice hockey and three hours of basketball each week, in addition to gym at school, he's certainly getting enough exercise. (Although he may enjoy an evening fast-walk with the rest of the family.) If your 5-year-old daughter takes one hour of dance each week and has only two hours of phys ed at school, she should be exercising more—maybe with you! "Normal play," such as running around the house or outside, playing tag, climbing trees, etc., does have benefits, of course, so keep an eye on how much of this activity your child is engaged in.

Look at the sports options open to your family, given the different ages of your children. When choosing sports, Dr. Flynn recommends picking "lifetime sports," or ones that can be practiced at any age, such as tennis, walking, running, cycling, and swimming, rather than team sports such as football, lacrosse, or gymnastics, which are rarely engaged in by adults. Sports can be seasonal, of course, so participation will change during the year (unless you're lucky enough to live in a warm climate).

If your children love to swim, join the YMCA or a local pool and set up weekly dates for family swims. If they like playing tennis, reserve a local court for Saturday or Sunday games. Try bowling or paddle tennis in the winter if these sports are available. Or consider setting aside two thirty-minute sessions every Tuesday and Thursday evening for video workout sessions—choosing a video that's specifically designed for family workouts. Many families invest in exercise equipment that simulates the action of rowing, cross-country skiing, stair climbing, etc., and use them effectively. (They may also be dangerous for young children, so keep them away or lay down strict rules for their use.) Something as modest as a chinning bar set up in a doorway can have value in building upper-body strength. The key to any successful exercise program is consistency—the family should attempt to work regularly at it.

As I've admitted, adhering to a family exercise program is not always easy. Children are often as busy as parents. As much as you can, try to create an environment in which child and adult do regular workouts and children are consistently encouraged and praised when they get involved in sports and fitness activities. Here are some other guidelines to help you encourage fitness in the family way:

■ TV is a major stumbling block for parents who would like their children to exercise more. A report from the U.S. Department of Health and Human Services states that while young people do sports or exercise activities only thirteen hours a week, Nielsen (the agency that reports on TV viewings) reports that kids watch TV an average of twenty-five hours per week. Although it may appear radical to some parents, I solved the TV problem years ago with the help of my son's third-grade teacher. She had posted a sign that read, "No TV during the school week." We've followed that rule ever since with the exceptions of educational and other specials and one or two favorite shows each week. The children do organized sports, play (or fight!), or even *read* for lack of anything better to do. (Thank you, Mrs. McCartney!) If TV is allowed, you might set limits and turn it off for periods to encourage free playtime, especially during daylight hours.

■ Each child responds differently to exercise programs. Sports and exercise have to be fun, or you will certainly see the ranks fade. Some youngsters need virtually no encouragement, while others are reluctant, uninterested, or uncertain about their physical abilities. Try to find the most entertaining sports or exercise for your children.

■ Remember that kids have shorter legs and less heart and lung capacity than adults. Although some children ski or run faster than their parents, others may have a hard time keeping up with adults or older siblings. Pace the sport to the speed of the slowest family member. Older kids can run ahead and then run back if they get impatient.

■ Try to keep the activity from becoming boring by setting time limits and having a goal. A family walk could end up in town for lunch, but don't reward sports accomplishments with candies or other sugary treats. This is self-defeating. When fitness goals are met, reward children with exercise-related prizes such as a new tennis racquet, a pro team T-shirt or cap, new sneakers, etc. Tickets to a professional basketball or baseball game can serve as a reward and will also educate. As a special incentive for the older child, you might consider offering a week or two at a sports camp in the summer. These camps can be a positive and fun experience for a child interested in a particular sport. Check out any camp by asking the camp for names of parents whose children have attended.

■■■■■■■■■■■■■■■■■■■■■■■■■■■■■■■■■■

Physical Education at School—Is It Adequate?

Not at all, according to York Onnen of the President's Council on Physical Fitness. "We make recommendations to the Senate for more phys ed classes and enhanced fitness programs at schools all the time," he says. "But it's like standing on top of a mountain and yelling and no one ever hears."

As I mentioned earlier, physical education is usually the first to go when budgets are cut. Only four states now require that students take gym in all grades, and only Illinois requires gym every day. Education is a state responsibility, and Mr. Onnen's plea at Capitol Hill is heard only as a recommendation—the federal government cannot impose physical-education standards. A further obstacle in your child's physical education at school is the lack of qualified gym instructors. York Onnen points out that the profession of physical-education instructor is perceived as a lower-level job in education, sadly enough, and many talented fitness experts are turning to other jobs in the exercise field, jobs such as personal training or kinesiology (the study of muscular movements of the body applied to physical conditioning).

How can you know about the quality of physical education at your child's school and whether he or she is getting the most out of it? The first person to ask is your child. What does she say about gym? Does she look forward to classes and are her attitudes toward the classes and instructor positive ones? The next step is a chat with the gym teacher, for whom I've compiled a checklist of questions. Look it over before a conference or refer to it when speaking over the phone:

1. Does the PE instructor have any comments to make about your child's physical fitness?
2. How often is gym class offered each week? (Our local elementary school offers gym only twice a week in elementary school, and only three times a week in the middle school, grades six to eight. I feel this is not enough and, like many other parents, have each of my three children participate in one, two, and even three extracurricular sports each season.) Each day, children need at least one-half hour of vigorous physical activity that produces a heart rate above 160 beats per minute.
3. Is the PE instructor satisfied with the school program, and how does it stack up against physical education programs in other school districts in your area?
4. What is the PE curriculum? Does the instructor emphasize sports skills and competition, or does she emphasize fun and participation? The latter is necessary for encouraging all children to participate, but some of the former is

obviously called for as well, with competition being the least important issue.

5. Does the school offer enough sports participation for girls? Does it provide activities for kids who are overweight or poorly coordinated? What about the physically handicapped? A program that ends up making some children feel physically inadequate and bad about themselves is flawed and needs upgrading.

6. Does the school offer instruction in "lifetime" sports, such as running, walking, bicycling, aerobic dancing, which have a good chance of being part of your child's recreational life for years to come?

7. Does the gym teacher look physically fit? Does she teach other classes in the school, or is this a full-time job?

If you are still concerned about the PE program, talk to your school principal. After that, consult with the Parent-Teacher Association. When the problem reflects a policy within the entire district, talk to the Board of Education. If enough parents feel strongly about changing the physical education program, there is a good likelihood that the school system will start to seek ways to enrich it.

■■■■■■■■■■■■■■■■■■■■■■■■■■■■■■■■

Age-Appropriate Sports—A Sample Guide

Should your 4-year-old start tennis this summer? Is a 9-year-old too young to try waterskiing?

While there are general parameters, it is difficult to accurately gauge just when a child should begin a certain sport. Skills such as eye-hand coordination (needed in sports such as baseball and soccer), a sense of balance (for sports like bicycling or gymnastics), and long concentration spans (for tennis) develop at varying ages.

Often, a child's body is simply not ready for a sport. A case in point is weight lifting. In my research I heard of many 9- to 12-year-old boys who were self-conscious about their smaller bodies compared to the more physically advanced girls of the same age or other boys who'd started puberty early. In a desperate bid to look like seniors in high school, they wanted to begin weight lifting, which is clearly not safe or effective at this age, or at least weight training (which involves machines, such as Nautilus, for resistance training). A policy statement from the American Academy of Pediatrics discourages boys who have not gone through puberty from taking up these forms of exercise. "Prepubertal boys . . . do not significantly improve strength or increase muscle mass in a weight training program because of insufficient circulating androgens," say the authors. They do add that "a recent report indicates that preadolescents have some improvement in strength of the abdominal and back muscles after weight training, but no significant change in strength of the limbs."

Elements of many sports can be dangerous for young children. Matthew Chaloux, sports and leisure director for the Darien, Connecticut, YMCA points to a few. "Most Little Leagues outlaw the throwing of curve balls in their games because they involve unnatural body movements and there is a great risk of injury to the muscles, ligaments, tendons, and growth plate in the elbow," he says. "In football, tackling with the head angled down—or 'spearheading'—is not only dangerous for school-age children but has also caused some catastrophic injuries in the pro leagues."

Dr. Flynn recommends letting common sense be the guide when your child wants to try a new sport. If your 3½-year-old wants to swim very badly, certainly help her try. Instruction is required—and you will probably have to put in a number of hours at the pool while she masters the sport. If you are the one who wants your child to learn a new sport, be careful not to push too hard. Even if all his 5-year-old friends are riding two-wheel bikes, your child may not be ready. (Some children don't develop bike-riding skills until age 11 or older.) Certainly wait until your child feels confident with a sport before making it a part of your fitness regime. The trick is to get your children involved in any sport or program while they are still young. In his book *Kid Fitness*, Dr. Kenneth H. Cooper asserts that ". . . it is *essential* that parents get children involved in some sort of structured aerobics program by this age (8 to 10 years old) because fitness begins to decline rapidly in many children after age 10 for several possible reasons. One is that many children don't develop good exer-

cise habits. Another is that the drop-out rate increases as both boys and girls become discouraged with or uninterested in team sports."

The following list shows various sports and approximately the best age at which to begin them. Obviously, older children can try all the sports listed for the younger age groups and younger children must be more carefully supervised during sports activities.

2- to 4-year-olds—toddler exercise classes, walking, tricycling, tag games, playground activities, ball play, pool and water play, sledding, short hikes.

4- to 6-year-olds—short runs, video exercises, gymnastics, ballet, tap dancing, ice-skating, biking, skiing, fishing, rope-jumping.

6- to 8-year-olds—swimming laps, Tee-Ball (a junior form of Little League wherein participants use what looks like a giant golf tee that places the ball at batting level), jazz dancing, soccer, tennis, cross-country skiing, ice hockey.

8- to 10-year-olds—horseback riding, sailing, baseball, softball.

10- to 12-year-olds—volleyball, field hockey, football, lacrosse, golf, diving, waterskiing.

AT AGES 4 AND 5, THESE GIRLS PARTICIPATE IN A DANCE RECITAL. THEIR FATHERS WAIT TO CONGRATULATE THEM WITH BOUQUETS OF FLOWERS. DANCE CLASS PROVIDES A STRUCTURE IN WHICH CHILDREN CAN LEARN TO MOVE THEIR BODIES TO MUSIC WITH GRACE AND PRECISION.

A Sampling of Popular Children's Sports

There are good things to be said about every sport and recreation, from hopscotch to playing pool, from kite flying to wind surfing. Here are a few of the sports that children love:

Ball Games (baseball, basketball, football, lacrosse, soccer): There's a wide range here. Sports such as basketball, lacrosse, and soccer keep kids racing up and down a court or field and get the heart pumping, which gives aerobic value. Baseball, as I mentioned earlier, is a different kind of game that calls for sharp eye-hand coordination. Football is an exciting game, but often involves violent contact with other players. Tackling is not usually allowed until players turn

11—at the secondary-school level, more injuries are sustained from playing football than from any other sport. Players age 8 to 13 have a slightly lower incidence of injuries.

Bicycling: Most children go through a series of bikes: the tricycle, the two-wheeler with training wheels, the mountain bike, and later, perhaps the serious touring or racing bike. As a recreation, cycling strengthens the heart and is an excellent overall body builder. But to promote real fitness, children should ride regularly—at least a half hour of vigorous cycling three times a week. Be sure the seat of the bike is set at the right height—setting the saddle too low can put a strain on the knees. Check with your local bike shop for correct seat height. Also make sure your child wears a safety helmet when he rides. Set a good example by wearing one yourself. Only 10 percent of adults and 2 percent of children now wear helmets! This is changing, however, thanks to increased awareness of the dangers of biking without a helmet. According to a study reported on in *Physician & Sportsmedicine* magazine (Vol. 16, No. 1, Jan. 1988) more than 1,000 bicycle riders, both young and old, are killed on the road every year, and 75 percent of biking fatalities result from head injuries. Good helmets are expensive but are well worth the investment, and luckily, kids now seem to want to emulate professional bikers with gear that makes them look like pros themselves. Lots of flashy and fashionable Lycra covers for bike helmets are available. Treat your child to one!

Bowling: Kids usually love to go bowling, and it's a relatively easy game for the entire family. The game won't do much to build stamina, but it does enhance motor skills. Use a smaller bowling ball for smaller hands.

Dancing: Whether it's ballet, tap dancing, or aerobic dancing, the physical benefits are enormous. Girls and boys love moving their bodies to music. Ballet teachers generally agree that children should be at least age 10 before they put on a toe slipper and attempt to dance en pointe—on their toes. Before age 10, the bones of the feet are too soft to withstand a child's weight and could actually become curved.

■ ■ ■ ■ ■ ■ ■ ■

THOUGH NOT AS PHYSICALLY DEMANDING AS OTHER SPORTS, FISHING CAN BE A WONDERFUL ACTIVITY. CHILDREN QUICKLY BECOME AWARE OF THE ECOLOGY AND ENVIRONMENTAL ISSUES WHEN SPENDING TIME ON THE WATER AND DEALING WITH WILDLIFE. CHRIS CAUGHT THIS BIG BLUEFISH IN THE LONG ISLAND SOUND AND SHARED IT WITH HIS FAMILY THAT NIGHT FOR DINNER.

Fishing: Some kids naturally gravitate to the nearest lake, stream, or beachfront to pit themselves against trout, muskie, even bluefish. As a sport, fishing's a fairly static activity and involves considerable waiting about. One of my sons has been a serious fisherman since the age of 2, while my other son is bored to distraction with the process. My personal theory is that it's genetic—four out of my five brothers would put fishing before power, sex, and money (and probably have). Fishing's a sport that—at the very least—gets children out into the open air. Anybody who has ever hooked into a large fish knows that pulling it in can be hard work and enormously exciting.

Gymnastics: Inspired by the Olympic gymnasts on television, hundreds of thousands of young girls and boys have taken up gymnastics. This is a great sport for building body strength and teaching balance and grace. Young girls are particularly adept at gymnastics because of their body flexibility. If you sign your child up for class, be sure at least one instructor is certified by the United States Gymnastics Safety Association and that the equipment in the gym is scaled down to child size, properly padded, and surrounded by mats.

Ice Hockey: This exciting sport will help kids get a terrific aerobic workout, and it's an excellent way to build stamina and balance. Children are often eligible to start in kindergarten. They gain great self-esteem from learning how to skate, and then have fun taking a puck from one end of the ice to the other. One terrific benefit: once children learn to skate, they are able to skate all their lives.

Jogging, Running, Fast Walking: Whether your child is racing down a track or walking briskly down a road, these sports add up to excellent exercise. They build endurance, encourage cardiovascular fitness, strengthen the legs, and tone the upper body. They are also great sports for the family while traveling if there are no other sports facilities available. Running is the most demanding of these sports and should be done under the supervision of a coach. Long-distance running among children is controversial because of the high number of epiphyseal growth-plate injuries (see pages 192–93) and other joint trauma. Children are also less tolerant of weather extremes than are adults. Jogging short distances is wiser for children; beginners should start by jogging slowly for a minute, then walking for a minute. Children can quickly build up their stamina to the point at which they can jog five to ten minutes at a time. Fast walking puts much less strain on the legs and feet than running or jogging, and is virtually injury-free. Swinging arms vigorously increases the aerobic value of this recreation.

Self-defense (karate, judo, tai kwan do): If your child has indicated interest in karate or judo, visit a nearby dojo (martial-arts school) with him and see what a class looks like. Classes should start with limbering-up exercises and calisthenics before the children begin practicing their kicks and falls. The attitude of the teacher is crucial: he is there to teach self-confidence as well as self-defense. Children should come out of the class knowing not only how to defend themselves, but how to back away from an encounter with another child without punching and kicking.

Skateboarding: To the dismay of many parents, one of the most popular recreations for kids age 8 and older is riding wildly decorated little boards on streets, sidewalks, steps, or

GYMNASTICS HELPS KEEP JOINTS LOOSE AND TEACHES CHILDREN TO MOVE WITH GRACE.

various homemade backyard ramps. According to industry officials, over 10 million children now own skateboards. Skateboarding is essentially a communal recreation: kids hang out in packs, practicing, exchanging skateboard lore, or watching videos of professionals in action. Adults rarely ride boards (part of its appeal, I suspect). As a sport, skateboarding builds stamina, agility, and balance, but many children take a lot of falls in the process. All skateboarders should wear a safety helmet, gloves, knee pads, and a mouthguard.

Skiing: For most recreational skiers, a day on the slopes is an opportunity to get together with family or friends while practicing skiing skills. Since the runs are usually short and punctuated by stops at different trails, the aerobic value is limited. Cross-country skiing is something else again. Using legs and arms (not gravity) to propel yourself with ski poles across a flat terrain builds overall body strength. Cross-country skiers also report significantly fewer injuries than their downhill counterparts.

■ ■ ■ ■ ■ ■ ■ ■ ■

JUGGLING REQUIRES EXCELLENT EYE-HAND COOR-
DINATION. TWELVE-YEAR-OLD MORGAN WENT TO
JUGGLING SCHOOL AND NOW ENTERTAINS AT
YOUNGER CHILDREN'S BIRTHDAY PARTIES.

Swimming: Swimming is one of America's most popular recreations; according to *USA Today*, over 100 million Americans swim. Regular lap swimming for older children is an excellent path to physical fitness, but it must involve getting in the swim a minimum of twenty to thirty minutes at least three times a week. For safety's sake, all children who are physically able should learn to swim. But wait till after the age of 3. According to the Academy of Pediatrics, children under the age of 3 do not have the physical and emotional skills to take group swimming lessons. Mother-child classes (after the age of 6 months) are fine for introducing children to the water, although babies prone to ear infections should not be started till age 3 or older.

Tennis, Paddle Tennis, Racquetball: These racquet-and-ball games can be learned and enjoyed by anyone from the age of 7 or 8 on. A fast, well-played game provides a good aerobic workout and demands considerable skill in returning and controlling the ball.

■ ■ ■ ■ ■ ■ ■ ■ ■

TENNIS IS A "LIFETIME" SPORT. THOUGH CHIL-
DREN MAY START CLASSES AS YOUNG AS 4 OR 5,
TENNIS IS A SPORT THAT REQUIRES SOME PHYSI-
CAL MATURITY AND LONGER ATTENTION SPANS,
OFTEN NOT REACHED UNTIL AGES 9 OR 10.

■ ■

Your Daughter in Sports—
Questions and Answers

How lucky we are that our daughters are enjoying more legal
and social freedom to participate in sports than ever before.
When I was about 9 years old, I remember outracing everyone in my class—including the boys—in a hundred yard
dash on field day at school. I was tall and did have an advantage. Was glory mine? Never! The boys (including the one I
had a crush on) teased me unmercifully and I quickly learned
that racing down the field sweating, face beet-red, was not
feminine, "cool," or ever rewarded in the 1950s. But today
the image is exactly the opposite. Today we see the most
glamorous women of our times on workout videos or in TV
commercials perspiring profusely, working their pecs, exhib-
iting their strong, well-toned bodies with the message that
working out and staying fit will get girls all the boys they'll
ever need.

   In a major leap for equality in the physical education
arena, the Federal Education Act of 1972 (Title IX) man-
dated that boys and girls have equal athletic facilities and
programs. Women have been allowed to compete in more and

Backyard Fun

If you have heard "There's nothing to do, Mom" one too many times, it's time to upgrade your backyard entertainment! No need to raid your money-market account to put in a tennis court, swimming pool, or skateboard ramp—the following games provide some relatively low-cost answers to the couch potato blues. If your backyard is the city park, you can often find portable versions of many outdoor games that are easily set up on a grassy knoll. Check your local stores for the myriads of other lawn games available. Here are some of the most popular:

Horseshoes: For children 6 and older. Throwing the "shoe" and hitting the metal stake can be quite an art, but who cares if you don't get a ringer—it's great family fun! The game won't melt away many calories, but it does have some value in improving eye-hand coordination.

Badminton: Badminton involves hitting a feathered shuttlecock back and forth over a net, using a light, long-necked racquet. Children love it—especially on days when the family's outside barbecueing or gardening. Incidentally, the game first became popular in the late nineteenth century in England and was named after Badminton, the estate of the Duke of Beaufort, where it was introduced to the gentry.

Volleyball: For older children—ages 8 and up. Volleyball can be easily set up in a park, backyard, or beach, and there are no limits on how many can play.

Frisbee: Flipping the Frisbee will happily involve adults, kids, and even the family dog. (Fido may execute marvelous acrobatic leaps in order to catch the Frisbee, but then may choose to run off with it—which usually leads to a mass family charge after the beast.) Kids quickly get the hang of flipping the wrist for a long, floating toss. An excellent game for building eye-hand coordination.

Croquet: This game, which has been around for at least two hundred years, consists of wooden mallets that are used to hit balls through a series of arches called wickets. Croquet calls for good eye-hand coordination and an ability to concentrate.

Swing Set: Even though it's probably the most expensive "toy" you'll buy for a young child, it's usually the best investment you can make toward helping your children stay fit. The younger your children are, the greater the return, since swing sets can be added to as your child grows. Slides, ladders, climbing ropes, platforms, and even enclosed clubhouses are often available for addition to many sets. Buying a good quality swing set that is anchored in the ground is very important, because light, flimsy swing sets tend to tip over or even collapse as children grow heavier.

Homemade Miniature Golf: For families with a little imagination, a lot of energy, and a garage or basement full of gadgets and tag-sale items, why not construct your own miniature golf course? This effort has amused children and grandchildren in our large family for decades. Use cardboard rolls or coffee cans for chutes. Hoses, boards, plastic bowls full of water all add to an interesting course for all the mini-golfers in your life.

more sport categories in the Olympics and the "tomboy" image is as happily dated as the 1950s. While our daughters have more freedom in sports, parents are still confused about a number of issues concerning girls in sports, including girls playing on boys' teams, sports injuries, and exercise's role in keeping girls healthy and slim.

WINTER WEATHER CREATES A PLAYGROUND FOR SPORTS SUCH AS ICE SKATING. THIS SPORT CAN BE MASTERED AT A VERY EARLY AGE. HERE, 4-YEAR-OLD SUSAN BRINGS UP THE REAR.

Q. *My 12-year-old daughter is a real athlete. She runs with her middle-school track team, swims on the swim team at the YMCA, and works out with a biking club on weekends. She loves it and seems to be getting good supervision. I've read that women athletes whose body fat gets low due to extreme exercise often stop menstruating. My daughter hasn't started menstruating, but my fear is that so much physical activity will keep her percentage of body fat low and her period may be delayed. What is the current thinking on this subject?*

A. Female athletes (and anorexics, by the way) low in body fat may stop menstruating. And female athletes whose percentage of body fat is low may start their periods later than other girls of the same ethnic background. According to research, athletes have a delayed onset of menstruation in all sports except swimming. This seems to produce no adverse effects in the long run, and these athletes suffer no more childbearing complications than the rest of the population. A study of 145 female athletes in the 1976 Montreal Olympic Games cited in an article on female athletes in the *Sports Medicine Handbook* found that the average age of "menarche," or onset of menstruation, was 13.7 years and that each group of athletes had a later menarche than that of the general population of their country of origin. The article reports that runners and gymnasts got their first periods the latest of all the athletes in the Olympics study group—at age 14.3 and 14.5, respectively. Swimmers got their periods the earliest,

13.1 years. "An earlier study showed the ages of menarche as 14.2 in a group of Olympic volleyball players," report the authors, "13.0 in high school and college athletes, and 12.2 in non-athletes." If they diet and exercise vigorously, ballet dancers seem to get their periods latest of all, at 15.6 years. Restriction of calories as well as excess stress and energy drain might be the reasons for delayed menstruation in this group. When these ballerinas stopped exercising and dancing for a few months or longer due to an injury or other reason, their periods arrived shortly thereafter.

Q. *My 6-year-old daughter wants to join the local ice-hockey team. (Her older brothers love it!) The league is open to girls, but are they strong enough to compete against boys at this age?*

A. The recommendation from the American Academy of Pediatrics in their *Sports Medicine Handbook* (1983) is that girls can compete against boys in any sport if they are matched in size, weight, degree of physical maturity, and skill. Hockey-league divisions usually have a two-year

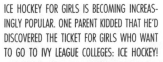

ICE HOCKEY FOR GIRLS IS BECOMING INCREAS-INGLY POPULAR. ONE PARENT KIDDED THAT HE'D DISCOVERED THE TICKET FOR GIRLS WHO WANT TO GO TO IVY LEAGUE COLLEGES: ICE HOCKEY!

age range, which is fine unless your daughter is very small for her age. "Checking," or bumping opponents, in ice hockey is usually not allowed until the children are age 12 or 13.

Until puberty, boys and girls are very similar in height and weight for any given age, with boys showing slightly greater heights and weights. Despite this size similarity to boys, girls seem to lag on performance of physical tests given by the President's Council on Physical Fitness in every area except flexibility. This may be due to the fact that boys are offered more sports opportunities by the parents and community.

Old cultural values and stereotypes may also play a role in keeping girls from participating in sports. At about age 11, girls get taller and heavier than boys for a period of about two years. Then it's the boys' turn: from age 12 to 15, the boys grow dramatically and end up taller, heavier, and stronger than girls, on the whole. After puberty, girls have higher fat content and less muscle mass per unit of body weight and should not compete with boys in heavy-collision sports because of the risk of injury, according to the American Academy of Pediatrics. Should an exceptional female athlete participate in direct contact sports with boys? Controversy still surrounds this question. The Academy's recommendation is to develop programs and athletics for girls rather than highlighting the exceptional female athlete on the boys' team.

For now, indulge your 6-year-old daughter's interest in ice hockey. (A checkup with the doctor before entering a sport is always advisable.) By age 13 or 14, when boys catch up and surpass girls' height and weight, your daughter may do better finding an all-girls ice-hockey league or else playing boys' teams that are younger and better matched in size and weight, or switching to another sport.

Q. *My daughter is 10 years old and ten pounds overweight. What sport will help her trim down in the shortest time?*

A. Any sport that interests her and that she considers fun. Why? Because stick-to-itiveness is all-important. Highly aerobic sports such as running, aerobic dancing, and singles tennis are terrific for toning up, whereas team sports, such as softball, in which players are active only for short periods, have only limited aerobic benefits.

Girls who are beginning to enter puberty can be self-conscious. If they are overweight, they may be especially so. If this is the case with your daughter, you may want to choose an exercise that is girls-only. Or your daughter may want to stay at home to dance to a video or work on an exercise machine—if she is disciplined and motivated enough. If she is willing to exercise in a group, check into exercise classes specially designed for overweight children. Your local YMCA may conduct these classes or may know of others. A registered dietitian, a nutritionist, or a hospital with a weight-loss clinic may also be able to direct you.

Q. *I'd love to have my 7-year-old daughter play Tee-Ball this year, but I'm afraid she'll get hurt. I'm particularly afraid of her getting injured in the chest or genital area. Is this crazy?*

A. This is a common fear of both mothers and fathers—fear that their daughters might somehow sustain an injury that would hurt their ability to bear children, or even get breast cancer from a blow to the chest area. The latter is untrue, as research has shown that there is no basis for believing that an injury causes or predisposes the affected area to cancer. Luckily, breast injuries in child and teen sports are relatively uncommon.

The reproductive area is well-protected, because it sits in the center of the pelvis. A cushion of fluid renders the ovaries relatively invulnerable. Boys' genitals should be well-protected in all heavy-collision sports. The only sport in which the female genitals are at risk for injury is waterskiing. A fall could allow water to enter the vagina at great force and tear the vaginal wall. However, these injuries are also rare.

Research on the number of sports injuries among children ages 2 to 12 is limited, but studies on teenagers show that girls tend to suffer no more injuries in sports than do boys. Protective gear should be worn faithfully when called for. A real concern for both boys and girls is injury and possible permanent damage to the epiphyses, or "growth plates," at the growing ends of the long bones—at the elbow or knee, etc. If these areas are injured, growth may be hindered, so that one arm or leg is shorter than the other. However, these deformities are rare. These areas are particularly vulnerable to injuries such as blows to the area, wrenching, or sudden pressure as in a fall. A friend's 10-year-old daughter injured an epiphyses in her elbow in a simple fall off a "horse" in her gym class. She has been doing therapy for nine months with mild improvement. She still cannot straighten her arm completely, but her prognosis is good. One study has shown that only 6 percent of all sports injuries among preadolescents are epiphyseal. They are usually successfully treated with pressure, traction, or therapy.

Coaching

Team sports among children and preadolescents are often run by nonprofessionals—i.e., volunteer parents who are willing to give their time and effort to create sports leagues. These parents and the overseeing organizations, such as the YMCA, the local parks and recreation department, and Little League of America, are responsible for seeing that the sport is played safely, fairly, and with the ultimate goal of having fun and getting a good workout. How can parents best prepare for their coaching roles?

Each group has its own program for the training of coaches. The YMCA's methods of training parents are a case in point. YMCAs vary from community to community to some degree, since each one is independent; however, all adhere to general standards set by YMCA of the USA, the national organization of YMCAs. Matthew Chaloux, of the Darien, Connecticut, YMCA, explains his own program. "The professional instructors from the YMCA who teach community volunteer coaches are trained by members of a group called 'The American Coaching Effectiveness Program,'" says Chaloux. "They teach YMCA instructors the latest information in sports medicine, sports science, sports management, and specific topics such as techniques and tactics in each sport. Our instructors then take this information back to volunteer parents,

along with teaching aids, such as videotapes. These clinics are followed by studies and tests that qualify parents to coach."

Chaloux reports that the older the children in each sport, the more extensive the coaches' training. For younger children, coaches are taught little tricks such as getting down on one knee, and looking into children's eyes when explaining various moves. A paid staff member from the YMCA, trained in first aid, CPR, etc., is present at practices and games.

The National Youth Sports Association is another program that, under the auspices of state representatives, helps train parents, again with the use of videotapes and books. "Our job is not to turn parents into real coaches," says Michael Pfahl, national executive director of the NYSA, a nonprofit organization founded in 1981, "but to make them aware of their roles and responsibilities when they choose to coach." NYSA's philosophy puts emphasis on fun and participation, rather than on winning at all costs. With certification from the NYSA, each parent not only learns how to coach children, but also receives insurance covering coaching liabilities. Cost is minimal. For more information, write:

National Youth Coaching Sports Association
2611 Old Okeechobee Road
West Palm Beach, FL 43409
Or call: (407) 684-1141

Your Child's Body: Healthy, Fit, and Beautiful

Right before our eyes, our children's bodies are growing, changing, responding not only to their inborn genetic blueprint, but also to the outside influences we are responsible for: their nutrition, the air they breathe, and the proper amount of exercise.

Although it will probably require some sacrifice in other areas of your life, helping your children stay fit is one of the most important gifts you can give them. A child who is physically fit needs no designer clothes, expensive haircuts, or perfect features to make him or her lovely. Physical fitness transcends these trappings to give children the glow that is the real essence of childhood beauty.

CHAPTER SEVEN

Fun Fashion for Kids

What magic clothes work for children! How easily they are transformed into what they wear! When my daughter pulls on her ballet tights and tutu, she becomes the Sugar Plum Fairy in the *Nutcracker;* when she dons her workout leotard and leg warmers, she's a mini–workout queen. "Macho" and "pumped-up" is the way my two sons look and feel in their hockey uniforms. And at Halloween time, children effortlessly enter their witch, tiger, and pirate personas.

Brand-new clothes seem to lift children's spirits the way they do ours. Dressed in Easter finery or holiday best, children are exultant—at least until they realize parents won't let them do cartwheels or wrestle all dressed up. Great-looking clothes provide an instant makeover. They improve children's looks—as they do ours—with no diets, no aerobics, and no plastic surgery. How easy!

Realize not only how clothes can make children look and feel great, but also how they will help them develop self-esteem and pride. When kids are younger, clothes are instrumental in helping them master certain motor skills, such as buttoning and snapping. As they grow, clothes help children learn about making choices, help them feel like part of the crowd, like they belong. Then, by picking up on style, fashion helps them express their personalities, take risks, and build self-confidence. And caring for clothes builds character and demonstrates maturity for children of all ages.

This chapter gives general guidelines to children's fashion. It won't give up-to-the-minute fashion looks for kids, since they change so rapidly. It does give an idea of what fashion means to each age group, and it's full of practical advice. Here you'll find some pretty looks and enter the exciting and sometimes bewildering world of children's fashion.

■ ■ ■ ■ ■ ■ ■ ■ ■

ANTIQUE CLOTHES WORN FOR THIS CHILDREN'S TEA PARTY WERE FOUND IN THRIFT SHOPS, FLEA MARKETS, AND VINTAGE CLOTHING STORES. DRESSING CHILDREN DURING THEIR YOUNG YEARS ALLOWS PARENTS TO INDULGE THEIR FASHION FANTASIES AND RELIVE THE MAGIC OF THE CHILDHOOD YEARS!

■■■■■■■■■■■■■■■■■■■■■■■■■■■■■■

Toddler Togs (2- to 4-Year-Olds) (*Or Dress Your Children in* Your *Favorite Fashions Before They Discover* Theirs!)

There are so many wonderful, fun clothes for the 2- to 4-year-old set that we are tempted to buy the unusual—and dress up the new little person in our lives to the nines. My advice is: Do it! Don't be practical, or sensible, or economical! Use this short period of your child's life to express your fashion whims. This is the only time you'll be able to assert your style on these rapidly developing egos. That's not to say it's fair to dress your child in something so outlandish it invites ridicule. But if you have a girl and love how she looks in dresses, keep her in as many fabulous frocks as you have the time and money to buy or the luck to borrow! By the time they are out of nursery school, girls may eschew dresses and want to wear pants and tops only—as do many a girl in the lower grades.

Some of these parents would love to see their daughters go to school in a pretty dress or a fun skirt and top at least once in a while, but no chance. The only dress one friend's 9-year-old daughter has worn since she was 4 was her confirmation dress last year. (She wore shorts underneath!)

And some of these young children will simply not tolerate Mama's choices. While some 2- to 4-year-olds are compliant about letting a parent choose their clothes, others have this strong sense of individuality in fashion from early on. They will pick a special T-shirt or a favorite pair of shoes as the *only* ones they'll wear to nursery school. Some children become fixated on particular items of clothing as *their* fashion statement. When one of my sons was 3 years old, he would engage me in daily fights to wear his cowboy boots to nursery school—a definite no-no for playground safety—and I admit I gave in more than once. His battle with me was symbolic— he wanted to gain control of the way he looked.

If your child is willing to wear the clothes you choose, take care not to overdo. " 'Dressing up' a child may have psychological implications," says Peggy Marble, nursery-

■ ■ ■ ■ ■ ■ ■ ■ ■

THEIR MOMS CHOSE THESE OUTFITS FOR THEIR TODDLERS. DRESS YOUR CHILDREN TO YOUR TASTE WHILE YOUR CHILDREN ARE STILL YOUNG—THEIR OWN FASHION IDEAS TAKE OVER SOONER THAN YOU THINK.

school director for Christ Church Day School in New York City. She advises parents not to "objectify" their young children by dressing them up the way one would dress a doll. Ms. Marble voices concern that, inadvertently, parents may be trying to create extensions of their own fantasies and expressing hopes for their children that are grounded in missed opportunities for themselves. She cites one mother she knows. Once a beautiful, slim woman, she is now fifty pounds overweight. While she dresses her 9-year-old daughter, Cynthia, in very expensive, very carefully chosen clothes and real jewelry, this mother goes about looking dowdy. One wonders: if the mother recaptured her self-confidence, would what Cynthia wore and how she appeared become less important?

■ ■ ■ ■ ■ ■ ■ ■ ■

CHOOSE CLOTHES THAT WILL NOT DATE AND COLORS THAT ENHANCE YOUR CHILD'S BEAUTY WHEN HAVING A PORTRAIT PAINTED. HERE, SAGE POSES FOR HER GRANDFATHER WHO IS CAPTURING HER IMAGE ON CANVAS.

MEDICAL ALERT
Sleepwear Safety

When research showed that most injuries caused by fire happened during the night to sleeping children ages 5 and under, a panel of authorities amended the 1953 Flammable Fabrics Act passed by Congress. The original Act stated that only certain children's clothing for daytime contain flame retardants. The new amendment required that by 1972, all *sleepwear* in sizes 0 to 6X be manufactured with either a flame retardant material or finish. In 1974, sizes 7 to 14 were added.

Dr. Abraham Bergman, director of pediatrics at Harborview Medical Center in Seattle, Washington, was part of this law-making panel in 1967. "The sleepwear law is one of the greatest triumphs in pediatrics," he says. "Burns caused by rapid conflagration of cotton or other untreated fabrics became rare almost immediately. It was like a miracle."

But there was another problem. In 1976, it was discovered that one of the flame-retardant finishes, called "Tris," was carcinogenic. Although Tris (used on about 25 percent of all sleepwear at the time) was banned, many frightened parents around the country switched to 100-percent-cotton sleepwear. Clothing manufacturers in the United States and abroad found ways to circumvent restrictions for sleepwear and produced what was, in effect, 100-percent cotton sleepwear. "Playtime Suits" is one of their many euphemisms. These clothing articles should *not* be used to sleep in. Look for required labels before you buy. Only items that meet federal standards can be called "sleepwear."

Nursery School or Day-Care Wear: How to Dress Kids for Preschool Success

OVERBUNDLING A TODDLER MAKES FREE PLAY DIFFICULT. GAUGE THE AMOUNT OF CLOTHES YOUR CHILD NEEDS TO KEEP WARM BY THE AMOUNT YOU WEAR.

What your child wears outside of school depends on you and your children's needs and lifestyle. When our family moved from New York City to the suburbs, we had to invest a small fortune in an entire fashion overhaul for my three children. Styles vary not only from state to state, but cross a town or neighborhood line—and fashions are often a world apart.

When it comes to preschool or day-care wear, there are some universal guidelines to follow that will help you dress young children for safety, ease, and independence—the last, an important consideration for the 2- to 5-year-old who is struggling for self-reliance and autonomy. Diane Berkely, a former nursery-school teacher in New York City, was consulted for the following tips for the preschool set:

■ For those obstinate fashion independents, those who must wear something of their own choice—whether it's plaid on plaid or a swimsuit in December—the answer is less selection. You can avoid confrontation by agreeing to allow your child her choice of one of two or three outfits, laid out the night before school, preferably color coordinated for last-minute switching. In this manner, she will be allowed to maintain the sense of control so important to her at this age and you are spared the early-morning conflict.

■ Choose clothes and accessories that simplify dressing. These clothes not only encourage self-reliance but also help children develop fine motor skills. Velcro fasteners on shoes are ideal for toddlers, while shoes with laces are more appropriate for 4- to 6-year-olds who are more capable of tying a bow. Choose clothes that have large necks and side openings so kids can easily slip them on and off. Big zippers, large buttons, etc., simplify tasks for small hands and give children a chance to practice getting dressed by themselves without the added frustration of trying to button small buttons or zipping small zippers. Overall-type fasteners are fine for 4-year-olds but sometimes difficult for 2-year-olds in a rush to undress to go to the bathroom; elastic waistbands are particularly good for young children who are being toilet-trained. Avoid belts for this age group. In order to make the classroom-to-playground transition easier for teachers and children, buy one-piece snowsuits for your 2- to 3-year-old. And finally, remember that it's a lot less difficult for young children to get their chubby little hands into mittens than gloves. Mittens should be fastened to the jacket with clips held together by a long string that slips through the jacket arms.

BEAUTIFUL FOR CHURCH, BUT NOT RIGHT FOR SCHOOL. BE CAREFUL NOT TO OVERACCESSORIZE AND "DOLL-UP" YOUR CHILD WHEN BOUND FOR NURSERY SCHOOL. PLAY CLOTHES AND SNEAKERS ALLOW YOUNG CHILDREN TO FEEL RELAXED AT PRESCHOOL.

■ Don't overdress your preschooler. First-time parents often don't realize that children get hot while playing indoors or outdoors if too bundled up. (I made this mistake with my first child, who'd go off to school looking like an Eskimo trapper!) Try to judge the layers of clothes needed for your child by what *you* wear, and have him wear the same. If you are walking your child to school in a stroller on a cold day, remember that he is inactive and very susceptible to the wind. Use a plastic wind-cover if your stroller accommodates it, or bundle your child up in extra wind-resistant blankets. Hat, scarf, gloves, and boots or other protective footwear should all be in place.

■ Dressing your beautiful little 3-year-old girl in a Dior dress or your 2-year-old boy in a white gabardine sailor suit is fun for you and everyone else to see. Nursery-school director Peggy Marble warns, however, that these fine clothes can cause problems for the young child in school or day care. "Wearing special clothes inhibits the free and spontaneous play preschoolers are naturally involved in," says Ms. Marble. "Dressy clothes look wonderful, as do jewelry and other accessories, but they do get in the way. Children are often reluctant to do their artwork or cooking projects for fear of getting dresses dirty." Ms. Marble says that it is easy to lose an accessory such as a bracelet or a headband, and that searching for these items uses up time that might be better spent on learning or socializing. Many a

■ ■ ■ ■ ■ ■ ■ ■ ■

FANTASY BECOMES REALITY. HALLOWEEN IS A DREAM-COME-TRUE HOLIDAY FOR CHILDREN, AS WHAT THEY WEAR IS WHAT THEY BECOME FOR A NIGHT. HERE, ADAM PLAYS PUMPKIN WHILE NOELLE IS THE LITTLE MERMAID.

storytime or other activity has been disturbed by children playing with a ring or headband. Some of these accessories can be dangerous, as well. Dangling earrings or loose bracelets can get caught while toddlers are engaged in rambunctious play at the playground or on the jungle gym. Ms. Marble suggests that parents dress their preschooler in clothes that he will be proud to wear—but will also feel sufficiently comfortable in which to participate in all activities.

■ Some nursery schools and day-care centers have banned "Superhero" clothes and accessories for fear that the costumes increase aggression and delude children. Parents hear the story about the child who jumped out a window wearing a Superman cape and T-shirt in full belief that he had taken on Superman's flying powers along with the clothes. Whether or not this is true, I know that the Superman T-shirt and cape were very important to my first son and his best friend when they were in preschool and that the Batman outfit was indispensable for much of my second son's third year of life. These outfits were worn *every* day, under regular clothes as though they were sacred vestments, in the belief that they lent important powers.

Although these particular fads have subsided somewhat, the media will always provide new superheroes, and the symbolic value of clothes cannot be underestimated. You know whether your young child is able to sufficiently separate fantasy from reality to judge how superhero or cartoon character clothes affect his behavior. If you see him losing social control while romping around in character clothes, simply tell him you'll have to put them away until he can behave. Clothes can inspire more mature behavior as well: witness the little rebel who puts on a velvet and lace party dress and is transformed, like Cinderella, into a gracious hostess.

■ The best footwear for toddlers at preschool or day care? Shoes with nonskid soles. Most pediatricians give well-fitting, comfortable sneakers high marks for everyday footwear for young children. Avoid sending your child to school in dressy shoes, high-heeled boots, sandals, and thongs. Accidents are common among children who wear these shoes.

You will make teachers' lives easier if you send your child to school in boots worn *without* shoes, and send shoes along in a bag. If you prefer rubber slipover boots, have your son or daughter wear plastic bags over shoes to ensure easy slipping on and off. (For more information on shoes, see page 222.)

■ Last, but not at all least, label all removable articles of clothing with either cloth name labels ironed or stitched on (for the organized parent among us) or names written in or stamped on with a permanent marker.

■■■■■■■■■■■■■■■■■■■■■■■■■■■■■■

Sizing

One of the more Byzantine systems that comes to light when one becomes a parent is the world of children's sizes. Says Jerry Kostic, boys' clothes buyer for the Darien Sports Shop in Darien, Connecticut, "I've been in this business for ten years, and I'm still confused." You may have experienced this same trouble early on, as I did when my eight-pound, eleven-ounce firstborn barely fit into a 0–3-month infant size coming home from the hospital! One simply cannot assume that a child's size matches the child's age—especially in our American system of sizing. To make matters worse, sizes vary from manufacturer to manufacturer—as is true of adult clothes. And while you find that your daughter may fit into a 3T size of a fine-quality line of children's clothes, the 3T size from another manufacturer (often of lesser quality) will be snug. European sizes usually run truer to age than American ones. This is particularly interesting in light of the fact that European children tend to be somewhat smaller than American children.

Listed below are some tips for the parent in quest of well-fitting clothes. If you are unsure of your child's size and don't want to take him on every shopping trip, use these tips to help you pick the right fit.

■ Measure your child's waist and chest and keep those figures handy. Knowing his height and weight will also be helpful. Use these measurements to help decide his size at the store—with the help of a salesperson, if necessary. Boys' pants are particularly difficult to buy without your son trying them on. Waist size and pant length will be your ultimate guide. Another tip: take a pair of your son's well-fitting pants to the store to help you buy a new pair. Bring along any item of clothing to match sizes with the one you want to buy.

■ Toddler sizes run larger in the waist and hip area to allow for diaper girth. Any size that has a "T" after it will be cut fuller in the middle. Toddler sizes (1T to 4T) are usually appropriate for ages 18 months to 4 years, although many children outgrow them by age 3.

■ Children's regular sizes, 2 to 6X for girls and 4 to 7 for boys, fit children ages 3 to 7 years and are cut slimmer than toddler sizes but still wider than children's sizes in the next category—7 to 14 for girls and 8 to 14 for boys. Children's sizes "S," "M," "L," and "XL" fit sizes 2 to 3 (S), 4 to 5 (M), 6 to 6X (L), and 6X (XL).

■ For boys, "slim" sizes and "regular" sizes are usually available in both 4 to 7 and 8 to 14. "Husky" sizes are harder to find. (Ask your salesperson for help in this quest.) Jackets and pants in sizes 16 to 20 often come in husky sizes.

■ Don't assume your child's size matches your child's age. Find the size that gives your child ease and comfort of movement, allowing leeway of about $\frac{1}{2}$ to 1 inch in fit. Don't dress your child in clothes one size too large for "growing into" (unless it happens to be a "big look" sweater, sweatshirt, or other stylish oversize clothes). One friend insists her son didn't get into the nursery school of her choice because his shirt was too large. "It was the only shirt he wanted to wear, and rather than risk a tantrum, I let him," she laments. "He ended up looking like the little rumpled Spanky in 'Our Gang'!" Whether this was the reason for the rejection or not, her mistake, she says, was allowing him to wear it so large in the first place.

Elementary-School Children— Growing with Style (Grades One Through Five)

All children, even toddlers, are conformists when it comes to fashion—kids feel most comfortable when they wear clothes similar to school friends' or their older siblings'. The desire to "belong" to an identifiable group is very urgent early on, lets up a little in the 4-to-8 age group, then really heats up in grades five through eight. Woe to the seventh-grade fashion maverick who wanders too far from the norm! This stray is quickly herded back to the fold through often merciless peer disapproval.

By the time children are in elementary school, parents can see expressions of personalities in the clothes children choose to wear. For better or for worse, their children are developing style. One 9-year-old I know seems to have been born with it. He says, "I always know what will look good on me." This stylish boy also takes fashion risks: confident, he dares to wear the newest style, whether it is a pair of bright-colored suspenders or a funny hat.

While you may not always love the results, 6- to 10-year-olds are very insistent about choosing their own clothes—at stores and for school. They are, by now, interested in looking "cool." Parents trying to steer their children toward classic looks such as plaid wool shirts, crewneck sweaters, and penny loafers may find their kids increasingly resistant. The child's desire to blend in and identify with children his age, or look "special" like a sports hero or a rock star, becomes much stronger than the desire to please you.

By all means let your child know that you hope she won't wear the purple patterned shirt with the orange polka-dot pants, because she is still looking for and respects your opinion. At the same time, give your child the benefit of the doubt. State that you are happy she has made this interesting choice—and that choosing one's clothes is an important part of growing up—but that you personally prefer to see patterns matched with solids, or orange set off with white and not purple, and would she select another blouse for the pants? You will be aiding the elementary school–age child by giving her valuable information about clothes, color, and design, and at the same time letting her have some control over her choices. Give lavish compliments as well when she picks a well-coordinated outfit or even a break-the-rules outfit that really does work. Children thrive on this kind of praise—and learn even more from positive reinforcement.

A glamorous look may appear on your elementary school–age child one day of the week, then abruptly change to a preppy look the next. Many children are great experi-

SOME CHILDREN HAVE A STRONG SENSE OF STYLE ALL THROUGH CHILDHOOD.

menters, trying out different outfits not only for themselves but to gauge the reaction of their peers. They are probably more experimental in grades one through four than grades five through eight, when conformity seems to peak. Lauren, a 6-year-old, often goes to first grade wearing a hot pink spandex workout outfit under her pants and T-shirt outfits. "Someday at gym I'm going to take off my pants and shirt so I can do my gymnastics really well," she says. She hasn't yet worked up the courage to peel off the top layer, but the pink spandex is a glamorous part of her personality that she would like to express in her own style.

■■■■■■■■■■■■■■■■■■■■■■■■■■■■■■

The "Dirt" on Stain Removal

Do all kids wear their clothes once, then expect their parents to wash them anew? I know my kids do. One friend believes kids throw their clothes into a hamper after one wearing because it's easier than folding them or hanging them up. This friend always checks the hamper, then leaves in her children's rooms the "clean enough" clothes.

Clothes that do need a wash are usually adorned with the stains and markings of childhood—grass, crayon, ketchup, chewing gum, etc. For these problems, I've provided a guide to the latest information on stain removal. The following treatments are for "washable" fabrics. Nonwashables are best left to dry cleaning experts. First, some general tips:

■ Sponge most stains with water or club soda as soon as possible.

■ Protein stains such as blood or food must be treated with cold water only, as hot water may "set" them.

■ When using a spot remover or other clothes cleaning product, test first on a hidden part of the fabric. Follow product directions carefully, since some chemicals used in some spot removers are flammable. Combining products can also be dangerous. Products such as ammonia and chlorine bleach in combination can cause noxious fumes.

■ Soak new spots for thirty minutes and old stains for two hours before washing.

What To Do If the Stain Is

Adhesives: For chewing gum, tape, etc, rub residue adhesive with an ice cube. Scrape away excess with dull knife. Wipe with cleaning fluid. Rinse. Launder in hot water.

Baby Formula: Pre-treat with an enzyme soak product for thirty minutes. Launder in hot water and laundry detergent.

Ball Point Ink: Do not use water. Try to remove spot with either fingernail polish, rubbing alcohol, or dry-cleaning solvent on front and back of fabric (check product on trial section of fabric). Rinse and wash with laundry detergent. Alternate method: spray spot with hair spray; blot with clean cloth and launder.

Blood: Wash in cold water. Then apply liquid detergent. If stain remains, apply an unflavored meat tenderizer and allow to sit for thirty minutes. Launder with fabric-safe bleach. Or use a small amount of hydrogen peroxide (pretest fabric) to bubble out stain. Rinse in cold water.

Chocolate Ice Cream: First soak in cold water for 30 minutes, then use a pre-wash stain remover according to directions. Launder. Or: rinse in cold water; rub hydrogen peroxide mixed with a few drops of ammonia on spot; soak for one half hour; then launder.

Coffee and Tea: Rinse with cool water immediately. Mix warm water and an all-fabric bleach for one half hour of soaking. If coffee or tea contained milk, and stain persists, sponge with a cleaning solvent. Rinse and launder.

Crayon: Rub liquid detergent directly onto soiled area. Leave overnight. Launder with hot water. Or, soak stain in enzyme pre-soak. Launder as above.

Egg: Rub stain in cold water. Soak in enzyme pre-soak product for thirty minutes. Make sure stain is removed before laundering in hot water—hot water will set the stain.

Grass: Rinse with cool water. Apply liquid detergent to stain and rub. Wash in machine with the hottest water possible allowed for fabric with a color-safe bleach. Or, pre-treat with an enzyme pre-soak product, then launder as usual.

Fruit, Fruit Juices, and Food Coloring: Do not use soap—this will set stains. Stretch stained area over a pan in the kitchen. Hold a container of hot water about a foot above the pan, then pour over stain. You may also use your spray apparatus with the hottest water possible. Then scrub area with liquid detergent. Or: soak in cool water for 45 minutes; work in a paste of all-fabric bleach and powder detergent; then launder.

Ketchup: Blot off excess ketchup. Soak in cold water for one half hour. Apply a pre-wash product, then launder with laundry detergent.

Mustard: Pre-treat with pre-wash stain remover according to product directions. Then soak in hot water and laundry detergent for at least two hours. If stain remains, try using a little hydrogen peroxide or white vinegar. Launder as usual.

Pencil: Erase residue pencil with soft eraser. Pre-treat with pre-wash stain remover. Launder.

Soft Drinks: Mix one tablespoon white vinegar in one gallon cold water. Soak stained area for fifteen minutes. Rinse. If stain persists, use one tablespoon enzyme pre-soak product to one quart cold water and soak for thirty minutes. Launder.

Urine: Rinse thoroughly with cold water. Rub liquid detergent on stain. Or: soak in cold water for thirty minutes. Pre-treat with pre-wash product. Ammonia or white vinegar may also be helpful if stain persists.

Vomit: Soak clothing in cold water to remove food particles. Use one cup salt to one gallon warm water and soak to remove smell. Launder as directed.

■■■■■■■■■■■■■■■■■■■■■■■■■■■■■■■■■■

How You Can Help Your 6- to 10-Year-Old Gain "Style" and the Confidence to Express It

Style appears to be one of those elusive qualities that one either has or doesn't have. I talked earlier about the boy who seemed to have been born with style. Some children do seem to have special fashion sensibilities, but *you* can also help your children develop style. How? Simply talk about the clothes other kids are wearing. When you watch TV or look at clothes catalogues together, discuss how kids are dressing. Ask them about what looks they like on some of their friends. If you are feeling brave enough, ask them what they think of the clothes Mom and Dad wear! Gently guide them in matters such as wearing the right outfit for the right occasion. Your son or daughter may love the "studied casual" look, but for a wedding or other formal occasion, pants and tops with sneakers would make everyone, including your child, feel uncomfortable.

If you help your child pick clothes that are durable, well-made, and have style (classics such as khaki pants and Irish knit sweaters are especially good-looking when mixed and matched with newer fashions), you'll be aiding her in establishing her own style in years to come.

■■■■■■■■■■■■■■■■■■■■■■■■■■■■■■■■■■

Purchase Power: How to Get the Most for Your Money

How can you stretch your children's clothing allowance? Will your daughter wear the English dress coat often enough to justify its expense? Is it necessary to buy name brands when you know the knockoff will make a fine substitute? Knowing where to make fashion investments will help.

Quality

Shop for quality clothes. Though they cost more, they will last longer and look better, and the finer fabrics and good workmanship usually justify the extra expense. Carol French of the Magic Window stores in New York City finds that her customers usually make the investments of one good dress coat and at least one good party dress for girls and one blazer for boys. These clothes are worn many times during the school year for the formal lifestyle led by many children in Manhattan.

Families with less formal lifestyles may find they need the deepest pockets when buying a good cold-weather jacket. Ice hockey is a popular sport in our area, and many children wear their team jackets three seasons a year. The jackets are made of corduroy with quilted padding, and the children add sweatshirts or sweaters in the winter. At a cost of about $60, this jacket is a great investment, since neither fall nor spring jackets are required. Other families spend larger amounts of their clothing budgets on durable name-brand clothes, such as good corduroy overalls, because of their quality and ability to last as a young child grows.

Quality clothes also mean finer fabrics that look good longer, clean well, and store better for use by a younger brother, sister, cousin, or friend. Pay particular attention to the fabrics of your son's pants. Hemlines will show on certain fabrics when they are let down. Pants that roll up are terrific for growing children. And remember that "feel" is all-important to most children. My children used to cry croco-dile tears when asked to wear pure-wool sweaters, even when separated from their skin by long-sleeved cotton shirts. (I quickly learned that 100-percent wool—"So itchy!"—was not for my kids. How do the Europeans keep their children in all that wool?) Clothes made of stiff or itchy fabrics are a poor investment if children won't wear them.

CERTAIN CHILDREN'S CLOTHES FIT A VARIETY OF NEEDS. SHAIN'S TURTLENECK, BLAZER, AND KHAKIS CAN BE WORN TO SCHOOL AND TO MORE FORMAL OCCASIONS.

CELEBRATING THE HOLIDAYS GIVES LIT-
TLE GIRLS THE CHANCE TO GET DRESSED
UP AND LOOK THEIR BEST.

Classics

Make classic clothes a major part of your child's wardrobe. Classics are styles and designs that have been time-tested. Sailor suits for young children, girls' smocked dresses, and navy-blue blazers are examples of classics. Even blue jeans, with their relatively short history, are now classics. Many of the finer European clothes with their darker colors and sophisticated cuts tend to look classic. Try not to buy too many "trendy" looks for your child's wardrobe—especially ones that make children look like small versions of adults. Dr. David Elkind, in his book *The Hurried Child: Growing Up Too Fast Too Soon*, reminds us that kids used to dress like kids, in knickers and other distinguishable children's clothes. He writes, "Today even preschool children wear miniature versions of adult clothing. From overalls to La Coste shirts to scaled-down designer fashions, a whole range of adult costumes is available to children. . . . When children dress like adults they are more likely to behave as adults do, to imitate adult actions." Certainly enjoy the full range of children's clothes available today, but skip the fedora for the 5-year-old!

▪ Color Coordination

Many parents build their children's wardrobe around one or two basic colors to simplify choices and to save money by mixing and matching easily. For example, if a child's basic color is navy blue, his parents always know which color to buy to match. White, yellow, red, etc., all go with the pants, the blazer, or the sweater of navy blue. Even if you don't use a basic color plan, review your child's wardrobe and have matching colors in mind when purchasing. An added benefit of color coordination is the child's role in picking out his own outfits each morning. This makes him feel independent and helps you avoid daily "style wars."

A child's wardrobe shouldn't be made up of all solid colors, of course—the exciting patterns and bright colors one sees among children's clothes are what makes buying and outfitting children so much fun. Plaids, patterns, prints, and unusual colors can all be practical buys when carefully considered for their versatility with what is already hanging in your child's closet.

▪ ▪ ▪ ▪ ▪ ▪ ▪ ▪ ▪

SMOCKED DRESSES AND OTHER PARTY DRESSES AT THIS 5-YEAR-OLD'S BIRTHDAY PARTY ARE CHILDHOOD FASHION CLASSICS.

Shopping with Your Children: Dos and Don'ts

When the old familiar refrain "Mom, I have nothing to wear!" is truly the case, make your buying excursion a fun activity, one you plan for and enjoy. How, you ask? Heed the following dos and don'ts to make back-to-school or anytime shopping not only bearable, but also an entertaining event.

■ *Do* prepare for your trip by looking through magazines or catalogues to see the latest styles. Make a list of what your child will need to add to his current wardrobe and which colors will look best and be the most versatile. If your child is old enough, discuss costs and the need to stick to a budget. Children enjoy this planning process and feel accomplished if they can exercise good judgment within specific guidelines.

■ *Don't* try to accomplish too much on a given day. For back-to-school shopping, for instance, some parents buy a few basics for the first month of school, and wait till Columbus or Election Day sales to buy the rest.

■ *Do*, if possible, take only one child shopping at a time. This allows you to concentrate on your one task at hand. It also allows quality time for both of you and makes each child feel special. One mother said that going out shopping with her daughter was like "having a date with my child." As you know, children act differently without siblings, and are bound to be on their best behavior without "little bro" or "big sis" around.

■ *Do* have your child wear clothes that are easy to get on and off. Have her wear clothes that are similar to those she is trying on.

■ *Do* agree on a place to meet at each store or each department floor if you get separated or she gets lost. Instruct even 18-month-olds about what you would like them to do if they cannot find you.

■ *Don't* push your child so hard that she starts dropping while shopping. This is especially true of toddlers and preschoolers, of course. Take frequent breaks in the lounge at the mall, or outside in a park. Bring juice, crackers, or fruit for little ones, whose systems can often break down in a matter of minutes. A restful lunch at a restaurant or in the park is essential for maintaining or restoring a good mood. It's also a perfect time to go over shopping lists and update the next assault on stores.

■ *Don't* (or try not to) get into battles over what you want your child to wear and what he wants to wear. While some mothers allow their children to choose all their clothes (especially older children) within reason, others feel they want more control over how they want their children to look. As I said earlier, clothes battles are more often than not a child's urge to separate from the parent, a fight for freedom of choice. Compromise is usually the key to success. Some families work out deals in which the parents choose the holiday and church clothes while children are allowed to choose school clothes; or parents choose school clothes while children get to wear what they want on weekends. Still other parents choose their child's outfits two days of the school week and the child has her choice for three. If push comes to shove over a particular item of clothing, remember that children will not wear something they hate, or if they do, will feel grumpy and unhappy in it.

■■■■■■■■■■■■■■■■■■■■■■■■■■■■■■■■

Cheapest Is Chicest: How to Keep Kids' Clothes Budget Pint-Sized

How can you keep your kids well-dressed throughout childhood without taking a second or third job? It's easy if you can put a little time into seeking out bargains. The list below shows where you can go to buy children's clothes at great savings while you kiss retail prices good-bye. (Clothes bought from many of these sources require careful checking

■ ■ ■ ■ ■ ■ ■ ■ ■

SINCE THEY ARE WORN SO INFREQUENTLY, GIRLS'
DRESS COATS AND BOYS' BLAZERS RARELY WEAR
OUT AND MAY OFTEN BE FOUND IN EXCELLENT
CONDITION AT THRIFT SHOPS. THE CLASSIC PLAID
COAT ON THE LEFT AND THE BOY'S BLAZER WERE
BOUGHT AT A SCHOOL CLOTHING SALE, AND THE
COAT ON THE RIGHT IS A HAND-ME-DOWN FROM
A FRIEND. THEY LOOK GREAT!

for stains, holes, broken zippers or buttons, and loose hems.
Pay attention to fabric quality and make sure you really need
an item before buying.) Watch your local paper for announce-
ments of these and other sales in your area.

■ Neighborhood clothes swaps

■ Tag or garage sales

■ Public- and private-school clothing sales

■ Church rummage sales or charity bazaars

■ Flea markets

■ Thrift shops

■ Consignment shops

■ Vintage clothing stores

■ Discount outlets

■ Catalog sales, including catalogs that carry discounted
clothing. (Catalogs save time, which is, of course, money.)

■ Relatives. If they haven't already offered, gently hint to
relatives that you'd love to borrow Niece Hannah's kilt
when she outgrows it, with the promise that you'll return it
in good condition or be responsible for replacing it.

■■■■■■■■■■■■■■■■■■■■■■■■■■■■■■■■■

Label Fever—Children Grades Five Through Eight (Ages 10 to 13)

Conformity is the watchword for children ages 10 through 13. It's been there all along, but reaches an all-time high in this age group. (Teenagers eventually develop greater individuality in dress, or at least go off into more numerous splinter groups.) Hold on to your wallets, too. Labels are in, so watch out when you come home with a key article of clothing for them in a knockoff brand. Some children are, mind you, less concerned with fashion and name brands than others. But for the parents whose preadolescents have already developed a sharp eye and sharp appetite for the "in" fashion, the jig is up!

There are ways to ameliorate this situation. Compromise with the child who must have this or that label by asking her to buy some larger item with a label, and smaller accessories, such as sunglasses, watches, gloves, and belts, in less-expensive versions. If your child wants the trendy "fashion forward" look, buy her a few outfits as an adjunct to her more classic clothes. Often, by age 11 or 12, children want to wear more adult clothes: they don't want to be considered children. You may be in love with the way your fifth-grade daughter looks in a pleated skirt and blouse, but if she's not interested in this look anymore, pass these clothes on to a friend or store them away carefully. (See Storing, page 224)

At this point it might serve to remind children not to judge each other by their clothes—or race, or parents' income, for that matter. This lesson becomes more difficult at this age when peer pressure is so strong, but it is one that needs reinforcing now. Many a good argument has been made for school uniforms—including the absence of peer judgment of clothes and lower costs. If the "in" fashion items of the year are beyond your budget, remind your child that not all children are wearing these items and that many boys or girls are wearing other clothes that look terrific. Children learn a great deal when parents don't accede to their every wish. Children are also happy to have some limits set for them. They can feel proud to accomplish the tasks of buying clothes at a reasonable price and sticking to a budget.

There are more lessons to learn about the value of money at this age: older children can do baby-sitting or other chores for money, which will enable them to buy something extra or contribute toward the cost of a more expensive label. Paying for their own clothes at this age brings new respect for clothes, and you can reinforce this new respect by reminding kids to hang up their clothes and care for them properly. My mother made all seven of her children do their own laundry by age 12. How else could she paint portraits and write her many books?

Colors

"Most parents know what colors look good on their children," says Carol French of the Magic Windows stores in Manhattan. "Color choices work much the same way for children as they do for adults." If you are uncertain about what looks good on your child, use the technique described in the popular book *Color Me Beautiful,* by Carole Jackson. Take swatches of different-color fabrics (or items of clothing) and hold them up under your child's chin. Simply eye the color next to her skin tone, hair, and eyes to determine whether or not it is flattering. Keep her "good" colors in mind when shopping.

And ask your child about his favorite color. When he is wearing a color that looks good with his special coloring, let him know. Take advantage of the dark colors that have become popular in children's fashion, influenced by European mode. They look surprisingly good on children. But also experiment with the large and exciting color range in children's clothes. Kids love the bright and dramatic colors that are usually not available in adult fashion—let them play the color field in children's fashion while they can!

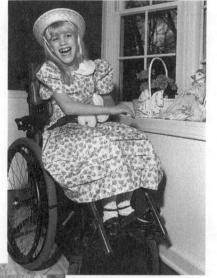

CERTAIN CHILDREN'S CLOTHES NEVER GO OUT OF STYLE. SEEN CLOCKWISE: EASTER DRESS-UP; FLANNEL SHIRT WITH A TURTLENECK; THE PATTERNED SKATING SWEATER; THE IRISH KNIT SWEATER; THE RUGBY SHIRT, JEANS SHIRT AND SUSPENDERS.

■■■■■■■■■■■■■■■■■■■■■■■■■■■■■■■

Trompe L'Oeil—How Your Heavy Child Can Look Thinner with Twelve Easy Fashion Tricks

Dressing the child who carries some extra baby fat can be a challenge. The bigger waist of the heavier child requires pants that are always too long, the crotch falling halfway to the knees. Shirt sleeves must often be hemmed, and the proportions of girls' dresses are way off because of the need to accommodate a bulkier middle. On the other hand, your son's or daughter's wardrobe can work wonders in making them look and feel good: the right fashion can create illusions that will slenderize and flatter your child's figure.

Victoria Mahkorn, a designer for Florence Eisenman, manufacturer of fine clothes for children since 1945, helped me with the following tips:

■ Take a good look at your child's body to understand where she carries her weight. Understand where her body is disproportionate: does she have a thicker waist than most girls her age, or are her shoulders narrower than average? Choose her clothes with these proportion problems in mind.

■ Make sure there is enough "ease" or "give" in your child's clothes. Tight fits on a heavy child are rarely flattering.

■ Layering, especially with thick articles of clothing such as a heavy sweater on top of a turtleneck, may add pounds by adding sheer bulk. Avoid.

■ Better fabrics look wonderful on all children, but especially so on overweight children. Avoid shiny or polished fabrics.

■ The old rule that applies to overweight adults also works for children: avoid horizontal designs and wear straight, vertical stripes or pleats. This adds height and has a slenderizing effect. If your child likes a shirt or a dress that has horizontal stripes, make sure it doesn't hit his or her body at its widest point.

■ Bold prints and big plaids give children a larger or broader look. Choose clothes whose patterns, prints, and plaids are small to effect a slimmer look. Avoid too many contrasting colors in one outfit.

■ Girls between the ages of 2 and 6 (sizes 4 to 6X) are typically sway-backed and have a protruding tummy. Designers for children's clothes work with these age-related body peculiarities in mind. For overweight girls who have even larger tummies, buy dresses that have less defined waists, such as those with waists set just above the waistline.

■ As girls grow, dresses in sizes 7 to 14 usually have definition at the waistline or lower. Avoid these dresses and opt for ones with appliqué, detail, etc., away from the waistline.

■ A-line dresses, the mainstay of Florence Eisenman's line in years past, look well on overweight toddlers and on up to age 5 or so.

■ A yoke running from armhole to armhole often takes the eye away from a large middle and refocuses it to this detail. The "princess line" seam running from each armhole and carrying it toward the center and down to the waist, resulting in a Y shape, is also slimming. For boys, suspenders provide vertical lines, which are also slimming.

■ A square or V-shaped collar can serve as a focal point to draw attention away from a larger waist. Contrasting colors at an arm cuff will do the same.

■ Creased pleats and trouser cuffs are very helpful in slimming out a heavy boy's silhouette. Blazers can look terrific on chubby kids if the jackets don't pull at the middle buttons. You may have to spend a little more, but making sure the jacket fits properly is essential in making your son look his best. Have it tailored if necessary.

■■■■■■■■■■■■■■■■■■■■■■■■■■■■■■■■

Dressing Your Thin Child

Refer to the rules on the two previous pages and do exactly the opposite! Here are some extra tips:

1. Select dresses with plenty of ruffles and petticoats.
2. Belts serve to broaden a child's middle.
3. Bow ties are cute and make little boys look broader.
4. Choose the heavier fabrics, such as sweat-type cotton or heavy corduroy, to create a fuller look on your child.

■■■■■■■■■■■■■■■■■■■■■■■■■■■■■■■■

"If the Shoe Fits . . ." Footwear for Kids

What shoes are best for children as they grow? Shoes that mimic the feeling of going barefoot, say the experts. Shoes that fit this bill are, of course, sneakers. They are usually roomy enough to allow foot muscles to work properly, they are flexible, and they are made of "breathable" material. Most pediatricians applaud the popular status of sneakers today. The right type of sneakers has been a status symbol for the middle-school set, and parents find that keeping kids in their favorite sneakers can cost hundreds of dollars each year.

Poor choices of footwear for kids are the following: inflexible or pointed shoes (which can promote the growth of bunions in adults); any shoe that has a high heel, such as a cowboy boot; shoes with slippery soles; shoes with very grippy soles. (Babies learning to walk often stumble if their sneaker soles are too grippy. Sneakers with smooth soles or high-topped leather shoes are good choices for babies' first walking shoes.) Footwear should be appropriate for weather conditions—provide protection for feet against cold, for example—and protect against glass or other harmful objects. (See page 203 for shoe wear in nursery and preschool.)

Make sure your child's shoes fit well before you buy. More than once I've bought a pair of shoes for one of my children that they've outgrown within a month. A growth spurt? Probably not—just poor measuring on the part of the

■ ■ ■ ■ ■ ■ ■ ■ ■

SISTERS HAYLEY AND ANNABELLE FEEL CLOSE
WEARING LOOK-ALIKE DRESSES. AS CHILDREN GET
OLDER, THEY MAY NOT BE WILLING TO DRESS
ALIKE, SO MATCH UP SIBLINGS NOW AND GET
YOURSELF A MATCHING OR COMPLEMENTARY
DRESS, TOO!

shoe salesman. Most salespeople who work with children's
shoes are well-trained and will not sell shoes that are too
small. How can you double-check the fit of your child's shoe?
Read on.

■ While the child is standing, look for ½- to ¾-inch spaces
between the big toe and the front of the shoe.

■ Make sure your child's foot does not slip out of the shoe or
fits so tight in the heel that it causes blisters.

■ The shoe should fit flexibly around the ball of the foot.

■ Dress shoes don't feel as good as sneakers, so allow for less
comfort when they are trying them on.

■ One mother asks her child if his shoes make him "feel
frisky." She also asks him to walk or run around the store.
If he indeed breaks into a run, the fit is perfect!

Pierced Ears—Are They Right For Your Child?

When should you allow your children to get their ears pierced? A sage pediatrician told me that the best time is before age 2 or after 13 because proper follow-up care is easiest to control in a baby, or more responsibly carried through by a teenager. Follow-up care is crucial because once ears are pierced, they are very prone to infection. For six weeks, two to three times a day, the child or parent must clean the fronts and backs of the earlobes with either rubbing alcohol or an antiseptic. The earring posts must be rotated daily. The earrings used to pierce the ears must have 14-karat gold posts and should not be removed or changed during these six weeks.

You probably know your child well enough to judge whether she is sufficiently mature to be careful about cleaning her pierced ears. If she has wanted pierced ears for a long time and has many friends who have pierced ears, you might think of letting her get her ears pierced now or on an upcoming birthday. One nursery school director I interviewed feels that earrings—even studs—inhibit children's free play and make them susceptible to school accidents—especially on the playground. Hoops and dangling earrings should not be worn to school by anyone under the age of 12. Heavy earrings are dangerous as well: one of my neighbors has a 19-year-old niece who must have plastic surgery performed. Her ears were pierced too low and a heavy earring pulled right through one lobe! Worn often, too-heavy earrings can also create an ugly permanent line on the lobes. Studs and other light earrings are the safest for young children.

Remember that once your child has pierced ears, a small indentation or scar will remain if you decide to let them close up. Black children may develop a darker coloration on the scar site, making a visible spot where the ear was once pierced. Closed-up pierced ears can also develop hard scar tissue where there was once a hole.

But pierced ears, properly cared for, can be fun for children—even today, for boys. Make sure the person who pierces your child's ears is experienced and uses sterile equipment. The piercing can be performed by experienced personnel at a hair salon, a jeweler's, or, of course, a doctor's office. It should be done with an ear-piercing gun (not with needles and ice in the school hallway!) and a local anesthetic may be used. Check the points at which the ear will be pierced, to make sure they are even and neither too high nor too low.

Eyeglasses

Some children love the look of glasses. My 12-year-old begged me to get him glasses. He thought he would look great in them—never mind they weren't needed. One optometrist reports that some children come in and fake eye exams to get glasses. One of the current high school fads is wearing glasses with clear lenses to achieve an intellectual, Ralph Lauren look.

For those children who hate their glasses, the best solution may be to tell them that they will have to treat glasses as one of the trials of childhood, like braces on teeth. Vision problems must be corrected—and most kids, after some time, adjust to their glasses. For active children, there are safety glasses that aren't easily broken. While some children may desire contact lenses, most ophthalmologists do not recommend them for children under age 12 because a child's vision can change rapidly. Children must also use great care in handling and wearing lenses.

Encourage your child to take part in choosing her glasses. Fit is extremely important, so encourage your child to speak up if they pinch or slip. If your daughter's favorite color is blue, let her try on blue frames. If her eyes are green, she may want to match them to the frame color. Metal frames are popular now, and they have the added benefit of great flexibility and durability.

■■■■■■■■■■■■■■■■■■■■■■■■■■■■■■■■

Storing Children's Clothes for Posterity

Whether you're putting away your son's outgrown T-shirts and shorts for younger siblings, or your daughter's expensive Belgian-import vyella dress for—gasp—grandchildren, the storage method is the same. If you want to protect your children's clothing in storage for anywhere from two to twenty years, precautions must be taken. Follow these tips:

■ Dry-clean or wash all soiled clothes, removing all stains before storing. Spots you never knew were there will appear after a period of storage if not cleaned before. Insects are attracted to dirt, another reason to inspect all clothes before packing them away.

■ Dry cleaner Michael Czegledi of Midway Cleaners in Rowayton, Connecticut, recommends storing clothes in cardboard cartons with tiny holes in the sides so that clothes can "breathe." If you have trouble with moths, silverfish, cockroaches, etc., close cartons tightly with tape. Trunks can be used to store clothes except when they are completely airtight, because lack of oxygen breeds mildew, says Mr. Czegledi. Use plenty of cedar chips to repel insects, but avoid mothballs. Their scent is so strong, you may never be able to rid clothes of it.

■ Store boxes in a cool, dark place, preferably in the main floors of the house, if space permits. Avoid basements where mildew is possible or attics where temperatures can go higher than 100 degrees or lower than freezing.

■ The name of the item, the size, and the season should be labeled on the outside of the carton. I often attempt to predict the year and season my second son will be ready to wear his older brother's clothes. (Unfortunately, by the time he's ready to fit into the clothes, the season is usually wrong or the clothes are no longer in style. Another great argument for classic clothes!)

■■■■■■■■■■■■■■■■■■■■■■■■■■■■■■■■■

Putting It All Together

Kids can have fun with fashion—it is an expression of their emerging personalities. Teaching your children about fashion—design, color, style, clothes care, clothes budgeting—is time well spent; dressing your children well during these formative years will pay off. You can be proud knowing that your positive influence in this area will probably be felt all of their lives.

Children feel not only self-assured but also "special" when they know that time and care has been spent on what they wear. They are learning every day that it takes effort to dress well and stay well-groomed. This care, by the parents and by the child himself, is a kind of celebration of his childhood, an expression of your mutual love.

■■■■■■■■■

BEST FOOT FORWARD. DRESSING WELL HELPS KIDS FEEL GOOD ABOUT THEMSELVES AND SHOWS OFF THEIR HEALTHY GOOD LOOKS.

ACKNOWLEDGMENTS

Medical information is the foundation of this book and I would like to thank the following doctors and medical professionals for their counsel and guidance. They are: Abraham Bergman, M.D., director of pediatrics at Harborview Medical Center, Seattle, WA; Ervin Braun, D.D.S., assistant clinical professor of prosthodontics, Norwalk Hospital, CT; Wendy Coren, D.C.M., Norwalk, CT; Martin J. Davis, D.D.S., director, division of pedodontics, Columbia University School of Dental and Oral Surgery, president-elect of The American Academy of Pediatric Dentistry; Dominick DePaola, D.D.S., dean, University of Medicine and Dentistry of New Jersey; Howard V. Dubin, M.D., clinical professor, department of dermatology, University of Michigan, Ann Arbor; Harry Dweck, M.D., spokesperson for growth and development section for The American Academy of Pediatrics; Michael Fenster, M.D., assistant clinical professor of dermatology, Yale University; Robert S. Fields, D.D.S., secretary-treasurer of The Society of Orthodontists; Barry Goldberg, M.D., Sports Medicine Institute, Lenox Hill Hospital, New York, NY; Richard Gregory, M.D., plastic surgeon, officer of The American Society for Laser Medicine and Surgery; Mutaz B. Habal, M.D., pediatric plastic surgeon, Orlando, FL; David Hendell, D.D.S., associate professor of dentistry, Columbia University; Walter Huurman, M.D., associate professor of orthopedic surgery, University of Nebraska; Sydney Hurwitz, M.D., clinical professor of pediatrics and dermatology, Yale University School of Medicine; Carden Johnson, M.D., pediatrician, Birmingham, AL; Ronald Kahan, M.D., assistant clinical professor of dermatology, Yale University; Steven Kahn, D.D.S., assistant professor, department of oral surgery, University of Illinois; Katherine Karlsrud, M.D., pediatrician, New York, NY;

Leonard Krassner, M.D., medical chief, Choate Rosemary Hall, Wallingford, CT; William Lattanzi, M.D., clinical professor of pediatrics, Yale University School of Medicine; Christopher Mangos, D.D.S., Washington University, St. Louis, MO; Alvin Mauer, M.D., past chairman for the council on nutrition for The American Academy of Pediatrics; Terry McDonald, D.D.S., chairman, Council of Orthodontists; Stephen Moss, D.D.S., chairman and professor, department of pediatric dentistry, New York University College of Dentistry; Terry Nagler, R.N., New York, NY; David Orentreich, M.D., assistant clinical professor of dermatology, Mt. Sinai School of Medicine; Norman Orentreich, M.D., clinical associate professor of dermatology, New York University School of Medicine; Barbara Z. Parks, M.P.H., The American Dental Association; Michael Pertschuk, M.D., psychiatrist, founder of The Center for Human Appearance at the University of Pennsylvania; Harrison Pierce, M.D., pediatrician, New Canaan, CT, Yale–New Haven Hospital; the late Virginia Pomerance, M.D.; Guy Rowley, M.D., director of the emergency department, Grant Hospital, Chicago, IL; Mary Lee Ruff, M.D., pediatrician, spokesperson for section on growth and development for The American Academy of Pediatrics; Cherilyn Sheets, D.D.S., Newport Beach, CA; Irwin Steuer, D.D.S., New York University; Robert Weiss, D.P.M.; William Weston, M.D., professor and chairman of dermatology, professor of pediatrics, University of Colorado School of Medicine.

Special thanks are in order to four doctors who read my chapters for medical accuracy, and I am deeply indebted to them for their time and good will. Dr. Thomas Flynn, a pediatrician in New Canaan, CT, read the chapter on exercise; Dr. Myron Genel, professor of pediatrics at Yale University School of Medicine, read the chapter on body image and growth; Dr. Angelo Milazzo, a pedodontist in Stamford, CT, oversaw the dentistry chapter; and Dr. Neil Sadick, assistant clinical professor of dermatology at New York Hospital–Cornell Medical Center, gave extra effort and read the two chapters on hair and skin. I am very grateful to them for their kindness.

Dr. Myron Genel wrote the Foreword for this book. He was a delight to work with, and I owe him a very special thanks for his time and incisive thoughts.

I sought and received great help from a number of people from nonprofit organizations. Their service was invaluable to me and they are to be commended for their work for the public. At the top of the list is the staff from The American Academy of Pediatrics, especially Leslie Williams. I would also like to thank Richard Asa of The American Dental Association, Karim Ahmed, formerly with the Natural Resources Defense Council, and Stephen Spencer of Rocky Mountain Orthodontics.

In the exercise field, I am grateful to have had generous assistance from the following experts: York Onnen, Washington, D.C.; Michael Pfahl; Don Collins, physical educator, Darien, CT; Dave Johnson, The American Coaching Effectiveness Program, Champaign, IL; and Matthew Chaloux of the YMCA.

I would like to express my appreciation to the hair experts. They are: Frederic Bouillerce, Lisa Bouillerce, and Sharon Gray of Frederic & Co., Rowayton, CT; Pamela Plummer, Shooting Star Salon, New York, NY; Pat Paz, New York, NY; Angela Johnson, Sweeney Todd Hair Salon, Stamford, CT; North Rebis, New York, NY; Latrinda Johnson, Savvy Hair Salon, Norwalk, CT; Kathy Hess, New York, NY; Ed Shulte, Elizabeth McAlloon, Ridgeway Hair Salon, Stamford, CT; and Philip Kingsley, Philip Kingsley Trichological Centre, New York, NY.

Fashion advice came from experts Carol French, owner of Magic Windows, New York, NY; Gerry Kostic and Steve Zangrillo of The Darien Sports Shop, Darien, CT; and Victoria Mahkorn, a designer with Florence Eisenman. They were extremely resourceful and I am grateful for their help. Michael Czegledi, owner of Midway Cleaners in Rowayton, CT, gave additional help for the fashion chapter.

I would like to say thanks to three educators who contributed ideas to this book: Peggy Marble, Diane Berkeley, and Dodi McCartney of The Buckley School, New York, NY. Naomi Sims, creator of Naomi Sims Skin Care System, deserves credit for her advice on black skin care.

I feel the special beauty of children was captured by photographer Susi Dugaw, and Fred Marvin's illustrations have added charm and whimsy. For her assistance and advice on matters visual, my gratitude goes to Barbara Cohen Aronica, this book's designer. Thanks also to my agents John Brockman and Katinka Matsen.

My editor at Bantam, Toni Burbank, gave me constant inspiration and support. Her talent is awesome.

I owe thanks to Blanche Parker and the rest of the energetic staff at the Darien Library for their help with research, with special kudos to Anne Carnahan whose enthusiasm helped me forge on during the difficult stages of writing this book.

The support of some good friends was essential in completing this book. Some babysat my children while I wrote, and others offered ideas and continual moral support. I am deeply indebted to: Kathi Van Voorhees; Gail Meckel; Lynn Ross; Jacqui and John Crocker; Mary Dowd; and the late Rosina Secco, whose special ability to see beauty everywhere was an inspiration for this book. My gratitude also to the lovely children who helped create the spirit of this book and to the parents who allowed me to photograph them.

In particular, I want to thank my large, wonderful family for all their help and support.

The experiences, knowledge, and wisdom of the hundreds of parents I interviewed for this book is the essence of *Bringing Out Their Best*—I am so grateful for their time and assistance.

Most of all, my love and thanks go to my husband, Geoffrey, and my children, Chris, Bryan, and Julia. Helping with every task from typing to modeling for the book, and often filling in in the kitchen while I was stationed in front of the word processor, they gave me touching support and tolerated my long absences—for the most part. Thank you, my dearest family. You are the best!

BIBLIOGRAPHY

■ **Chapter One: All About Your Child's Hair**

Barth, Julian H., and Rodney P.R. Dawber. "Acquired Disorders of the Hair and Scalp." *Textbook of Pediatric Dermatology.* Philadelphia: Grune and Stratton, 1989.

Berg, Barbara. "Nit-Picking." *New York* magazine (November 12, 1984).

Brown, Warren. "Conair Seeks Hair-Dryer Rule Waiver." *The Washington Post* (July 3, 1991).

Budd, Elaine. *You and Your Hair.* New York: Wildfire Books, Scholastic, Inc., 1978.

Cappugi, Pietro, and Maria Luisa Battini. "The Normal Skin From Birth to Adolescence." *Textbook of Pediatric Dermatology.* Philadelphia: Grune and Stratton, Inc., 1989.

Dvorine, William. *A Dermatologist's Guide to Skin Treatment.* New York: Charles Scribner's Sons, 1983.

Gignac, Louis, with Jacqueline Warsaw. *Everything You Need to Know to Have Great-Looking Hair.* New York: Viking Press, 1981.

Gregor, Carol. *Basic and Exotic Braids Made Easy.* New Rochelle, NY: Valco Publishing Co., 1985.

Guralnik, David B., ed. *Webster's New World Dictionary.* Second College edition. New York: World Publishing Co., 1970.

Hanle, Dorothea Zack. *The Hairdo Handbook: A Complete Guide to Hair Beauty.* New York: Doubleday, 1964.

Heloise. *Heloise's Beauty Book.* New York: Arbor House, 1985.

Klein, Arnold W., M.D., James H. Sternberg, M.D., and Paul Bernstein. *The Skin Book: Looking and Feeling Your Best Through Proper Skin Care.* New York: Macmillan Publishing Co., Inc., 1980.

Litt, Jerome Z., M.D. *Teen Skin From Head to Toe.* New York: Ballantine Books, 1986.

Littlefield, Robin Wiest. "The ABC's of Grooming." *American Health* (June 1990).

Lord, Shirley. "The Seven Ages of Hair." *Vogue,* Vol. 178, (July 1988). 216, (3).

McCarthy, Laura Flynn. "In an Age of Environmental Awareness, Many Companies Are Taking an All-Natural Approach to Hair Care." *Vogue* (May 1990) 150.

———."Mane Events: They smell wonderful, feel luxurious and

they're being relied on more and more to restore the condition of hair. Botanical treatments are gaining a following of devoted fans." *Harper's Bazaar.* (January 1991).

McGrath, Judith. *Pretty Girl: A Guide to Looking Good Naturally.* New York: Lothrop, Lee and Shepard Books, 1981.

Orentreich, Norman, M.D. "Disorders of the Hair and Scalp in Childhood." Pediatric Clinics of North America, Vol. 18, No. 3 (August, 1971).

Schmid, Judith. "Hair Rx: Less than healthy hair can be a clue: not to your stylist, but your doctor." *Vogue.* (July 1988).

Troesch, Doris Daily. *Home Haircutting Made Easy: A Step-by-Step Guide.* New York: Beekman House, 1984.

Zizmor, Jonathan, and John Foreman. *Superhair.* New York: G.P. Putnam's Sons, 1978.

■ Chapter Two: Your Child's Skin

Bark, Joseph P., M.D. *Skin Secrets: A Complete Guide to Skin Care for the Entire Family.* New York: McGraw-Hill Book Company, 1987.

Begley, Sharon, with Kate Robins. "Erasing Port-Wine Stains: A new laser makes birthmarks vanish." *Newsweek* (February 27, 1989).

Brody, Jane. "Higher Cancer Risk Seen in Childhood Sunburns." *The New York Times.* (August 10, 1989).

Burg, Dale. "Two Bad Habits You Can Break." *Woman's Day.* (October 1987).

Cappugi, Pietro, and Maria Luisa Battini. "The Normal Skin from Birth to Adolescence." *Textbook of Pediatric Dermatology.* Philadelphia: Grune and Stratton, Inc., 1989.

Dvorine, William, M.D. *A Dermatologist's Guide to Home Skin Treatment.* New York: Charles Scribner's Sons, 1983.

Glieck, James. "Treaty Powerless to Stem a Growing Loss of Ozone." *The New York Times.* (March 20, 1988).

Griffith, H. Winter, M.D., Howard Mofenson, M.D., and Arnold Greensher, M.D. *Pediatrics for Parents: A Guide to Child Health.* New York: New American Library, 1983.

Hurwitz, Sidney, M.D. *Skin Cancer Foundation Journal* (Vol. V).

Jacobson, Lauren. "Children's Art Hazards." The Natural Resources Defense Council, Inc. (brochure)

Karlsrud, Katherine, with Dodi Schulz. "About Birthmarks." *Parents* (June 1987).

Klein, Arnold W., M.D., James H. Sternberg, M.D., and Paul Bernstein. *The Skin Book: Looking and Feeling Your Best Through Proper Skin Care.* New York: Macmillan Publishing Co., Inc., 1980.

Lance, Kathryn. *Sportsbeauty.* New York: Avon Books, 1984.

Laude, Teresita. *Dermatologic Disorders in Black Children and Adolescents.* New Hyde Park, NY: Medical Examination Publishing Co., 1983.

Litt, Jerome Z., M.D. *Teen Skin From Head to Toe.* New York: Ballantine Books, 1986.

Lord, Shirley. "The Seven Ages of Skin." *Vogue* (January 1990).

Morgan, Elizabeth, M.D., F.A.C.S. *The Complete Book of Cosmetic Surgery: A Candid Guide for Men, Women, and Teens.* New York: Warner Books, Inc., 1988.

Noyes, Deborah. "Your House May Be Hazardous to Your Health." *Parents* (November 1987).

Parrish, John A., M.D., Barbara A. Gilchrest, M.D., and Thomas B. Fitzpatrick, M.D. *Between You and Me: A Sensible and Authoritative Guide to the Care and Treatment of Your Skin.* Boston: Little, Brown and Company, 1978.

Riedman, Sarah R. *The Good Looks Skin Book.* New York: Julian Messner, 1983.

Stern, Lorraine, M.D. "When a Kid's Habit Bugs You." *Woman's Day* (June 1987).

U.S. Dept of Health and Human Services. "Asbestos Exposure: What It Means, What To Do." Public Health Service. National Institutes of Health (brochure).

Verbov, Julian, M.D., and Neil Morley, M.B. *Color Atlas of Pediatric Dermatology.* Philadelphia: J.B. Lippincott, 1983.

Wasco, James. "What Your Hands Say About Your Health." *Woman's Day* (2/6/90).

Wells, Linda. "Babes in Makeup Land." *The New York Times.* (August 13, 1989).

Weston, William, M.D. *Practical Pediatric Dermatology, Second Edition.* Boston: Little, Brown and Company, 1985.

Yarrow, Leah. "Nail Biting, Hair Twisting, Thumb Sucking and Other Nasty Habits." *Parents* (June 1989).

Zizmor, Jonathan, M.D., and John Foreman. *Super Skin: The Doctor's Guide to a Beautiful, Healthy Complexion.* New York: Berkley Medallion Books, 1977.

Chapter Three: Your Child's Teeth

American Dental Association. "Raisins, Granola Bars Head List of Cavity-Causing Snacks." ADA News Release. (October 1984).

———."Diet and Nutrition Play Key Roles in Dental Health," ADA News Release (August 1984).

———."Juvenile Periodontal Disease: A Threat to Children's Teeth." ADA News Release (August 1984).

Brody, Jane E. "A Child's Routine of Sound Daily Dental Hygiene Habits Should Be Initiated in Infancy." *The New York Times* (August 21, 1985).

———."Personal Health: With Cavities on the Decline Flossing Is the Key Weapon in Battle for Dental Health." *The New York Times* (October 18, 1990).

Callahan, Maureen. "Hold That Smile! With new dental techniques, a dazzling set of pearly whites can be yours." *Parents* (April 1988).

Edmondson, Daisy. "Open Wide!" *Parents* (March 1987).

Fredericks, Carlton, Ph.D. "Organized Dentistry's Poisonality." *Let's Live* (February 1988).

Gallo, Nick. "Tooth Truths: Brush Up on the Latest Dentistry News." *Better Homes and Gardens* (February 1989).

Heitler, Susan. *David Decides About Thumbsucking.* Denver: Reading Matters, 1985.

Ibsen, Noreen, ed. "Learning the Advantages of Veneers." *Journal of Cosmetic Dentistry* (Spring 1985).

Leary, Warren E. "Survey Finds Sharp Drop in Tooth Decay in Young." *The New York Times* (June 22, 1988).

————."Overly Secret Weapon Against Tooth Decay: Plastic Sealants." *The New York Times* (March 30, 1989).

Morrissey, R.B., M.S., B.D. Burkholder, and S.M. Tarka, Ph.D. "The Carcinogenic Potential of Several Snack Foods." *Journal of the American Dental Association* (October 1984) 589–90.

U.S. Dept. of Agriculture and Dept. of Health and Human Services. "Dietary Guidelines for Americans." (1985.)

U.S. Dept. of Health and Human Services. "Seal Out Dental Decay." Public Health Service; National Institutes of Health.

Webb, Denise, Ph.D., R.D. "Smile, America. Diet and Cavities: The Good News." *McCall's* (February 1987).

Zezima, Jerry. "Are Your Fillings Dangerous?" *The Stamford Advocate* (January 22, 1991).

▪ Chapter Four:
Diet and Nutrition for the Growing Child

Brody, Jane. "Sorting Out Data on Diet and Cancer." *The New York Times* (September 30, 1987).

Bowen, Otis R., M.D., ed. *1988 Surgeon General's Report on Nutrition and Health.* Washington, DC: U.S. Government Printing Office. U.S. Department of Health and Human Services, 1989.

Burros, Marian. "Plain Talk About Eating Right." *The New York Times* (October 6, 1991).

Columbia University School of Public Health. "Nutrition During the Growing Years." *Health and Nutrition Newsletter.* Institute of Human Nutrition Health. (December 1986).

Findlay, Steven. "Diets for Kids: Pondering the Ice Cream Question." *U.S. News and World Report* (February 15, 1988).

Forbes, Gilbert, M.D., ed., and Calvin W. Woodruff, M.D., assoc. ed. *Pediatric Nutrition Handbook.* Elk Grove Village, IL: Committee on Nutrition, American Academy of Pediatrics, second edition, 1985.

"How Safe is Aspartame?" *Wellness Letter.* University of California, Berkeley, (February 1987).

MacNeil, Karen. "Diet Soft Drinks: Too Good to Be True?" *The New York Times* (February 4, 1987).

Marotz, Lynn R. ME.D, B.S.N., R.N., Jeanettia M. Rush, M.A., B.S., R.D., and Marie Z. Cross, Ph.D, MS, KBS. *Health, Safety, and Nutrition for the Young Child*. Albany, NY: Delmar Publishers, 1985.

Natow, Annette, and Jo-Ann Heslin. *No Nonsense Nutrition for Kids*. New York: Pocket Books, 1985.

National Academy of Sciences. "Recommended Dietary Allowances." (1980.)

Probber, Jonathan. "Avoiding Fatty Snacks." *The New York Times* (November 12, 1986).

"Prudent Life-style for Children: Dietary Fat and Cholesterol." *Pediatrics*. Vol. 78, No. 3 (September 1986).

Smith, Lendon, M.D. *Foods for Healthy Kids*. New York: Berkley Books, 1981.

——. *Feed Your Kids Right*. New York: Dell Publishing Co., Inc., 1979.

Udall, John N., Jr., M.D., F.A.A.P. "Why You Should Know About Cholesterol." *Healthy Kids 4–10* (Fall 1991).

■ Chapter Five: Body Image

Adams, Gerald R., and Paul Crane. "An Assessment of Parents' and Teachers' Expectations of Preschool Children's Social Preference for Attractive or Unattractive Children and Adults." *Child Development*, 1980. Society for Research in Child Development, Inc.

Arnold, Caroline. *Too Fat? Too Thin?* New York: William Morrow and Company, 1984.

Beard, Lillian McLean, M.D., with Susan Satlow. "Is Your Child Overweight?" *Good Housekeeping* (September 1990).

Briggs, Dorothy Corkille. *Your Child's Self-Esteem: The Key to Life*. Garden City, NY: Doubleday/Dolphin, 1970.

Brody, Jane. "Fat or Fit? Study May Confirm Suspicion It Is in the Genes." *The New York Times* (January 23, 1986).

——. "Personal Health: Parents' attitudes toward diet can contribute to obesity in children and adolescents." *The New York Times* (May 27, 1987).

Callahan, Maureen. "Feeding Kids in the Nineties—An Update. Giving Kids a Choice of Foods Is the Key to Good Nutrition." *Parents* October 1990, pp. 133–34.

Clark, Matt. "Why Kids Get Fat: A new study shows obesity is in the genes." *Newsweek* (February 3, 1986).

Cohen, Mindy, M.A., Louis Abramson, and Ruth Winter. *Thin Kids: The Proven, Healthy, Sensible Weight-Loss Program For Children*. New York: Beaufort Books, 1985.

Davis, Andrea R. "Fat Facts: Being Overweight Can Hurt a Child's Emotional and Physical Well-Being." *Essence* (June 1990), p. 95.

Elkind, David, Ph.D, "Eating Disorders." *Parents.* (April 1988).

Epstein, Leonard H., Ph.D., and Sally Squires, M.S. *The Stoplight Diet for Children.* Boston: Little, Brown and Company, 1988.

Ferrell, Tom. "Tall is Better." *The New York Times Magazine* (April 17, 1988), p. S102.

Hirschmann, Jane R. and Lela Zaphiropoulos. *Are You Hungry? A Completely New Approach To Raising Children Free of Food and Weight Problems.* New York: Random House, 1985.

Howell, Mary, M.D. "Obesity is Easier to Prevent than Alter. Still, there are some steps to take." *Working Mother* (December 1985).

Johnson, Marcia Corliss. "Parent and Child: Buddy Up to Fight Fat." *Weight Watchers Magazine,* (March 1988), pp. 56–61.

Kutner, Lawrence. "Weight Loss; Emotions Count More Than Calories. *The New York Times* (October 13, 1988).

———. "When Appearance is Truly a Concern." *The New York Times* (December 13, 1990).

Lansky, Vicki. *Fat-Proofing Your Children . . . So That They Never Become Diet-Addicted Adults.* New York: Bantam Books, 1988.

Lee, Sally. *New Theories on Diet and Nutrition.* New York: Franklin Watts, 1990.

Marks, Jane. "We Have A Problem." *Parents* (August 1988).

Mendelson, Robert A., M.D., F.A.A.P, and Lottie Mendelson, R.N., PNP. "Help For Your Overweight Child: Control Your Child's Weight by Encouraging Proper Eating and Exercise." *Healthy Kids 4–10* (Spring-Summer 1991).

Millar, Thomas P., M.D. "How Do You Give a Child Self-Esteem?" *Children Today* (September-October 1983).

O'Connell, Joseph B. "Pediatric Plastic Surgery: State of the Art 1992." *Fairfield County Kids* (November 1991).

Satter, Ellyn, M.S., R.D. *How To Get Your Child to Eat . . . But Not Too Much.* Palo Alto, CA: Bull Publishing, 1987.

Seligman, Jean. "The Littlest Dieters: Many normal-size kids are counting calories." *Newsweek* (July 27, 1987).

Shelov, Steven P., M.D., F.A.A.P, ed. *Caring for Your Baby and Young Child.* American Academy of Pediatrics. New York: Bantam Books, 1991.

Shuker-Haines, Franny. "Should You Buy Your Child a Better Body Image?" *Child* (October 1991).

Silverstein, Dr. Alvin, and Virginia B. Silverstein with Robert Silverstein. *So You Think You're Fat?* New York: HarperCollins Publishers, 1991.

Stunkard, Albert J., M.D., et al. "An Adoption Study of Human Obesity." *New England Journal of Medicine* 314 (January 23, 1986).

Weinhouse, Beth. "Health: You and Your Child: Teasing's No Joke." *Redbook* (November 1991).

Werth, Barry. "How Short Is Too Short?" *The New York Times* (June 16, 1991).

Wolf, Naomi. *The Beauty Myth: How Images of Beauty are Used Against Women.* New York: William Morrow and Co., Inc., 1991.

■ Chapter Six: Exercise

American Academy of Pediatrics Policy Statement. "Weight Training and Weight Lifting: Information for the Pediatrician." (July 1982).

Burke, Edmund R., Ph.D. "Safety Standards for Bicycle Helmets." *The Physician and Sportsmedicine* (January 1988).

Carey, John, Mary Hager, and Joanne Harrison. "Failing in Fitness: The health and exercise boom eludes America's kids." *Newsweek* (April 1, 1985).

Committee on Pediatric Aspects of Physical Fitness, Recreation and Sports. "Fitness in the Preschool Child." *Pediatrics.* Vol. 58 (July 1976).

———. "Competitive Athletics for Children of Elementary School Age." *Pediatrics* (June 1981).

Cooper, Kenneth H., M.D., M.P.H. *Kid Fitness: A Complete Shape-Up Program From Birth Through High School.* New York: Bantam Books, 1991.

Friedman, Nancy. "Testing the Fitness Tests: Are kids in better shape than we think?" *Parenting* (February 1987).

Galton, Lawrence. *Your Child in Sports: A Complete Guide.* New York: Franklin Watts, 1980.

Howell, Mary, M.D. "Play It Safe with Sports." *Working Mother* (May 1986).

Kardong, Don. "Getting Our Kids in Shape." *The Runner* (May 1985).

Kantrowitz, Barbara, and Nadine Joseph. "Building Baby Biceps: How toddlers keep fit at kiddie gyms." *Newsweek* (May 26, 1986).

Krantz, Paul. "Health Update: Bikes for Tykes." *Better Homes and Gardens* (November 1988).

Kunz, Jeffrey, R.M., M.D., and Asher J. Finkel, M.D. *The American Medical Association Family Medical Guide.* New York: Random House, 1987.

Monahan, Terry. "Family Exercise Means Relative Fitness." *The Physician and Sportsmedicine* (October 1986).

Neifert, Marianne, M.D. "Too Young For Pierced Ears?" *McCall's* (February 1987).

Reiff, Guy G., Ph.D. "National School Population Fitness Survey." The President's Council on Physical Fitness and Sports, 1985.

Rich, Celia R. "Lawn Games Make for a Backyard Olympics." *New Haven Register* (July 1, 1988).

Smith, Nathan J., M.D., ed. *Sports Medicine: Health Care for Young Children.* Evanston, IL: Committee on Sports Medicine, American Academy of Pediatrics, 1983.

Toufexis, Anastasia. "Getting an F for Flabby: U.S. youth comes up short on endurance, strength and flexibility." *Time* (January 26, 1987).

◼ Chapter Seven: Fun Fashion for Kids

Chapman, Eugenia, and Jill C. Major. *Clean Your House and Everything in It.* New York: Grosset & Dunlap, 1982.

Cruse, Heloise. *Heloise Around the House.* Englewood Cliffs, NJ: Prentice-Hall, 1965.

Elkind, David. *The Hurried Child: Growing Up Too Fast Too Soon.* Reading, MA: Addison-Wesley, 1984.

"Flame-Retardant Sleepwear: Today's Baby Sleeps in Safer Jammies." *American Baby* (May 1988).

Gray, Charlotte. "Designer Clothes: What To Do When Kids' Tastes Exceed Your Budget." *Chatelaine* (November 1988).

Jackson, Carole. *Color Me Beautiful.* New York: Ballantine Books, 1984.

Kane, Sheryl. "Take Me Along—Shopping? Sure!" *Connecticut Parent* (November 1986).

Koontz, Katy. "Caring For Your Clothes." *Redbook* (March 1986).

Neifert, Marianne, M.D. "Shoes for a Toddler." *McCall's* (March 1989).

Rhoads, Geraldine, and Edna Paradis. "Out With Spots! A Practical Guide for Getting Rid of Almost Any Stain." *Woman's Day* (April 2, 1991).

Schnurmberger, Lynn. "Shopping Without Tears (Or Tantrums)." *Parents* (May 1987).

Schultz, Dodi. "Best Foot Forward." *Parents* (November 1985).

INDEX

ABOUT THE
AUTHOR

WENDE DEVLIN GATES is a coauthor of *Newborn Beauty: A Complete Beauty, Health, and Energy Guide to the Nine Months of Pregnancy and the Nine Months After,* as well as a coauthor of two juvenile books. She was formerly entertainment editor of *Glamour* magazine and a staffer at *Vogue.* Ms. Gates has also written for *Redbook, McCall's, Bride's,* and *Harper's Bazaar.* She lives with her husband and three children in Darien, Connecticut.